100
YEARS
SIMON &
SCHUSTER

STOP People Pleasing

And Find Your Power

Hailey Magee

Simon & Schuster

New York London Toronto Sydney New Delhi

SIMON & SCHUSTER

1230 Avenue of the Americas
New York, NY 10020

First Simon & Schuster hardcover edition May 2024

SIMON & SCHUSTER and colophon are registered trademarks of Simon & Schuster, LLC

Simon & Schuster: Celebrating 100 Years of Publishing in 2024

For information about special discounts for bulk purchases, please contact Simon & Schuster Special Sales at 1-866-506-1949 or business@simonandschuster.com.

The Simon & Schuster Speakers Bureau can bring authors to your live event. For more information or to book an event, contact the Simon & Schuster Speakers Bureau at 1-866-248-3049 or visit our website at www.simonspeakers.com.

Interior design by Ruth Lee-Mui

Manufactured in the United States of America

1 3 5 7 9 10 8 6 4 2

Library of Congress Cataloging-in-Publication Data has been applied for.

ISBN 978-1-6680-5354-6
ISBN 978-1-6680-6532-7 (Int Exp)
ISBN 978-1-6680-5356-0 (ebook)

To Aaron,

for teaching me I don't need to be less

to be loved.

CONTENTS

INTRODUCTION

It was mid-August in Boston. The sun was unrelenting as I stood on the sidewalk of a busy thoroughfare, my arms filled with brown grocery bags. All I wanted was to return to my apartment and sit in front of the air conditioner, but instead, I strained to hear the Greenpeace canvasser who had stopped me ten minutes earlier to tell me about the plight of the polar bears.

I did my best to maintain an appropriately concerned expression as sweat dripped down my brow. I liked polar bears—who doesn't?—but I didn't have the time, or the money, to spare. I had a phone meeting in thirty minutes, and I was certain to be late. But I was rooted in place by politeness. I didn't want this stranger I'd probably never see again to think I was rude.

When she finally made her ask—"So, do you have thirty dollars to spare to keep our furry friends alive?"—I reached for my wallet, unable to resist the tug of guilt. Just then, my grocery bag split, and canned goods cascaded to the sidewalk. I apologized profusely, and when I finally collected the last of the cans, the canvasser had already moved on to someone else.

Let me paint you another picture.

A few weeks later, I was at a music venue where my friend's band was performing. But I was stuck at the bar. It had been thirty-five minutes—I'd been glancing at the clock every five, so I was certain of it—and a man I didn't know was *still* talking to me, in excruciating detail, about his twelve guitars. For the first few minutes I'd given him my full attention—I was always happy to have a brief chat with a friendly stranger—but by the end, I was using every cue I could think of to convey my disinterest. I glanced at my phone. I looked around the room. I gave one-word answers. Still, he went on.

I was not intimidated or threatened by this man; by all measures, he was harmless. But somehow, I couldn't muster the courage to say, "It's been nice talking to you, but I'm going to listen to the band now."

I couldn't find my voice. Instead, I waited for him to set me free.

A month or so later, I went on a first date with a man I'd met online. Right away, I knew that we weren't compatible. He didn't look like the photos in his profile. We shared few interests. He interrupted me constantly. Over dessert, I received a long lecture on the intricacies of the stock market.

When the date finally ended, I climbed into my Uber, flooded with relief. *Well, at least that's over*, I thought. Not an hour later, I received a text: **That was really fun. When can I see you again?**

I didn't know what to say. The thought of replying honestly—**Thanks for the date! I didn't feel a spark, but I wish you the best**—felt mean. I simply couldn't do it. I didn't know how. So I didn't reply.

Three days passed. Then another text: **You know, it's incredibly rude for you not to reply to me,** he said. **We had a great dinner—which I paid for, by the way—and you owe me an explanation.**

I didn't stop to question his entitlement. I didn't stop to consider whether this transactional point of view aligned with my feminist ethos. All I knew was: I felt guilty. So instead of answering honestly, I made up an excuse—**So sorry, I've been busy!**—and agreed to meet for a second date. It was four dates until I finally found the courage to bid him farewell.

For most of my life, people-pleasing was the air I breathed. It came so naturally to me that I didn't even have a word for it. When somebody wanted something from me—be they family, friend, lover, or stranger—I gave it, no matter how uncomfortable, exhausted, or resentful I felt inside.

It didn't matter if I was late to a meeting; it didn't matter if I was missing my friend's band; it didn't matter if I never wanted to see them again.

I was a people-pleaser. I put everyone else first. I couldn't say no.

In my romantic relationship, I listened to my partner's choice of music, hung out with my partner's friends, and had arguments on my partner's terms. In my family, I felt like others' emotions were my responsibility; I monitored and tended to them with far more dedication than I did my own. In my friendships, I struggled to share from the heart; convinced that I was "uninteresting," I was far more comfortable being a listener. In my community, I was known as the "happy one" who was "always smiling," and while these labels were intended as praise, they belied a deeper sadness: a painful feeling that nobody *really* knew me, or even cared to.

After years of therapy, I came to recognize the circumstances in my life that led me to become a people-pleaser. But I didn't know how to turn that knowledge *into action* to tangibly break the cycle. My morning journal entries were punctuated by exasperated questions: "How can I speak up for myself?" "How do I stop saying yes when I mean no?" "When am I finally going to put myself first for a change?" And, on one particularly difficult day, the following, written dramatically in angry red pen: "If I can learn to speak up for myself before I die, I will die a happy woman."

I still have this journal entry. I look back on it from time to time when I need a reminder of how far I've come.

Not long after I penned these frustrations, breaking the people-pleasing pattern became my personal mission. I went through a devastating breakup with a partner in whom I'd lost myself completely, and in his absence, I felt a searing clarity that I would never find contentment if I continued basing my self-worth solely on others' approval. I realized—painfully, suddenly, viscerally—that nobody was coming to "save me" from my people-pleasing. *I had to take responsibility for my own happiness.* This wasn't a duty I could outsource to others.

In the years that followed, I slowly and intentionally connected with my own feelings, needs, wants, and dreams. At first, they were shy with me—they'd learned through years of neglect that I could not be trusted to take care of them—but the more attention I paid them, the louder they became. The more I tended to myself, the more comfortable I became using my voice with others. The more I respected my needs, the more it felt imperative that I invested in relationships with people who *also* respected my needs. Slowly, I learned the art and craft of boundary-setting, making it clear what I would and would not tolerate in my connections with others.

It was empowering, and liberating, and uncomfortable. I felt awkward asking others to show me care in the specific ways I needed; I felt guilty setting hard boundaries with my loved ones; I felt grief as I outgrew relationships that were not a good fit for who I was becoming. But beneath every growing pain, like a slow and steady drumbeat, was the knowledge that after all these years, I was finally standing up for myself.

As I began to touch a freedom and self-trust I'd never known, I felt certain that I wanted to help others do the same. My goal was to help people who, like me, were ready to turn their desire for change into action: to take tangible, real-life steps to break the people-pleasing pattern.

Coaching, as a discipline, is designed for this. It asks and answers the question: "Where do I *most* want to go—and how, specifically, do I get there?" So I enrolled in a training program certified by the International Coaching Federation. When I graduated a year later, I knew I wanted to help others break the people-pleasing pattern, set empowered boundaries, and master the art of speaking their truth.

In addition to my one-on-one client sessions, I began writing about people-pleasing and sharing my work online. I was surprised by how deeply it resonated with people all over the world. I received messages from recovering people-pleasers in the US, India, Yemen, France, Afghanistan, New Zealand, Sudan, and more. They said, "I thought I was the only one who struggled this way." I told them, "I thought I was the only one, too."

With every new follower and subscriber, I felt a sense of solidarity: *We are in this together. We are not the only ones.*

Five years later, my writing has reached millions, and my workshops on people-pleasing and boundary-setting have welcomed thousands of participants from around the world. *Stop People Pleasing and Find Your Power* is the distillation of years' worth of research, coaching, teaching, and hundreds of one-on-one conversations with recovering people-pleasers. It offers an action-based approach to breaking the people-pleasing pattern, grounded in research and psychology, with practical tools that will help you find your voice and step into your power.

In Part 1: Find Yourself, you will learn how to discover—and prioritize—your own feelings, needs, values, self-concept, and wants. These are your five foundations of self, and only when you consistently tend to them can you confidently self-advocate in your relationships with others.

In Part 2: Stand Up for Yourself, you'll learn how to honor your needs in your relationships, make requests of others, set self-protective boundaries, and reconnect with your own power and agency. We'll also unpack how people-pleasing differently impacts various groups based on their social locations and degrees of privilege.

Part 3: Take Care of Yourself is a companion for the growing pains we all face as we break the people-pleasing pattern. You'll learn how to embrace bravery and become resilient toward guilt, fear, anger, loneliness, and grief; how to navigate the challenges of outgrowing relationships and facing difficult transitions; and how to reframe these challenges as powerful opportunities for growth and transformation.

Part 4: Enrich Yourself shows how breaking the people-pleasing pattern will make your life better. You'll learn how to stop playing small in your relationships with others; how to eradicate people-pleasing from your sex life; how to reconnect with play; how to approach your healing with nuance and discernment; and how to discover the joys of giving from a genuine and self-respecting place.

When I began writing this book, I knew I wanted it to expand the conversation about people-pleasing in two key ways: by offering nuance and acknowledging the inevitable growing pains of this important healing work.

As concepts like people-pleasing and self-care become more mainstream, complex ideas like boundaries are often diluted in ways that ultimately discourage us from building healthy relationships. We're told that if someone doesn't bring us "love and light at all times," we should "cut them out." We're told that if someone disagrees with us, we should leave them behind to "protect our peace." We're told that if someone can't meet *every single one* of our needs, we "deserve better."

These one-dimensional platitudes ignore the reality that human relationships are complicated. They impede our healing by encouraging us to seek an unattainable standard, and they prevent us from looking inward to assess how *we* may be contributing to our own unhappiness or disempowerment.

That's why *Stop People Pleasing* incorporates nuance to help you break the people-pleasing pattern while also encouraging sustainable and realistic relationships. This book takes seriously questions such as: What is the difference between kindness and people-pleasing? How can we have self-compassion for the painful circumstances that led to our people-pleasing while also taking personal responsibility for breaking the pattern? When is it appropriate to compromise on our needs, and when is it appropriate to hold firm to them? And how can we distinguish between when other people are violating our boundaries and when we're violating our *own* boundaries by giving more than we're comfortable giving?

I believe this nuance is where our true healing lies. By the same token, I believe that we must speak to the emotional nuances of healing: the fact that this inner work is not only empowering and freeing, but also difficult and, at times, deeply uncomfortable. As we break the people-pleasing pattern, we often feel afraid to make requests of others, no matter how reasonable those requests are. We often feel guilty after setting boundaries, no matter how necessary those boundaries may be. We often feel grief when we leave behind toxic relationships, no matter how harmful they were to us.

It's not only normal, but inevitable, that we face these growing pains as we leave people-pleasing behind. If we don't acknowledge them, we can't soothe ourselves through them—and if we don't soothe ourselves through them, we're more likely to renege on our boundaries and retreat, once again, into silence. For this reason, *Stop People Pleasing* offers practical tools for normalizing, and self-soothing through, guilt, fear, anger, uncertainty, and grief as we step into our power.

Remember that years-ago version of me who stood on that busy Boston street, who listened to that man at the bar, who went on that godawful series of soul-crushing dates?

She would have never, in a million years, believed that, one day, I would be sitting here, typing this introduction on my laptop, really, truly feeling like I've left people-pleasing behind.

Ridiculous, she would have said. *Impossible.*

But it *is* possible. I've witnessed it within myself; I've witnessed it from hundreds of my clients; I've witnessed it from thousands of individuals worldwide who have taken the time to email me and say, "I never thought I could do this, but I did."

This healing isn't a one-time event; it is a process of rededicating ourselves *to* ourselves, over and over again. Every time we redirect our attention back to our feelings, our desires, and our dreams, we are healing. Every time we soothe ourselves through our guilt instead of reacting to it, we are healing. Every time we use our voice where we would have once stayed silent, we are healing.

I owe my thanks to the hundreds of recovering people-pleasers who gave me permission to include their personal stories in this book. While names, ages, and other identifying information have been changed to preserve their privacy, the vignettes you'll read are real stories from real people around the world.

I hope that *Stop People Pleasing* serves as your companion, support, and cheerleader as you break the people-pleasing pattern. This work is not easy, but I can assure you: it is worth it a hundred times over.

—Hailey Magee, Seattle, WA

1

FIND YOURSELF

1

PEOPLE-PLEASING: WHAT IT IS, WHERE IT COMES FROM, AND WHY WE'RE LEAVING IT BEHIND

People-pleasing is the act of chronically prioritizing others' needs, wants, and feelings at the expense of our own needs, wants, and feelings. As people-pleasers, we struggle to speak up for ourselves in our relationships. We give past our limits to be liked by others; have immense difficulty setting boundaries; struggle to identify and leave toxic environments; and become involved in many one-sided relationships that are all give and no take. Often, we feel defined by how helpful, useful, and supportive we can be to other people.

Though people-pleasing manifests in our relationships with others, it stems from a disconnected relationship with ourselves. You might think of it as a form of self-abandonment. *Even in the absence of others*, many of us avoid tending to our basic needs; discount our own emotions; feel uncomfortable in our own company; and become disconnected from play, creativity, wonder, joy, and delight. Cut off from a sense of self-worth, we may engage in perfectionism, self-shaming, and self-judgment; struggle with distress tolerance, self-soothing, and emotional regulation; or even engage in compulsions or addictions to avoid feeling our emotions.

People-pleasing is a pattern of behavior, not a mental illness or diagnosis. For most, it isn't a conscious choice moment to moment, but an ingrained way of interacting with others that was instilled in childhood. In this chapter, we'll explore where the people-pleasing pattern comes from; how it affects our relationships; what differentiates it from kindness; and how we can use this knowledge to begin to break the pattern.

FOUR PORTRAITS OF PEOPLE-PLEASING

The people-pleasing pattern affects people of all genders, ages, ethnicities, and income brackets, but it doesn't manifest the same way for everyone. Some feel completely confident and authentic at work, but become passive in their romantic relationships. Others have no trouble speaking up for themselves with friends, but struggle to set boundaries with family members. Still others feel that people-pleasing colors every area of their lives: work, romance, friends, family, and community.

People-pleasing can look like:

Tanya

Tanya, forty-five, is a corporate lawyer in New York City. She is fierce and uncompromising in the courtroom, but in her personal relationships, she feels inconsequential and powerless. She resentfully subsidizes her unemployed partner's expenses while he seeks work at a snail's pace. Each weekend she travels upstate for a long visit with her recently widowed mother, whom she describes as "narcissistic and overbearing." She has a couple of casual friends in the city, but their coffee dates quickly turn into therapy sessions when her friends dump their personal problems into her lap—and show no curiosity in return.

A sense of obligation and resentment pervades all of Tanya's relationships. She over-gives and under-receives in every single one of them, but she doesn't know how to shift this dynamic.

Aaron

Aaron, thirty-five, is engaged to be married, but family complications are threatening his engagement. His father died when he was a child, and ever since, Aaron has been very close to his mother, Jada. Whenever Jada needs anything, he's there in a flash to provide it. She calls him multiple times a day to chitchat about everything from the weather to the recent football game. Even when Aaron and his fiancée, Issa, are on dates, he steps away to take phone calls from his mother.

He feels smothered by his mother's insistent presence, and even Issa has expressed hesitation about becoming the third wheel to Aaron and Jada's enmeshed relationship. But ever since his father died, he has felt responsible for his mother's emotional well-being. He wants to create space, but he doesn't know how—and he's terrified of hurting her feelings.

Lena

Lena, twenty-nine, was born into an Orthodox Jewish family. As she's gotten older, she's become uncomfortable with certain aspects of her faith—particularly its rigid gender roles—and after many months of reckoning, she decides that she can no longer participate in the religion and disaffiliates.

Newly uninvolved in the Orthodox community, she notices how much her upbringing has prevented her from finding and using her own voice. In social situations, she always defers to the men in the group; in conflicts with friends, she immediately becomes passive and accommodating. Without a religious community to guide her, she has no idea what she wants, what her dreams are, or who she is. Lena wants to follow her inner compass, but she doesn't know where to find it.

Zoe

Zoe, a nonbinary twenty-four-year-old, is a lively, talkative graduate student in a theater program. Zoe makes friends effortlessly; their social calendar is always filled with coffee dates, happy hours, and weekend adventures. But despite their many friends, Zoe feels disconnected and fundamentally unseen.

At a young age, Zoe learned that being permanently cheerful was a surefire strategy to get attention from their distant parents, so they use the same method now to make friends in adulthood. Zoe is always bubbly and agreeable, and though they make fast friends, those friendships never deepen; Zoe never shares when they're going through a difficult time, and never asks anyone for support. They crave connection and wish to be seen and known—but their people-pleasing prevents them from building intimate friendships.

Tanya, Aaron, Lena, and Zoe may have different backgrounds, but they share the struggle to speak up for themselves and the desire to express themselves authentically in their relationships. All four want to identify and assert their needs, set healthy boundaries, and make decisions based on their own values and priorities.

The first step in breaking the people-pleasing pattern is understanding its origins in our own lives. Doing so helps us develop both self-awareness and self-compassion as we learn how we originally developed this pattern as a coping mechanism to stay safe.

THE ORIGINS OF PEOPLE-PLEASING

We develop the people-pleasing pattern as a way to manage our experience of unsupportive, unsafe, or unpredictable environments. Many of us learn to people-please in childhood in order to get safety or affection from preoccupied, unavailable, or abusive caregivers. For marginalized groups—such as people of color, LGBTQ+ people, or neurodivergent people—people-pleasing can also be a survival strategy to avoid stigma, harassment, or harm.

Trauma

Those who have experienced trauma are more likely to develop the people-pleasing pattern. In 2003, psychotherapist and trauma expert Pete Walker expanded the well-known "fight, flight, or freeze" stress response model to include a fourth addition: fawn. When threatened, a person with the fawn response will try to please, gratify, or accommodate the source of threat instead of fighting back, running away, or shutting down.

The fawn response is particularly common among those who experienced childhood abuse. Walker explains that, in childhood, these people likely learned that protesting mistreatment led to even more severe retaliation, so they "relinquished the fight response, deleted 'no' from their vocabulary, and never developed the language skills of healthy assertiveness."

If fawning helped someone avoid harm as a child, they may cling to this coping mechanism long after it stops keeping them safe. As adults, when confronted with situations that provoke fear or anxiety, they may behave in ways that they think will earn others' approval: appearing kind and lighthearted, giving compliments, or even agreeing to activities they have no interest in. Walker explains that those who fawn "seek safety by merging with the wishes, needs, and demands of others. They act as if they unconsciously believe that the price of admission to any relationship is the forfeiture of all their needs, rights, preferences, and boundaries."

Trauma can also lead people to develop lifelong hypervigilance, carefully monitoring others' moods for subtle shifts and signs of danger. Often, survivors of trauma become experts at reading others' emotions, but struggle to identify their own. Over time, many become completely disconnected from their own inner worlds. In this way, trauma's long-term effects can leave a person less able to access their feelings and needs, say no, and practice healthy assertiveness in moments of stress.

How We Were Parented

Not all people-pleasing has its origins in trauma. Sometimes, we develop the pattern as a result of how we were parented.

Our caregivers teach us how to interact with the world. They teach us whether our emotions and needs are acceptable; they teach us whether we deserve love, and under what conditions. In the 1960s, clinical psychologist Diana Baumrind identified four distinct parenting styles: permissive, neglectful, authoritative, and authoritarian. Both authoritarian and permissive parenting can lead children to develop the people-pleasing pattern.

Authoritarian parents are punitive, controlling, and have unreasonably high expectations of their children. Though they meet their children's material needs, they rarely provide affection or emotional support. Authoritarian parents offer few explanations for their rules and offer no room for compromise: their control is paramount. Having such rigid rules in an emotionally barren environment leads many children to believe that the only way to gain others' approval is to do everything right. They become externally motivated, anxiously seeking their worth in the validation of their parents, teachers, and peers. Terrified of disapproval, they tend to be chronically anxious and extremely critical of themselves. Many grow up to be perfectionists who can't tolerate making mistakes. So preoccupied with meeting others' expectations, they struggle to identify their own feelings and desires. Though many become hardworking and successful adults, they often enter therapy seeking help for low assertiveness, guilt, depression, anxiety, and low self-esteem.

On the opposite side of the spectrum lie permissive parents: those who are highly responsive to their children emotionally, but inconsistently enforce expectations, rules, and consequences for unruly behavior. Some permissive parents act less like parents and more like friends to their children. They may overshare intimate details of their lives, inappropriately demand their children's emotional support, or position their children as allies during parental conflicts. This reversal of roles often results in parentified children who assume more responsibility than is appropriate for their age. These children learn that the love they get is based entirely on how emotionally supportive they can be—a mentality that often pervades their relationships in adulthood.

When children play the role of supporter and confidante for a parent, they often struggle to develop their own sense of identity. It's easy for them to see their parents' needs and feelings, but they have a hard time identifying their own. As a result, adult children of permissive parents often find themselves playing the role of savior, helper, fixer, or martyr in their adult relationships.

Likewise, emotionally immature caregivers—those who can't regulate their own emotions—struggle to recognize, validate, and be present with their children's emotions. These children never learn that their feelings and experiences are meaningful; their inner worlds go unacknowledged. Children of emotionally immature parents learn to neglect their own feelings and needs, often becoming chronic listeners, helpers, and fixers as adults.

Finally, caregivers may also instill people-pleasing in their children by role modeling people-pleasing themselves. As children, we learn what's normal behavior by watching our caregivers. We notice their mannerisms, their decisions, how they spend their time, and how they treat and speak to themselves. If we had a caregiver who was deferential, passive, self-sacrificial, or unable to set boundaries, we may unintentionally replicate these behaviors as we get older.

Being Raised alongside Addiction

Sometimes, caregivers' emotional limitations prevent them from giving their children the support they need. However, caregivers struggling with addiction—or preoccupied by another family member's addiction—may also fail to offer their children adequate support, presence, and encouragement.

Typically, families containing addiction become hyper-focused on the addict. Family members monitor the addict's behavior, urge them toward recovery, try to manage their erratic moods, and grapple with the fallout of their unpredictable behavior. Children learn that tending to the addict is their primary responsibility, and they don't receive the support they need to identify or communicate their own basic feelings and needs.

Many children raised alongside addiction become hyper-independent and hyper-responsible adults. They believe that they're worthy of love *to the extent that they can be of value to others*. Research shows that adult children of alcoholics tend to feel personally accountable for any negative occurrence at home or in the workplace. As they did when they were children, they feel responsible for managing everyone around them. Strangers even to themselves, adult children of addiction frequently surround themselves with addicts or emotionally unavailable partners, inadvertently re-creating dynamics from their childhood.

A Response to Gender Norms

Family dynamics often plant the seeds of people-pleasing, but gender norms can also play a major role. Despite significant advancements toward gender equality within the last century, women are still seen as the caretakers of our culture. Jobs with nurturing at their center—like nursing, teaching, and social work—are disproportionately done by women. In the home, women perform four hours of caretaking and household work daily compared to men's two and a half hours. Psychologist Marshall Rosenberg writes: "For centuries, the image of the loving woman has been associated with sacrifice and the denial of one's own needs to take care of others. Because women are socialized to view the caretaking of others as their highest duty, they learn to ignore their own needs."

Even in interpersonal relationships, women are still encouraged—implicitly or explicitly—to prioritize others first. Women, more often than men, find themselves responsible for emotional labor: the unpaid and undervalued work of maintaining relationships, managing people's emotions, and keeping people happy. Research shows that women apologize far more often than men, and are more likely to label their own behavior as offensive or apology-worthy. Women are even more likely to be called "bossy" when expressing confidence or assertiveness.

These days, it's less common to *explicitly* instruct women to be silent and self-sacrificial, but these norms are deeply embedded in our culture. We may not always say them aloud, but they continue to play a significant role in our society's expectations of women and women's expectations of themselves.

Men face different gender norms, but those norms can also foster people-pleasing by encouraging men to suppress their emotions, show no weakness, and give past their limits. Across the board, men are still expected to be stoic, unfeeling, and emotionally unexpressive; a 2019 study found that 58 percent of men feel like they're expected to be "emotionally strong and to show no weakness," and 38 percent have avoided talking to others about their feelings to avoid appearing "unmanly." This caricature of the Unfeeling Man creates two painful disconnections. First, many men become cut off from their *own* feelings and needs because they've been discouraged from having any at all. Second, many men become disconnected from *others* because it's difficult to build intimate, supportive connections if you were never allowed to be vulnerable.

Many men also feel pressure to give past their limits at work. Despite women's surging participation in the workforce, many men still feel obligated to prove their worth by playing a traditional breadwinner role in their families. Denying their own needs for rest and restoration, many men find themselves overworking to attain this masculine ideal, suffering elevated stress levels and reduced sleep along the way. Gender norms can prohibit men from embracing their emotions, building intimate connections, and honoring their own needs for rest and recuperation.

A Response to Culture

Behavior deemed "people-pleasing" in one culture may be commonplace and celebrated in another. Ultimately, what constitutes a healthy versus unhealthy amount of giving is culturally determined.

Individualistic cultures, like the United States, the United Kingdom, and South Africa, encourage people to set self-directed goals rather than fulfill others' goals for them. (Though, as we saw in the previous section, women and marginalized groups still face societal pressure to subjugate their own needs to care for others.) Individualistic cultures place less emphasis on family and group affiliations and more emphasis on autonomy, individuality, and self-actualization. As a result, some members of these cultures feel a sense of freedom and agency; others feel unmoored and disconnected.

Meanwhile, collectivist cultures, like China, Korea, Japan, and India, encourage members to prioritize the group or family above the individual. (Many organized religions also operate as collectivist cultures.) Emphasizing conformity, obedience, and loyalty, collectivist cultures assert that family and group affiliations are of the utmost importance. As a result, some members of collectivist cultures feel a sense of belonging and security; others feel restricted and confined.

Some from collectivist cultures—especially those who immigrate to individualistic cultures—feel conflicted between their culture's ideals and their personal desire to prioritize their own needs, passions, and dreams.

A Response to Stigma and Oppression

For many marginalized groups, people-pleasing, shape-shifting, and masking one's authentic self are methods for survival. If your society taught you that people like you weren't worthy of basic care, dignity, and respect, acting deferentially—especially toward those in authority—can be a way to protect yourself from harm. When acts of violence and harassment against members of your identity group are commonplace, becoming as small and unnoticeable as possible is a survival strategy.

Various marginalized groups face distinct pressures to people-please. This topic is broad and deserves a chapter of its own, so we'll discuss how systemic oppressions impact individual people-pleasing patterns in chapter 13.

Safety Is the Common Thread

Though the people-pleasing pattern has many origins, a common thread connects them all: the pursuit of safety. Safety doesn't necessarily mean safety from physical harm or violence, though it can. It can also mean safety more broadly:

- **Social safety:** "I belong" or "People approve of me."
- **Emotional safety:** "I am known and understood" or "I am loved" or "I matter."
- **Material safety:** "My basic needs are met."

People-pleasing may have kept us safe in childhood, but now, as adults with agency and independence, using our voices—not silencing them—becomes a far more effective strategy to ensure that we get what we want and need in our lives.

People-Pleasing in Psychology

While people-pleasing is not a formal mental illness or diagnosis, many schools of psychology examine the pattern of neglecting the self to put others first—and various forms of therapy provide helpful interventions to break the pattern.

Aaron Beck, the founder of cognitive behavioral therapy, coined the term *sociotropy*: a personality trait characterized by over-reliance on others' approval and an excessive investment in one's relationships. People who score higher on the sociotropy scale feel the need to please others; are nonassertive and overly nurturant; have trouble asserting their needs; and fear criticism and rejection. Sociotropic people are more likely to develop depression, and cognitive therapy—which challenges negative thought patterns about the self and the world—has been shown to mitigate these depressive effects.

Meanwhile, the Bowen family systems theory promotes the concept of *differentiation*: the ability to know where we end and others begin. Highly differentiated people have a strong and independent sense of self, while less differentiated people rely heavily on the approval of those around them. People who are less differentiated tend to adjust their actions to please others; avoid saying no; and struggle to maintain their own opinions in the face of difference. Bowen family therapy helps people increase their level of differentiation and create healthy boundaries so that they can better manage their relationships.

Attachment theory can also help us understand the people-pleasing pattern. It asserts that our childhood relationships with our caregivers affect how we interact with others as adults. People with an anxious attachment style generally had caregivers who inconsistently tended to their needs. As adults, they tend to feel uncertain about the state of their relationships, crave deeper intimacy, and seek excessive reassurance from their partners. More than anything, anxiously attached individuals fear being abandoned and are hypersensitive to threats to the relationship. Fueled by insecurity and low self-esteem, anxiously attached people anticipate rejection and will go to great lengths to avoid it—including sacrificing their own needs, wants, or feelings. Attachment-focused therapy helps clients understand their attachment style and modify their behaviors in their relationships.

Finally, the addiction field offers the concept of codependence. Originally popularized in the 1980s to describe the self-sacrificial characteristics shared by many spouses of alcoholics, the term *codependent* has evolved to describe any person—involved with an addict or not—who chronically self-neglects and over-prioritizes others. Codependents tend to have trouble identifying their feelings; avoid communicating their needs; struggle to make decisions; remain in harmful relationships for too long; and believe others are incapable of taking care of themselves. The twelve-step program Co-Dependents Anonymous was created to help people recover from codependency, and many addiction treatment centers offer codependency recovery programs as well.

Those with depression, anxiety, social anxiety, and various forms of neurodivergence may also struggle with people-pleasing. Though no data exists on the prevalence of people-pleasing specifically, the ubiquity of trauma, addiction, depression, anxiety, social injustice, and the pattern's other origins indicate that it affects millions of people around the world.

Despite how common people-pleasing is—and how many frameworks exist for addressing it—many still hesitate to label their chronic over-giving or self-sacrifice as people-pleasing. Some say, "Prioritizing others' feelings and needs sounds like something everyone should do. . . . That just sounds like kindness to me." And they're right; caring about others' needs and feelings *is* a form of kindness. But kindness becomes people-pleasing when we chronically neglect ourselves in the process.

KINDNESS VS. PEOPLE-PLEASING

On its face, people-pleasing may resemble kindness. After all, generosity, loyalty, compassion, and dedication are cornerstones of healthy relationships. But there's a difference between people-pleasing and being kind.

Psychologists have found that kindness (which they call "healthy altruism") and people-pleasing (which they call "pathological altruism") have entirely different motives. The very same action that's people-pleasing for one person might be kindness for another; it all depends on why you're doing it and whether it negatively impacts you.

Psychologists define pathological altruism as "the willingness of a person to irrationally place another's perceived needs above his or her own in a way that causes self-harm." Pathological altruists often neglect themselves in pursuit of others' well-being, and researchers have found that their actions are motivated by the desire to gain others' approval and avoid rejection.

At their core, people-pleasing behaviors are rooted in:

- **Transaction:** "I'm giving you this so you will give me something back."
- **Obligation:** "I'm doing this because if I don't, I'll feel guilty."
- **Compulsion:** "I'm doing this because I have no idea how *not* to do this."
- **Loss-aversion:** "I'm doing this because if I don't, I fear I'll lose you."

For many, this pattern is based upon a covert contract or unspoken agreement: "I will over-give and trespass my own boundaries for you, and in return, you will make me feel loved, wanted, and needed." The problem is that others never agreed to this transaction. We may over-give and cater to others' needs believing they will then be obligated to give us the love and attention that we crave. This transactional mentality imbues our relationships with piles of invisible debt.

After over-giving, people-pleasers often feel exhausted, frustrated, and resentful. When others don't respond to our giving as we wish they would, we might even demonize them as "rude," "self-centered," or "taking advantage of us." As a result, people-pleasing often leaves us feeling disconnected from the very people we're trying to "help."

Gwen is moving out of her apartment. The night before she's scheduled to move, she texts her friend Hazel and asks if she's available to help the following day. When Hazel receives the text, she's immediately overwhelmed: she's on a tight work deadline and already has plans the following evening with friends. She doesn't *really* have the time to help, but she feels guilty telling Gwen no; she doesn't want to fall out of her good graces. So instead, she agrees and tells Gwen she'll be over tomorrow at 10:00 a.m.

For the rest of the night, Hazel feels stressed and resentful. *This is a huge ask to make of a friend less than twenty-four hours beforehand*, she thinks. *I can't believe I have to spend tomorrow moving heavy boxes instead of making progress on my deadline.*

Hazel's agreement isn't kindness, but people-pleasing; she agrees to help from a place of obligation ("I'll feel guilty if I say no") and loss-aversion ("I don't want to fall out of Gwen's good graces"). As we'll explore more in the following section, the subsequent resentment that Hazel feels is a clear sign that she's giving past her limits.

Kindness and Healthy Altruism

Psychologists define healthy altruism as the ability to "experience sustained and relatively conflict-free pleasure from contributing to the welfare of others." Healthy altruists gratify their own needs while *also* taking steps to enhance others' lives; they don't sacrifice their own well-being in the process. Research shows that healthy altruism is motivated by the desire for new experiences and personal growth.

Acts of kindness are rooted in:

- **Desire:** "I want to give this to you."
- **Goodwill:** "I'm eager to increase your quality of life because I care about you."
- **Choice:** "I don't *have* to do this—I *want* to do this."
- **Abundance:** "I'm giving you this because there's enough to go around."

When we give out of kindness, it's because we could say yes or no, and choose, of our own free will, to say yes. We aren't necessarily expecting anything in return. Our generosity isn't motived by others' reactions, but by the *internal satisfaction* that comes from acting in accordance with our values. Importantly, how we act publicly aligns with how we feel privately. After giving to others in this way, we may be tired or spent, but alongside the fatigue are typically feelings of happiness, goodwill, and connection.

After Gwen texts Hazel, she also texts her friend Gabriel for help. Gabriel checks his schedule to see if he has time the next day. Right now, his only plan is to meet a friend for pickup basketball at 3:00 p.m.; he's happy to help beforehand. Gabriel texts back: **Yes—I can help until 2:45. I'll be there at 10 with my truck!**

After Gabriel replies, he feels a sense of satisfaction at agreeing to help a friend in need. His agreement was based on desire ("I want to help Gwen") and choice ("I don't *have* to do this—I *want* to do this"). Because he offered to give to the extent that he was comfortable giving, his actions didn't negatively impact him. He was being kind, not people-pleasing.

Pathological and healthy altruism differ in both the motivation behind the altruistic acts and the extent to which they cause personal harm. Psychologists Scott Barry Kaufman and Emanuel Jauk encourage those seeking to move from pathological to healthy altruism to increase their level of "healthy selfishness": the idea that "it's healthy and even growth-fostering to take care of oneself and enjoy life's little pleasures." We'll discuss how to begin tending to ourselves this way in chapter 2.

HOW PEOPLE-PLEASING HARMS US

A single instance of people-pleasing—like helping a friend move when you don't really have the time—may not cause you any serious harm. But in the long term, these small acts of self-neglect accumulate, negatively affecting our well-being, relationships, and dreams for the future.

After years of people-pleasing, we become strangers to ourselves; we are highly attuned to others' moods and feelings and woefully unmoored from our own. When others ask us what we want or dream of, we may be disturbed to find that we have no idea. Instead of designing our own lives, we become mirrors, reflecting back others' desires.

Chronically prioritizing others' needs leaves us little time or energy to care for ourselves, and as a result, our physical and mental health may suffer. We may neglect our physical needs for rest, healthy meals, or doctor's appointments; neglect our financial needs by lending money we don't have; or neglect our emotional needs by entering relationships with emotionally unavailable partners and friends. These neglects take a toll. Suppressing our own emotions can lead to higher rates of anxiety, depression, and stress. Research also shows that emotional suppression can contribute to physical illness, increasing the likelihood of heart disease, gastrointestinal health complications, and autoimmune disease.

When we people-please, we struggle to build intimacy in our relationships. True intimacy requires letting ourselves be seen for who we really are, and people-pleasing is like wearing a mask. We are the ever-cheerful ones and the easygoing ones; we are the ones who say yes, no matter what. We don't speak up when we've been hurt, and we aren't honest about what we need. Though these ways of interacting may reduce the potential for conflict in the short term, they are not conducive to true intimacy over time. The more we people-please, the more we feel painfully unseen and unknown.

For many, people-pleasing also breeds resentment. Our resentment stems from the fact that, like Hazel, we're uncomfortable stating our limits and boundaries. Often, we expect others to "just know" our needs, feelings, and limits, even if we've never communicated them before. Instead of saying no when we're overcommitted, we agree when others ask favors of us, smiling on the outside while shrieking on the inside, *They should just know how busy I am!* Instead of telling others when we've been hurt by their behavior, we stew silently, thinking, *They should just know how that made me feel!* Instead of asking for help when we need it, we suffer in quiet frustration when others don't automatically offer it, thinking, *They should just know what I need!* Instead of expressing how we want to be cared for, we hold our loved ones to an invisible standard, feeling angry when they don't attain it: *They should just know how to take care of me!*

In these ways, we outsource our responsibility for our own needs and feelings to other people. Unspoken expectations put our family members, partners, and friends in the unfair position of failing tests they didn't realize they were taking.

Unfortunately, these patterns of behavior often have a ripple effect, and we may model people-pleasing for others without even realizing it. Many of us know this ripple effect all too well from watching our own caregivers model self-sacrifice and self-denial in their relationships. Whether we're parents, bosses, leaders in our communities, or beyond, we have people looking up to us. We are teaching them, through our behavior, how to value themselves, how to express themselves, and what to expect from—and accept in—their relationships with others. We can either model people-pleasing, self-sacrifice, and deference—or confidence, self-advocacy, and self-respect.

IT'S TIME FOR A CHANGE

If you're reading this book, you've probably begun to suspect that the costs of people-pleasing outweigh the benefits. You're probably tired of feeling unseen, unheard, and cut off from yourself and others. You're probably sick of always being at the whim of others' moods, demands, and desires.

You're ready to take charge of your own life. You're ready to become the protagonist of your own story. You want to feel strong, free, and self-respecting. You want to step into your power.

Understanding the origins of our people-pleasing is a critical first step in breaking the pattern, but to truly change, we need to accompany our knowledge with action and dedicated practice. That's why this book offers an *action-based* approach to breaking the people-pleasing pattern, grounded in research and psychology, that gives you the practical tools to get from where you are now to where you'd like to be.

Your Deepest Why

Breaking the people-pleasing pattern is a challenging but deeply rewarding endeavor. At the outset, it helps to determine your Deepest Why: the most important, most heart-stirring reason you're embarking on this journey. If you find yourself grappling with fear, uncertainty, or self-doubt along the way, your Deepest Why is the North Star that will guide you through.

To uncover your Deepest Why, you might consider: What's the most important reason I want to break this pattern? What version of myself am I most eager to become? Who do I want to role model for?

I've posed this question to thousands of people in my workshops, and I'm always struck by the beauty of their responses. They've said:

- "I want to be a strong role model for my children. I want them to have a mother they respect. It's my dream that they know how to speak up for themselves, have healthy relationships, and set healthy boundaries."
- "I'm tired of feeling like a shadow. I've never felt like anything in my life was truly mine, you know? I'm ready to change that. I want to feel like I'm living a life that *I* chose, not a life others chose for me."
- "I want to develop the assertiveness and strength I need to follow my dreams. I have an incredible vision for a business I want to build, but right now I don't have the self-confidence to make it happen. I want to build this business and feel proud of what I've accomplished. I want to do everything in my power to bring it to life."
- "I come from a long line of women who self-sacrificed. Some were in abusive relationships. Some just never took the plunge to pursue their own dreams. It kills me to think about all of the women in my family whose voices went unheard. I want to break my family's intergenerational pattern of women staying silent. I want to create a new way."

What is your Deepest Why? Write it down and hold it close as you embark on this transformative process of self-discovery. Through any difficult moments that may arise, you will have this clear reminder of how breaking the people-pleasing pattern will radically transform your life and the lives of those you love.

2

FINDING OUR FEELINGS

As people-pleasers, we become disconnected from ourselves after years of prioritizing others' needs, feelings, and wants at the expense of our own. For this reason, the very first step in breaking the pattern isn't setting boundaries or speaking up: it's reconnecting with *ourselves* so that we can advocate for those selves in our dealings with other people. After all, how can we assert our needs if we don't know what they are? How can we speak our truth if we don't know what we feel? How can we set boundaries to protect ourselves if we're cut off from the selves we're supposed to be protecting?

This is why part 1 offers a road map to connect with our five foundations: our feelings, needs, wants, values, and stories of self. After years of self-neglect, prioritizing these five foundations is not only deeply healing, but a prerequisite for bringing more of ourselves into our relationships with others.

Feelings are our first foundation because they occur within our bodies even when we've developed the habit of ignoring them with our minds. Their visceral and immediate nature makes them a convenient starting point as we learn to attune within. Our feelings are like compasses that point us in the direction of our needs, wants, and values; they are the base upon which we'll build the remaining four foundations.

In this chapter, we'll explore how we commonly defend ourselves against our feelings; discuss how we can use our bodies as tools to identify them; examine how to increase our tolerance for difficult emotions; and create a supportive daily practice of reconnecting to our own feelings, even when doing so feels strange or unfamiliar.

KAYLEIGH'S STORY

Kayleigh, forty-eight, begins our session by giving me a detailed list of the ways that everyone else in her life is struggling. Her husband, Dave, is stressed at work as an important deadline approaches; her daughter, Casey, is having trouble adjusting to her freshman year at college; her mother, Ruth, was recently let go from her position as an elementary school teacher; and her father, Paul, is slowly losing his hearing.

"They're all going through so much," says Kayleigh. "These are supposed to be my parents' golden years, but instead they're getting fired from work and battling with their health. And Casey is *really* struggling at school. She was so excited to leave home, but now all she wants to do is come back."

I nod, hearing the empathy in Kayleigh's voice.

"That's a lot of hardship to face all at once," I affirm. "How are you coping with all of this upheaval?"

"Oh, I'm fine," Kayleigh responds automatically, batting my question away like a pesky mosquito. "It's really them I'm worried about," she emphasizes, skillfully redirecting our conversation away from the uncomfortable territory of her own emotions.

For Kayleigh, "I'm fine" is an old refrain. Like many people-pleasers, she's "the strong one," the one who, no matter the circumstances, can "handle it all." For clients like Kayleigh, connecting with her *own* suffering feels vulnerable—and selfish—when those close to her are in distress.

"I know how much you care about your family," I offer, wanting Kayleigh to know I understand. "And this time is for us to focus on *you*."

Kayleigh rolls her eyes. She's heard this spiel from me before.

"I know, I know," she huffs. "It's just that my feelings seem so small in comparison to what everyone else is going through."

I nod and say, "How about this: when our session is over, you can get right back to focusing on others' feelings. But just for the next thirty minutes, what if you gave yourself permission to look inside and ask: How do *I* feel about being the one who always supports everyone else when they're struggling?"

Kayleigh takes a deep breath. She's quiet for a few moments as she returns to the unfamiliar terrain of her own emotions.

"Umm . . . Look, I don't know. I'm not really sure," she says.

I sense that Kayleigh is getting frustrated—for people-pleasers, trying to access our own emotions can feel like peering into a murky crystal ball—and I want her to know that this is completely normal.

"It can be hard to tune in at first. There's no rush," I encourage. "Let's just take a moment and sit with what you notice."

Kayleigh is quiet again. Ten seconds pass. Suddenly, she bursts out: "I'm sad! And tired!" Her words ring out in the silence, and she seems momentarily stunned by her own admission. "I love my family—I obviously adore my husband, and my daughter, and my parents—but it gets hard sometimes, because I'm hurting, too."

She goes on, gaining speed: "I'm scared that my parents are getting older. I'm sad that Dave and I are empty nesters now. And truthfully, I feel . . . lonely. Not physically lonely—Dave is there in the house with me—but emotionally lonely. I want to feel like someone is really *with me* in this. I hate holding it all alone."

She exhales. A tear rolls down her cheek.

By giving herself permission to tune inward, Kayleigh moved from "not knowing" her emotions to knowing, and naming, quite a few: hurt, fear, sadness, and loneliness. She gave herself permission, if only temporarily, to stop being the one who has it all together for everybody else.

Though it's painful for Kayleigh to acknowledge these difficult emotions, we can now spend the remainder of our session identifying the needs that lay beneath: emotional support to soothe the fear, companionship to soothe the loneliness. By the time the session is over, Kayleigh has made two commitments: one to share her sadness and fear with Dave so that she doesn't have to hold it alone, and another to text her two closest friends and say that she could use some company over the coming weeks.

If Kayleigh hadn't given herself permission to connect with her feelings, she wouldn't have been able to identify her needs—and she wouldn't have been able to advocate for those needs in her relationships with her loved ones.

HOW WE HIDE FROM OUR FEELINGS

People-pleasers are emotionally intelligent, deeply feeling, and highly empathic—when it comes to others. But when it comes to our own emotions, it can be hard for us to name them and even harder to actually *feel* them. After years of prioritizing others' feelings, it takes dedicated practice to come home to ourselves.

Accessing our own emotions can be especially challenging when, like Kayleigh, our caretaker impulse is activated: when someone close to us is hurting, struggling, or disappointed. Many of us learned to prioritize others' feelings during similar moments in childhood, when our own safety depended on the moods of those around us. Psychologist Tian Dayton, author of *Emotional Sobriety*, explains: "Children who are worried about their parents may become anxious little caretakers of them, constantly scanning their parents' faces and moods for what they need or want. These children may develop a habit of scanning other people's moods in order to establish their own equilibrium and balance. This interferes with developing a sense of self because our sense of self, over time, becomes enmeshed with that of another person."

As adults, many of us find ourselves in this enmeshed place, caretaking others' feelings at the expense of our own. Sometimes, overfocusing on others' emotions can also be a defense against experiencing our own feelings in all their potency. In addition to chronic caretaking, we might avoid our emotions by drinking, smoking, taking drugs, or engaging in other addictive behaviors; compulsively pursuing productivity, success, and achievement; constantly consuming TV, podcasts, and social media; or spending all our free time with other people to avoid being alone.

These habits act like roadblocks, preventing us from noticing, naming, and feeling our feelings in their totality. We deploy these defenses with good reason; many of us never learned how to self-soothe through our difficult emotions, and sometimes we worry that they will engulf us. Psychologist Hillary McBride, in her book *The Wisdom of Your Body*, explains that defenses "protect us from emotional experiences that we feel unable to tolerate alone or experiences we feel scared to move toward; they also protect us from emotions that we have been shamed or punished for feeling in the past, either by those close to us or by cultural scripts."

The first step in breaking down our defenses is to simply recognize that we're avoiding our feelings. When we notice ourselves engaging in the habits listed above, the simple question "What am I afraid to feel right now?" can offer powerful insights into the emotions that lie beneath the surface.

BEGINNING WITH THE BODY

If we struggle to identify our emotions, we can connect with them through the portal of the body. After all, our emotional experience isn't just happening in our minds—it's happening throughout our chests, stomachs, shoulders, and legs.

Unfortunately, many Western societies discount the wisdom of embodied emotions. In the seventeenth century, philosopher René Descartes popularized the theory of dualism: the idea that the mind and body are two separate entities. The body, he believed, was flawed, while the mind was perfect. It quickly became a staple of Western thought that we needed to control our primal, "unevolved" bodies with our pure, "evolved" minds.

We see this attitude today in one of the most popular defenses against our emotions: intellectualization. When we intellectualize, we put our feelings into thoughts, using reason, logic, or research to avoid the *felt experience* of the emotion within our bodies.

When I went through a painful breakup in my early twenties, I intellectualized my grief because I didn't want to feel it. I made bullet-point lists of why being single was better; I listened to podcasts about the science of healing from heartbreak; I read endless articles to understand my ex-partner's psychology. I filled every spare moment with reason and thought because being in my body and actually *feeling* my sadness felt too threatening.

Around this time, I took up a group meditation practice, hoping to find moments of relief from my heartbreak. The first session was held at an old, impressive church in Cambridge, Massachusetts. Moments after I settled onto my cushion, the meditation leader invited us through a body scan: we slowly and deliberately paid attention to every part of our bodies, one by one. I noted that my stomach was clenched; my chest was tight; my throat was closed tight in a vice grip.

"Now," invited the meditation leader, "if your body could tell you something, what would it say?"

My answer was immediate and visceral: *It. Hurts.* I burst into silent tears as the grief I'd been intellectualizing flooded me. For the first time in days, I let myself *feel* my feelings instead of trying to think them away.

It was painful. I wrapped my arms around myself as I silently cried. When the intense wave of emotion passed about five minutes later, I was surprised to find that I felt stiller and calmer than I had in days.

While intellectualizing our emotions is popular in the Western world, this is not true elsewhere. Anthropologist Roy Grinker explains in his book *Nobody's Normal: How Culture Created the Stigma of Mental Illness* that most people outside of Western industrial societies actually experience their emotional suffering through the body first and foremost: "They feel anxiety as stomach pain, sadness and hopelessness as a burning or prickling sensation in one's limbs, and so on." Despite centuries of messaging to discount the body's wisdom, those of us in Western societies *do* still feel our emotions in our bodies; we just have to learn to listen. In 2018, a team of Finnish neuroscientists set out to understand where, exactly, our emotions live in our bodies—and whether those emotional signatures were universal for everyone. They recruited over one thousand participants from various cultures and conducted experiments to gather information about their experiences of one hundred distinct feelings.

In one of the experiments, participants considered one feeling at a time and, along with a blank outline of a human body, were asked to color the areas where they sensed the feeling most. After compiling the data, the research team definitively concluded that almost every feeling was associated with a unique bodily sensation. Anger, they discovered, is felt most potently in the chest and upper body. Love and happiness are felt like a strong flood throughout the entire body, while depression is associated with a decrease in sensation overall.

Fascinatingly, these emotional signatures were reproducible among study participants from various cultures, demonstrating that, wherever we come from, we all experience emotions similarly in our bodies—and we can all use our body's cues to recognize those emotions.

How to Tune In

We can begin attuning to our embodied emotions at any time. We might pause, set our phones aside, and close our eyes, turning our attention to the interior of our bodies. Then, as I did during the group meditation, we can ask ourselves: *What feelings are these sensations communicating to me?*

We might take just thirty seconds to observe: Do we notice a clenching in the chest? A pressure in the temple? A feeling of expansiveness in the heart?

Happiness and love are often experienced as lightness in the heart, spaciousness in the chest, or a flood of energy through the body. Anxiety is often experienced as a clenched chest, racing heart, or roiling stomach. Anger often coincides with tension in the chest, constriction in the neck and shoulders, and bursts of energy through the arms and legs. Fear and excitement are often accompanied by a pounding heart and a hyperawareness of vision, sound, and scent.

We can also work backward, recognizing that we're feeling a certain emotion—say, happiness after attending a birthday party—and then connecting that feeling with our body's sensations. When we notice an emotion, Hillary McBride encourages us to ask: "What *tells* you that you are feeling that way?" She suggests paying attention to "anything that stands out, such as temperature, tightness, openness, or movement of energy (swirling, rising, pressing, weighing, undulating, sinking, etc.)."

Over time, we begin to notice common patterns in our body's responses. We may feel an expansiveness after spending time with dear friends, or a tightness in the chest before work presentations. We may notice that interactions with certain people leave us feeling warm and open, while interactions with others leave us feeling clenched and tired. The more we pay attention to our embodied experience, the more we realize that our bodies are sending us emotional information all the time; we just need to pause and listen.

INCREASING OUR TOLERANCE FOR DIFFICULT FEELINGS

If we've spent a lifetime disconnected from our emotions, sitting with our own anger, grief, sadness, resentment, or anxiety can feel scary and, at times, overwhelming. We can increase our tolerance for these difficult states by setting a time limit; offering ourselves a loving reminder; physically self-soothing; and expressing ourselves to another.

To illustrate these tools, we'll use Rava's story. Rava, thirty-six, hangs up the phone after a long, tiring conversation with her domineering mother. Typically after these calls, Rava does anything she can to distract herself: answer some emails, clean the house, or drink a glass of wine. The rest of the day tends to pass by in a blur, with Rava moving from task to task as quickly as she can to outrun her feelings. Now Rava practices increasing her tolerance for difficult emotions:

Set a Time Limit

At first, sitting with a difficult emotion for an extended period of time can be uncomfortable. Instead, try setting a timer for just two or three minutes. Sit comfortably, take a deep breath, and notice the emotion within your body. It can help to name the sensations out loud as they arise: "Clenching in my chest," "Racing in my heart," "Tightness in my temple."

Remember that during these moments, the goal is not to change the difficult emotion. The goal is to simply practice staying with your emotional experience instead of distracting, numbing, or leaving yourself behind.

Instead of reaching for the wine, Rava takes a deep breath and sets an alarm on her phone for five minutes. She sits in a chair at her kitchen table and closes her eyes, paying attention to her body. She notices anger flaring in her chest as she recalls her conversation with her mother. The anger burns brightly for a minute or two, and then gives way to a cooler, softer sensation of fatigue and sadness. She notices her temptation to stop the exercise, but gently encourages herself to stay until the timer rings.

Offer a Loving Reminder

When our difficult emotions are strong, it can be helpful to put them in context with a gentle reminder. We can soothe ourselves in the throes of anger, fear, or anxiety by offering a reassuring phrase: "I'm here with you," "I will not abandon you," "This is hard, but I am resilient," or "This feeling will not last forever."

When Rava finishes observing the sensations in her body, she realizes that she's never paused to appreciate how strongly these calls with her mother affect her. She feels a surge of self-compassion as she recognizes that she—and her body—are clearly suffering. She offers herself a loving reminder: *This emotion is painful, but I've got you. I'm not going anywhere.*

Physically Self-Soothe

Simple gestures like placing a hand on our racing heart, running our hands gently over our arms, or breathing deep into our bellies can remedy the physical intensity of our emotions. After sitting with an intense feeling, it can be helpful to discharge any residual energy through movement: stretching, going for a run, taking a walk, dancing to loud music, or even hitting a pillow like a punching bag.

After sitting with her emotions, Rava feels like she needs to discharge some of the energy flowing through her body. She changes her clothes and heads out for a short run.

Express It

As we'll discuss in the coming chapters, expressing a difficult emotion offers us a release valve; it decreases the intensity of our experience like taking air out of a balloon. We might express our difficult feelings by writing about them in our journal, talking them out with a friend, or sharing them with our therapist. We might turn them into art with a song, dance, or painting. Simply naming an emotion aloud to ourselves—"I'm so *angry* right now, I can hardly stand it!"—can help regulate us, making what we're feeling less overwhelming.

After her run, Rava decides to call her sister, Rachel, to vent about the phone call she had with her mother. Rava and Rachel are close; she knows her sister will understand her frustrations better than anyone else. They chat briefly, Rachel offering a few words of support and some sisterly humor, and when Rava hangs up, she feels less alone in her anger.

After going through these steps, Rava contrasts how she usually responds to her emotions—by burying them under emails and wine—with how she responded to them today. Normally after a call with her mother, she would feel distracted and hyperactive, with a simmering anger on the periphery that would persist for hours. Today, however, she notices that her anger flared up, but also died down—and she realizes that she befriended her emotions instead of trying to outrun them through a flurry of activity.

Through this process, she's teaching herself that she can withstand, and feel resilient toward, her own difficult feelings. In the coming chapters, we'll explore how she can take this understanding of her anger and use it to inform the needs, requests, and boundaries she expresses to her mother in future phone calls.

An Important Note on Trauma

Sitting with potent traumatic memories without the support of a therapist can overwhelm your nervous system. The practices I suggest here are for difficult emotions surrounding less intense experiences. A trauma therapist can help guide you through difficult emotions at a slow and sustainable pace to help you build tolerance for trauma-related distress.

EXERCISES FOR FINDING OUR FEELINGS

Learning to attune to our feelings is a long-term practice, not a one-time goal. We get better at it with time, intention, and repetition. Here are a few simple exercises you can include in your daily routine to strengthen your connection with your feelings:

Set an Alarm

Set an alarm to go off three times throughout the day. Each time the alarm rings, check in with yourself: *What am I feeling at this very moment?* Document your responses. If for some reason setting an alarm isn't feasible for you, you can make a habit of asking yourself this question every time you check your phone, open the refrigerator, or step outside.

This is a busy season for Audrey. Work is picking up, her three teenagers are involved in multiple extracurricular activities, and her sister needs support as she heals from an operation. In the past, Audrey would become completely disconnected from herself during busy times like this, only paying attention to others' emotions and needs. But this time, as she works to break the people-pleasing pattern, she's committed to staying present with her emotions. She sets her alarm to ring at 10:00 a.m., 2:00 p.m., and 6:00 p.m. every day.

The first few times her alarm goes off, she's taken by surprise. She's typically mid-task, and the alarm notification—*What am I feeling at this very moment?*—is jarring. Her mind is so preoccupied with others' problems that, at first, it takes her a while to find her own emotions: *Stressed. Overwhelmed. Resentful.* By acknowledging her feelings, she can get curious about what needs they may be signaling and take steps to meet those needs.

The more Audrey's alarm rings, the more quickly she finds language for her feelings. By the fourth day, she anticipates the alarm before it even goes off, asking herself at various intervals: *What am I feeling right now?* Through this practice, she becomes more skilled at acknowledging her own emotional reality—a challenging feat for a recovering people-pleaser with a busy schedule.

Use the "How Are You?" Cue

When a friend or acquaintance asks, "How are you?" pause and check in with yourself emotionally: *How am I, really?* Whether you choose to share this authentic answer with them is up to you; what matters is that you're naming it for yourself.

Take a Moment Alone

Sometimes, social situations—like spending time with a friend, going to a party, or visiting family members—can activate our people-pleasing tendencies. We're surrounded by others' emotions, others' problems, and others' energies, and it's easy to become disconnected from ourselves. The next time you're in a social situation, briefly step away—perhaps walking outside or going to the restroom—and take a moment to attune to your own emotions. Now that you're alone, notice if you have any emotions that you've been suppressing or ignoring when you're with others. Remember that you can use your body to gather information about what you're feeling, too.

Lars recently went through a divorce, and for the first time since he was married, he decides to visit his parents for the holidays. On Christmas Eve, his parents host their annual family party, the house bursting with aunts, uncles, cousins, and friends. Lars loves his extended family, but as an introvert, he finds these big gatherings overwhelming. While his parents are bringing out dessert, he manages to steal away to his childhood bedroom and gently shuts the door behind him.

After hours of socializing, smiling, and trying not to think about his divorce, Lars can finally relax his facade and simply be. He takes a deep breath and listens to his body, noticing that his shoulders are tight and his jaw clenched. Lars rubs his jaw gently, loosening the muscles there, and lets out a big sigh, allowing himself to acknowledge that, yes, he is sad about his divorce, and, yes, he does miss his ex-wife.

Though these emotions are painful, he also feels relieved as he lets himself drop the mask of people-pleasing and simply be sad. Taking physical space to allow his emotions to surface is a powerful act of self-care. Now that he is in touch with his feelings, he can listen for any messages they might be giving about what he needs in this moment.

3

DISCOVERING OUR NEEDS

Our feelings are like signposts, directing our attention to the needs that lie beneath. Happiness, peace, and pleasure can indicate that our needs are being satisfied. Difficult feelings like resentment, frustration, and overwhelm may signal that, in this moment, we're not getting what we need.

Breaking the people-pleasing pattern requires us to become comfortable identifying and tending to our own needs. After all, if we haven't taken the time to prioritize our needs ourselves, it will be immeasurably more difficult to advocate for them with others. However, many people-pleasers tend to see *need* as a dirty word: a sign of weakness or dependency. If our needs weren't appreciated by our caregivers in childhood, we may have learned to be ashamed of them, hiding behind a veil of independence and self-sufficiency. Many of us now take pride in "how little we need," preferring to pay attention to others' hardships instead. We may feel that having needs makes us high-maintenance, burdensome, or selfish.

Though we may believe that our needs are unimportant, neglecting them has ruinous impacts on our physical and mental health over time. When our requirements for rest, sustenance, and genuine connection go unmet, we become unhappy, depleted, and chronically burned-out: a state with which many people-pleasers are painfully familiar. At the extreme, our self-neglect can result in poor hygiene, physical or mental illness, or impoverishment. The consequences of neglecting our own needs can be severe, which is why needs are perhaps the most important of our five foundations.

For people-pleasers, the idea that prioritizing our own needs is selfish can be hard to shake. If you still need convincing, remember this: ironically, prioritizing ourselves enables us to become better friends, partners, and family members. Research shows that those who practice healthy selfishness—who have a healthy respect for their own needs, health, and happiness—report more positive relationships and more loving attitudes toward others. When we're depleted, we are distractable, frustrated, and fatigued; it's hard to be a caring and attentive companion when we're chronically on the brink of collapse. But when our needs are met, we can properly show up for ourselves *and* others. Learning how to prioritize our own needs is, in fact, a win-win situation.

In this chapter, we'll discuss what constitutes a need; explore how to use our feelings as messengers that point to our needs; unpack five common ways we discount our own needs; discover how to relate to our needs in new ways; and lay the groundwork for a daily practice of attuning to our needs.

NEEDS ARE ABOUT WELL-BEING, NOT JUST SURVIVAL

Many of us believe that something only counts as a need if we require it for our immediate physical survival. However, in truth, our needs are more comprehensive than this. *Merriam-Webster* defines a need as a physiological or psychological requirement for the well-being of an organism. Needs aren't just about subsistence; they're about maintaining a sense of physical and emotional well-being.

People-pleasers tend to ignore or discount needs that aren't acute or life-threatening. Even when we have the financial resources required to take care of ourselves, we may think: "My back's been giving me a lot of trouble lately, but I don't really *need* to get it looked at by the doctor," or "My depression is getting really bad, but I don't *need* therapy; I can tough it out," or "I would love if my husband showed *any* appreciation for all the housework I do, but I don't *need* it. He says he loves me and that should be good enough."

Discounting our needs has tangible negative impacts on our well-being. Physical comfort, financial security, mental health, and relational reciprocity are absolutely required to feel well, strong, and whole. They're not mere desires; they're necessities. As we break the people-pleasing pattern, we begin to believe that we are worthy of not just survival, but of living well, too.

The List of Basic Needs

Some basic needs that all people share include:

Physical Needs

- Shelter
- Food
- Clean water
- Clean air
- Sleep
- Relaxation
- Sexual touch and expression
- Medical care
- Mental health care
- Connection to the earth

Interpersonal Needs

- Community
- Acceptance
- Belonging

- Support
- Love
- Communication
- Respect
- Empathy
- Compassion
- Kindness
- Reciprocity
- Honesty
- Acknowledgment

(We'll explore a list of more specific interpersonal needs in chapter 7.)

Independence Needs

- Autonomy
- Self-worth
- To matter
- The freedom to make one's own decisions
- A sense of control over one's life

Meaning Needs

- Purpose
- Peace
- Balance
- Creativity
- Play
- Time to grieve and celebrate

I recommend bookmarking "The List of Basic Needs," as we'll refer back to it in the chapters to come.

FOLLOWING OUR NEED SIGNPOSTS

We may have spent so many years discounting our needs that now we struggle to identify what they are. As we stop people-pleasing, our work is to excavate our needs from underneath layers of other-focus. This practice becomes habitual over time, and a few strategies can support us in the process:

Begin with the Body

The simplest way to begin attuning to our needs is to start with our physical needs. Instead of relational needs, which rely on others' participation, physical needs are typically ones we can meet ourselves, which makes them a less daunting place to begin.

Daily, we might ask ourselves: *Am I cold or overheated? Do I need a sweater or blanket? Am I hungry? Is there food in my refrigerator? Do I need to go shopping? Am I thirsty? Am I tired? Do I need to rest? Am I getting enough sleep? Is my body restless? Do I need to move or go for a walk? Are my shoulders tense? Do I need to do some stretching or yoga?*

For six months, Amit has been taking care of his elderly mother as she battles late-stage Parkinson's disease. Tending to his mother's needs is physically and emotionally demanding, but Amit is happy to do it; it's important to him that his mother spends her last few months comfortably at home instead of in a senior care center.

One day, Amit's younger brother, Rohan, flies into town to relieve him. "You need a break," says Rohan. "Go take care of yourself for a few days. I've got things covered here."

Amit agrees, packing a bag and returning to his own apartment for the first time in months. But minutes after walking through the door, he feels unsettled; without his mother to care for, he has no idea what he needs.

He sits in his armchair and decides to pay attention to his body. It takes a few minutes for his mind to quiet enough for him to focus, but when he does, he recognizes a few potent sensations. First, he's cold: he forgot to turn up the thermostat when he arrived. Second, he's hungry: he can't remember the last time he sat down for a full meal. And third, beneath it all, he recognizes a bone-crushing weariness; he realizes suddenly that he hasn't slept more than four hours at a time in days.

After months of focusing entirely on his mother, Amit feels a refreshing sense of connection with himself as he acknowledges his needs this way. He gets up from his chair, turns up the thermostat, and orders takeout from the Chinese restaurant down the street. He reassures himself that tonight, his only job is to eat a full meal and sleep as deeply as he can. Now that he senses the severity of his own hunger and exhaustion, he realizes how important it will be for him carve out time—even when he's with his mother—to tend to these needs however much he can.

Meeting our basic physical needs may seem like a small thing, but by tending to these needs time and time again, we slowly increase our sense of self-trust: we learn that we can rely on ourselves to take care of ourselves in a fundamental way. From here, accessing deeper needs—like those for connection and meaning—feels more doable.

Our Feelings Are Need Signposts

Despite their unpleasantness, uncomfortable feelings are signposts that direct us toward our unmet needs. This is why learning to sit with our uncomfortable feelings is so important: only then can we hear the messages they convey.

As we sit with our uncomfortable emotions, we might learn that we feel anxious when we need more security, or depressed when we crave more community. We might notice resentment when we don't receive reciprocity in our relationships, or fatigued when we spend time with someone who drains our energy. Simply asking ourselves, *What do I need right now?* in the face of a difficult emotion is a powerful practice for attuning to our needs.

HOW WE DISCOUNT OUR NEEDS

Once we start recognizing our needs, we also start recognizing the ways we discount them. After years of settling for the bare minimum, it makes sense that bringing our needs into the light may, at first, provoke some resistance. Common ways that we discount our own needs include:

We Judge Ourselves for Having This Need

Kelly and Amma have been friends since grade school. Kelly regularly reaches out to Amma to coordinate plans, and though Amma is always willing, she never takes the initiative herself. Kelly feels insecure. She needs Amma to put effort into their relationship, but she judges herself for having this need. *Amma is always happy to spend time together, isn't she?* thinks Kelly. *I shouldn't be so sensitive.*

We Think We're "Too Strong" to Have This Need

Ever since graduating college six months ago, Marco's mental health has been struggling. His job is demanding, he feels disconnected from his college friends, and he's been fighting a lot with his partner, Cedric. Marco wants to talk to a therapist, but when the idea crosses his mind, he judges himself for weakness. *Your parents were immigrants who never complained,* he tells himself. *You're strong enough to do this on your own.*

We Use Others' Struggles to Discount Our Need

Mel and her husband, John, have been married for five years. They generally have a happy marriage, but there's one thing Mel can't stand: the way John occasionally makes jokes about her weight. Mel laughs along, but the truth is, she finds his comments terribly upsetting. When she considers addressing it with him, she thinks about her friends, one of whom is in a physically abusive relationship and the other who is struggling with dating. *At least I don't have to go through all of that,* Mel thinks. *I should feel lucky to have John at all.*

We Anticipate That Our Need Will Go Unmet

Rory works at a prestigious marketing firm. Her manager, Kenny, recently assigned her some high-profile, high-paying clients, and while Rory is excited for the opportunity, her new tasks leave her with daily questions. She would benefit from a weekly meeting with Kenny to address her uncertainties, but she knows his schedule is busy. Rory worries that if she were to ask, Kenny wouldn't have the time—so she continues to struggle with her client load in silence.

We Reject the Need as "Too Much Work"

Leena has been sleeping on the same mattress for ten years. At first it was comfortable, but over time, it has lost its firmness; she wakes with an aching back and spends the morning doing stretches to relieve the pain. A new mattress is within her budget, but at the thought of doing research, going to the store, making a selection, and having it delivered, she waves her hand. *Too much work,* she thinks. *I can just deal with it the way it is.*

YOU'RE ALLOWED TO NEED

Notice the ways you discount your own needs. What stories do you repeat about what you deserve and what you must tolerate? Do these stories sound familiar—perhaps like stories you heard from your caregivers in childhood? Do they sound like stories you heard from past partners or friends?

Often, without even realizing it, we repeat old, negative messages about our needs. If we were told in childhood that we "should just deal with it" or that we were "too sensitive," those messages can become the soundtrack of our judgments toward ourselves. Likewise, if a past partner told us that we were "overreacting" or "demanding" every time we expressed a simple need, their words may echo long after their departure.

Breaking the people-pleasing pattern requires us to rewrite these narratives. Our old stories judged, shamed, and belittled us for having needs. Our new stories will normalize our needs and celebrate us for doing the hard, necessary work of prioritizing them.

Our new stories might include:

- After many years of self-neglect, prioritizing my physical and emotional needs is how I show myself care, love, and respect.
- I am allowed to need more than just the bare minimum required to survive. I am allowed to need things that contribute to my sense of overall well-being.
- Other people's struggles do not discount the fact that I, too, have needs. Tending to my own needs does not mean that I'm dismissing others' hardships.
- Taking care of myself gives me the energy and strength I need to show up as a good friend, partner, and family member.

At first, these new stories may feel uncomfortable or downright untrue—but we don't necessarily need to believe them in order to act on them. We can ask ourselves: *If I believed this new story fully and completely, how would I act?* Our answer offers a guide for how to move forward.

As we'll explore in chapter 5, sometimes we need to act our way into a new way of feeling instead of waiting to feel our way into a new way of acting. Bit by bit, our vestiges of self-judgment are replaced with the satisfaction and self-respect that arise when we trust ourselves to prioritize our needs.

EXERCISES FOR TENDING TO OUR NEEDS

As you practice identifying your needs, consider incorporating some of these simple exercises into your daily routine:

Listen to Your Difficult Emotions

Make a list of any difficult emotions you've felt within the past week: anger, sadness, frustration, resentment, etc. For each occasion of that emotion, see if you can identify an unmet need beneath it. You can reference "The List of Basic Needs" earlier in the chapter (see page 37) to support you.

Combat Procrastination

If you have a habit of procrastinating meeting your needs, consider: *Specifically, which physical, emotional, or interpersonal needs do I regularly postpone?* Write down the needs you identify.

Your list might include things like scheduling doctor appointments, buying houseware items, getting fresh groceries, turning up the heat when it's cold, or buying seasonally appropriate clothing. From your list, pick just one need that you regularly delay and commit to prioritizing it this week.

Lorraine is a nurse at a busy hospital. After her twelve-hour shift ends, she's exhausted; she grabs some granola bars from the break room for dinner, stops on the way home for a bottle of wine, and falls asleep in front of the television still in her scrubs. On her days off, she usually helps babysit her twin sister's two young children. Lorraine genuinely loves other people and is exceptionally good at caring for them, but she struggles to invest the same energy in her own care.

The past few months, Lorraine has been feeling more and more sluggish and depleted. She senses she's on the verge of burnout. On her next day off, she considers the needs that she habitually postpones or delays. She rarely goes grocery shopping; her refrigerator is always empty. She has a backache that has gotten worse over the past few months; she needs to see her doctor. And she can't remember the last time she took a day to herself to recuperate from the busy week.

Right after compiling her list, Lorraine capitalizes on her momentum and picks up the phone to call her doctor. Once her appointment is scheduled, she feels an unfamiliar sense of pride at accomplishing a task she'd postponed. This feeling of pride is so satisfying that it motivates her to walk to the nearby grocery store and fill her refrigerator, too.

Like Lorraine, we benefit from tending to needs we've long delayed. When we procrastinate our needs, we feel a sense of broken trust with ourselves: there is something we need to do that we haven't done, which can leave us feeling self-critical and, ironically, more overwhelmed than we'd feel if we were to simply complete the task. By taking the time to meet a single need, we teach ourselves that we can take care of ourselves, which inspires us to do so even more.

Recognize Old Stories

Notice if there are any needs you feel uncomfortable admitting. Perhaps you need more affection in your romantic relationship, more rest in your busy schedule, or more time away from your friends and family. For each, ask yourself: *Why do I believe I'm not entitled to this need?* Notice if your responses echo messages you received from your caregivers early in life. Then practice replacing this old story with one of the new stories you devised earlier in the chapter.

Ever since she was a child, Maia has been sensitive to loud noises and bustling environments; they make her feel overwhelmed. Now, as a young adult, she finds that many of her friends enjoy clubbing and attending live concerts, both events that she struggles to enjoy.

When her friend Tessa suggests they go clubbing on Friday night, Maia feels insecure about telling her that she needs quieter environments. She asks herself, *Why do I believe I'm not entitled to this need?*

For Maia, the answer is obvious. When she was a little girl, she would often cry when her parents took her to loud places like the mall, a busy restaurant, or a holiday party. Instead of soothing her, Maia's parents would scoff, telling her that she was "too sensitive" and "just needed to relax." She's internalized the idea that her sensory needs aren't really *needs*; they're just undesirable aspects of herself that she needs to fix.

Now, however, she's trying to honor her needs. She replaces this old story—I'm a problem because I'm sensitive—with her new one: *I'm allowed to need more than just the bare minimum required to survive. I'm allowed to need things that contribute to my sense of overall well-being.*

Maia takes a deep breath, acknowledges the nervousness she feels, and sends Tessa a text: **Actually, I find the club overwhelming—too loud! Can we get drinks instead? Would love to be able to talk and catch up.** She is pleasantly surprised when Tessa replies: **Oh no worries! Yeah, for sure. Let's go to the place down the street.**

Track Your Progress

In your journal or phone, document the times you meet particularly challenging needs. Examples could include prioritizing a medical or dental appointment you'd been neglecting, purchasing a household item you'd been needing, or carving out time for rest amid a busy schedule. Be sure to review your list when you need a reminder of your own progress.

4

UNEARTHING OUR VALUES

Once we establish a baseline of self-care by honoring our feelings and needs, we can deepen our connection with ourselves by unearthing our values. Just like our feelings and needs, our values are alive within us, even if we've never paid them much attention before. Values are the core principles that guide our actions; they can include things like loyalty, authenticity, strength, freedom, and kindness.

People-pleasing prevents us from embodying our values because we're constantly adapting our behavior to appeal to others. We may *claim* to value honesty, assertiveness, and self-respect, but when push comes to shove, we don't have conviction; gaining others' approval feels more important than acting in our integrity.

For the recovering people-pleaser, reconnecting with our values is important for three key reasons. First, research shows that acting in accordance with our values offers us a greater sense of connection with ourselves. Second, while our feelings change based on the day, our mood, and our circumstances, our values are consistent *over time*, which makes them more reliable tools to guide our decision-making. And third, aligning our actions with our values has been shown to make stressful situations more manageable; our values help us move through bumps in the road and maintain our motivation to break the people-pleasing pattern.

Ultimately, our values are like anchors, grounding us firmly in ourselves even when our feelings, circumstances, and relationships change. In this chapter, we'll explore why values matter; distinguish group values from personal values; explore how to unearth the values we *already* practice and the values we *wish* to practice in the future; and investigate how values help us build visions for the future, make difficult decisions, and stay grounded within ourselves.

PUTTING OUR VALUES TO WORDS

We all have values, but many of us go through life without explicitly identifying them. A person who works as a school counselor and volunteers with the elderly on weekends probably values service and compassion; a person who is self-employed and lives alone might value independence, autonomy, and individuality. Our values are like points on our personal compass, illustrating what really matters to us. The list of common values below will be a reference point throughout this chapter; take note of any that resonate strongly with you.

COMMON VALUES

Acceptance	Challenge	Cooperation
Accomplishment	Charity	Courage
Accountability	Commitment	Creation
Achievement	Communication	Creativity
Adaptability	Community	Curiosity
Awareness	Compassion	Decisiveness
Balance	Confidence	Dedication
Boldness	Connection	Dependability
Bravery	Consistency	Determination
Brilliance	Contentment	Devotion
Candor	Conviction	Dignity

Discipline
Drive
Efficiency
Empathy
Endurance
Energy
Enjoyment
Enthusiasm
Equality
Fortitude
Freedom
Fun
Generosity
Grace
Gratitude
Greatness
Growth
Happiness
Harmony
Health
Honesty
Honor
Hope
Humility
Independence
Individuality
Innovation
Inspiration
Integrity
Intelligence
Joy
Justice
Kindness
Knowledge
Leadership
Learning
Liberty
Logic
Love
Moderation
Motivation
Openness
Order
Passion
Patience
Peace
Persistence
Playfulness
Poise
Power
Presence
Respect
Responsibility
Serenity
Service
Simplicity
Sincerity
Skillfulness
Solitude
Spirit
Spirituality
Stability
Status
Stewardship
Strength
Success
Tolerance
Toughness
Tranquility
Understanding
Uniqueness
Unity
Vigor
Vision
Vitality

GROUP VALUES

We can hold values at the group level and the personal level. As we break the people-pleasing pattern, we might experience some dissonance between the group values we were raised with and the personal values we're currently unearthing.

Nations, cultures, religions, organizations, communities, and even businesses have values that inform what they prioritize. The United States, for example, values independence, liberty, and freedom; Quakers value simplicity, peace, and community; Alcoholics Anonymous values recovery, unity, and service.

Families also have their own values. Some value humor; some value faith or hard work; some value aesthetics or perfection. From the moment we're born into a family or culture, we adopt their values as part of our socialization into that group. Once adopted, our values are relatively fixed over time. However, they can and do change throughout our lives, especially when we experience major life events, leave old communities, and halt old cycles of unhealthy behavior.

Unearthing Our Family Values

Many of us spent years unthinkingly embodying our family's values; they were hidden motivators driving our actions, decisions, and beliefs, often without our realizing it. Now, as we carve out an independent sense of self, we begin to see how our personal values may, in fact, be quite different.

In some families, values are made explicit with statements like "In this house, we take pride in our hard work" or "It's selfish to put your own well-being before others'." Most often, however, family values are implicit in the rules that govern the family; how family members spend their time; which actions garner praise and which garner punishment; which traits are celebrated and which are rejected; and which stories are told and retold to create a family mythology.

To help you uncover your family's values, reflect on your early years and consider: What were the most significant rules in your family? What accomplishments were given the greatest attention and praise? Who were the "heroes" and the "black sheep" in your family? What memories or stories were regularly repeated by your caregivers? For each response, see if you can unearth the implied values beneath.

Corbin's Story

Corbin, thirty, reached out to me shortly after he left the Mormon Church. He had been a devout Mormon all his life, but he'd begun to question the stricter aspects of the faith—specifically its insistence on chastity, sobriety, and traditional gender roles.

As Corbin got older and began interacting with people outside of the Church, he began to discover his own free-spirited nature. The more he got in touch with his values of individuality, open-mindedness, and exploration, the more he felt at odds with Mormonism's values of tradition, obedience, and chastity. Eventually, the tension became too much to bear, and he disaffiliated from Mormonism altogether.

This process was painful for Corbin. Disaffiliating ended some of his friendships, and he was no longer welcome in the community he'd called home his entire life. For a few months, he floated in the disorienting liminal space between the end of old connections and the beginning of new ones. (We'll talk more about this space in chapter 16.)

However, Corbin took steps to put this time to good use. When colleagues asked him out to happy hour after work, he accepted their invitations. In the spirit of open-mindedness, he attended gatherings about alternative spirituality: meditation circles, sound baths, and a plant medicine ceremony. He even went on dates with women outside the Mormon faith. Bit by bit, he began to feel a sense of self-connection as he embodied his personal values. And best of all, he no longer felt the inauthenticity that had plagued him when he feigned enthusiasm about Mormonism.

Even if we've never left a faith, many of us can relate to Corbin's story. We might feel a sense of dissonance between our group and personal values when we leave an old community, neighborhood, or workplace; move out of our hometown into a new, unfamiliar city; or begin adult life outside of our family of origin and witness new ways of living and thinking about the world.

PERSONAL VALUES

Our personal values can be divided into two categories: embodied and aspirational. Our embodied values are those we already practice on a regular basis. Our aspirational values are those we hope to practice in the future but currently lack.

Unearthing Our Embodied Values

By taking stock of our own lifestyle, habits, and relationships, we can identify our embodied values.

Review the "Common Values" list earlier in the chapter and consider the six to eight values that you practice most. To support yourself in this exercise, you might consider:

- What is your chosen line of work? What values does that imply? A teacher might value service, community, or compassion; a musician might value creativity, authenticity, or self-expression; a lawyer might value justice, prestige, or power.
- How do you spend your free time? What values do those activities imply? Someone who plays recreational sports might value play, determination, or fun; someone who gardens might value balance, stillness, or connection with the earth; someone who reads might value learning, curiosity, or solitude.
- What qualities do you embody in your relationships? What values do those qualities imply? Someone who is loving and attentive might value compassion, empathy, or love; someone who is the life of the party might value connection, humor, or adaptability; someone who is quiet and thoughtful might value introspection, understanding, or presence.
- After your baseline expenses are covered, what do you spend your money on? What values does this imply? Someone who spends money on travel might value novelty, adventure, or

exploration; someone who purchases home decor might value beauty or luxury; someone who purchases new technology might value innovation, growth, or productivity.

- What topics most pique your curiosity? What values do those topics imply? Someone who's interested in religion might value devotion, spirituality, or faith; someone who's interested in outer space might value discovery, learning, or adventure; someone who's interested in personal growth might value self-awareness, integrity, or balance.

Identifying Our Aspirational Values

Our aspirational values are those we want to embody but haven't attained yet. As we break the people-pleasing pattern, many of us are eager to begin practicing values like authenticity, self-respect, assertiveness, honesty, and integrity.

Review the "Common Values" list and consider the six to eight values that you most wish to embody in the future. For help, consider these questions:

- Imagine that it's many years in the future and you're on your deathbed, taking stock of your life. As you look back, how do you *most* want to have lived—and what values does this imply?
- Think about two people you deeply admire. What, specifically, do you most admire about them? What values do these qualities demonstrate?
- Think of a time you were willing to get into trouble or be disliked for something important to you. What was that important thing? What value(s) does this imply?

VALUES HELP US BUILD VISIONS, MAKE DECISIONS, AND STAY GROUNDED

Once we've identified our values, we can use them as tools to guide our vision, make difficult decisions, and stay grounded in our commitment to heal.

Using Values to Guide Our Vision

As we stop people-pleasing, we release old patterns for new and unfamiliar ways of being. At times, it feels like stepping into uncharted territory. Building a clear vision of what we're aiming for—and who we'd like to become—helps us find inspiration in the process.

Our values offer a strong foundation for a vision of our future self. Select one item from your aspirational values list and imagine a five-years-later version of you who fully embodies this value. Consider: What does your life look like? How do you spend your free time? How has your relationship with yourself changed? What do your relationships look and feel like? How do you navigate conflict?

Lola, a massage therapist and mother of two, aspires to *self-respect,* so she imagines a five-years-later version of herself who is fully self-respecting in all areas of her life. Future Lola's life is free and expansive. She sets clear boundaries around her work hours and raises her rate to match the value she offers. When her husband makes a comment that upsets her, she speaks up. Instead of spending all her spare time scrolling through social media, Future Lola enjoys her long-hidden passions of painting with watercolors and playing the piano.

As you go through this exercise, notice what excites you about your answers. What do you love about this future version of you? What aspects of their life do you find most inspiring?

Using Values to Make Difficult Decisions

Our values don't just help us imagine the future: they help us navigate the present. Our aspirational values offer a road map for living, pointing us in the right direction when faced with difficult decisions or unfamiliar situations.

CONSULT AN ASPIRATIONAL VALUE

When deciding how to handle a difficult situation or interaction, select one of your aspirational values and ask: *If I were to fully embody this value, how would I proceed?* Your answer may illuminate a path forward that you wouldn't have considered otherwise.

When I was first breaking the people-pleasing pattern, my friend Lori hosted a potluck so that her friends could meet Jerome, whom she'd been casually dating for six weeks. I'd known Lori for years, and I was excited to meet her new beau. It was a great meal—everyone cooked to impress—but I noticed that over dinner, Jerome made some backhanded jokes about Lori's appearance and even criticized the (delicious) dish she'd made.

I didn't say anything that night, but the next morning, I got a text from Lori. It read: **What did you think of Jerome? Be honest.** After the potluck I had major reservations, but I wasn't sure whether to be sincere and risk upsetting Lori or simply feign approval. I considered integrity—the aspirational value I'd been working hardest to embody—and asked myself: *How would I proceed with integrity?*

To me, integrity meant being honest, consistent, and acting the same way on the outside that I felt on the inside. Through this lens, it became immediately obvious that the path of greatest integrity was to offer Lori honest feedback in a loving way. I responded by saying, **To be totally honest, I didn't like the way that Jerome criticized you last night. It made me feel skeptical about whether he can give you the respect you deserve.**

Lori received my feedback appreciatively. In fact, she revealed that she'd been feeling the same way about Jerome, but had wondered if she was just being too sensitive. Had I been dishonest and said, "I loved him!" she might have second-guessed her own intuition.

CONTRAST TWO VALUES WHEELS

Alternatively, we can consider how a course of action aligns with multiple values. This can be more difficult, because different values may point us in different directions. We may find ourselves torn between generosity and balance, assertiveness and harmony, or conviction and open-mindedness. When confronted with situations like this, we can contrast two values wheels to discern which path better aligns with the majority of our values.

To illustrate this exercise, we'll use the case of Denae: a thirty-year-old woman who recently had a big argument with her older sister, Michelle. Ever since Denae was a teenager, Michelle's made judgmental comments about her lifestyle and relationships. After years of taking Michelle's snark in stride, Denae finally told her the truth about how it made her feel, and a fight ensued. The sisters haven't spoken in three months, and their annual family reunion is right around the corner.

Denae doesn't want to stomach the discomfort of being in Michelle's presence, but she worries that she'll let her family down if she skips the reunion. She decides to contrast two values wheels to see which option is most aligned with her integrity.

To contrast two values wheels, follow these steps:

1. Draw a circle and divide it into eight slices like a pizza. Write your values around the edges of each slice. This represents Decision A.
2. Create an identical circle beside it and write your values around the edges. This represents Decision B.
3. Begin with Decision A. For each value around the wheel, ask yourself: On a scale from 1 to 10—10 being the most and 1 being the least—how much does Decision A embody this value? (If your value were kindness, for example, you'd ask yourself: On a scale of 1 to 10, how much does Decision A embody kindness?)

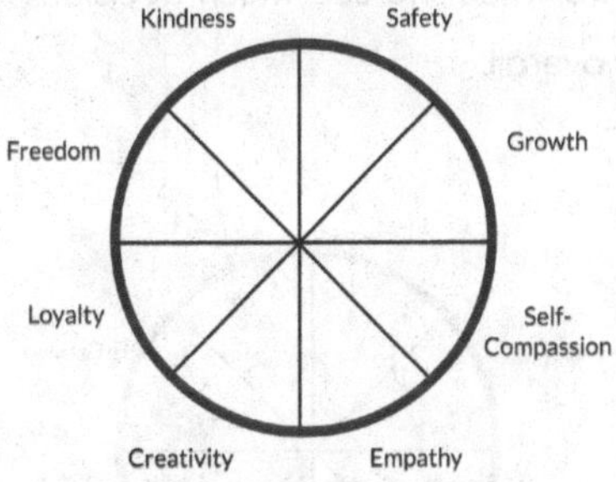

Go to the Reunion

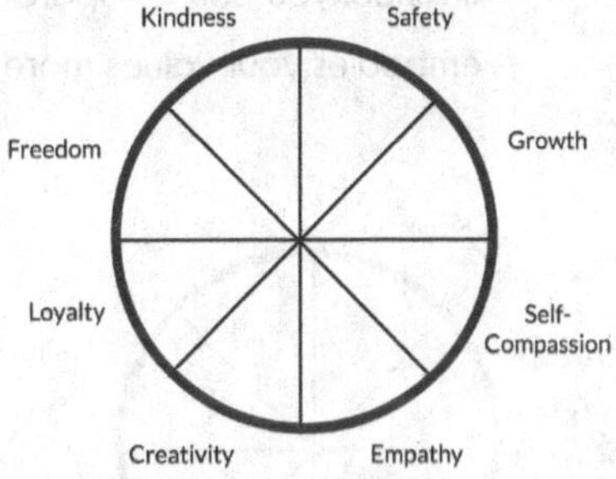

Skip the Reunion

4. Based on your answer, shade in the slice from the inside out. A ranking of 10 means the slice will be entirely filled in; a ranking of 5 means the slice is filled halfway. In the example here, kindness may have received a 9 out of 10, but safety received a 2 out of 10.

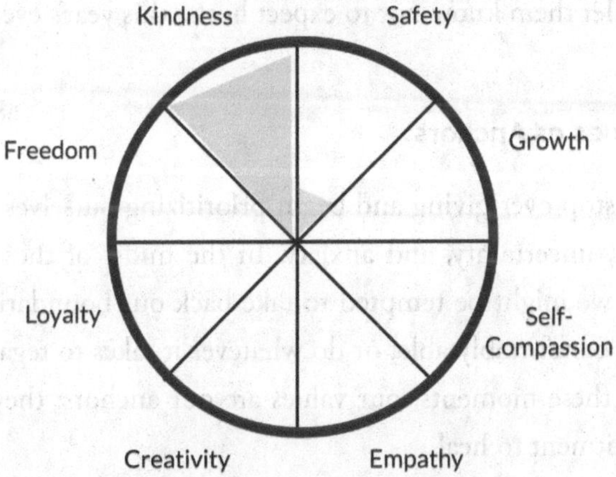

Go to the Reunion

5. Go through this process for every slice on Decision A. If you can't see how a value applies to the current decision, shade it in with lines. By the end, you will have a visual representation of to what extent Decision A embodies your values.
6. Then go through the same process for Decision B. When you've

finished, you can compare the two wheels to see which decision embodies your values more fully overall.

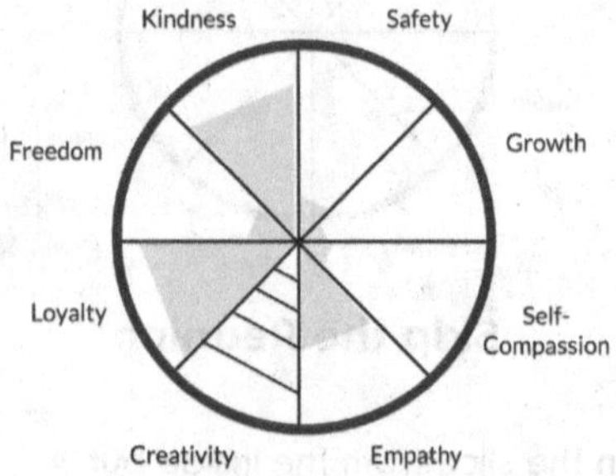

Go to the Reunion

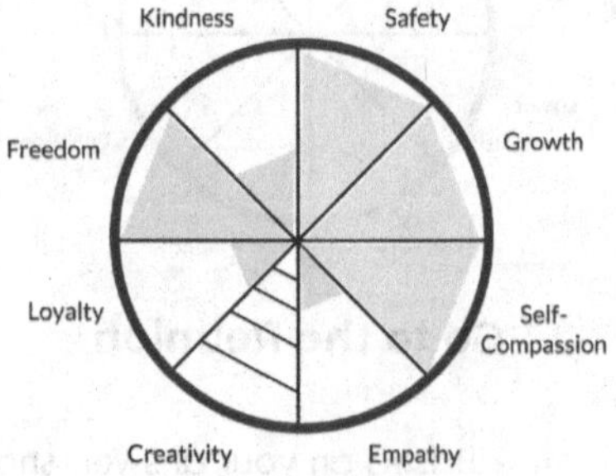

Skip the Reunion

As Denae reviews her two wheels, she sees that skipping the reunion better aligns with the majority of her values. She sends off a text to her parents to let them know not to expect her at this year's event.

Using Values as Anchors

When we stop over-giving and begin prioritizing ourselves, we may face fear, anger, uncertainty, and anxiety. In the midst of these tumultuous emotions, we might be tempted to take back our boundaries, give more than we're comfortably able, or do whatever it takes to regain others' approval. In these moments, our values are our anchors: they tether us to our commitment to heal.

Leann recently got a new job. She sets a gentle boundary with her friend Gina, telling her that she can't get together as frequently as they used to because her new position is stressful and she needs time to rest. By setting this boundary, Leann embodies her own values of honesty, balance, and integrity. Unfortunately, Gina responds poorly, and Leann leaves the conversation feeling guilty.

If Leann were judging this scenario based only on *feelings*—Gina's sadness, or her own guilt—she might conclude that she did something wrong. But difficult emotions don't always mean we made the wrong choice; in fact, they're often necessary growing pains as we break old patterns of over-giving. If Leann were to judge this same scenario based on her *values*, she would find that she acted in a manner she respects. Using our values as anchors helps us sustain our progress through moments of emotional turbulence.

EXERCISES FOR UNEARTHING OUR VALUES

As you begin unearthing your values in your daily life, consider some of these practices:

Review Your Aspirational Values Daily

Practice referring to your values to help you celebrate your progress. At the end of each day, review your list of aspirational values and ask yourself: *What's one way I embodied honesty today? What's one way I embodied bravery?* No action is too small to be counted!

Rewrite a Memory

Consider a recent situation in which you didn't embody your aspirational values. Ask yourself: *If I could rewrite this experience having fully embodied (a specific value), what would I have done instead?* Write down your answer, being specific about how you would have acted or what you would have said. Feel free to write down more than one scenario if there are multiple ways you could have handled the situation.

Jessie is eating lunch in the company break room with her colleagues Mark and Rudy. Mark begins gossiping about the office secretary, Veronika, making crude jokes about her personal life and criticizing her outfits. Uncomfortably, Jessie laughs along; she finds Mark's comments distasteful, but isn't sure what to say.

Later that night, Jessie feels frustrated with herself; she's been trying to practice integrity and wishes she'd done a better job during lunch. In her journal, she takes a moment to rewrite the experience:

Scenario 1: I'm sitting with Mark and Rudy at lunch. Mark begins making crude comments about Veronika. I feel a little bit awkward, but I say: "Come on, Mark. Veronika can wear what she likes and live how she wants. Anyway—have you guys heard anything about the new manager?"

Scenario 2: I'm sitting with Mark and Rudy at lunch. Mark begins making crude comments about Veronika. I say, "I really don't like gossiping like this. It makes me feel bad. Let's talk about something else."

Scenario 3: I'm sitting with Mark and Rudy at lunch. Mark begins making crude comments about Veronika. Instead of participating in the conversation, I stand up and say: "I think I'm going to finish this at my desk. See you guys later."

When she's done writing, Jessie reviews her three scenarios. It's helpful to see her options laid out before her; seeing them written out makes them feel less impossible to implement. Jessie knows she can't rewrite the past, but if a similar situation comes up in the future, she feels more comfortable having brainstormed how she might respond.

Envision an Upcoming Interaction

Consider an upcoming interaction that you're nervous about. It might be a conversation with your boss, an interaction with a difficult family member, or a stressful social situation. Pick one aspirational value that you'd like to embody in this situation. Then spend some time journaling: *If I were to fully embody this value during this situation, how would I act and what would I say?* Be as specific as you can in your response.

Apply Your Value Within

Take some time to explore how you can more fully embody a value in your interactions with yourself. For those of us breaking the people-pleasing pattern, this can be especially helpful when our values include generosity, empathy, compassion, kindness, acceptance, or respect. You might inquire: *What is one specific way I can bring more of this value into my interactions with myself today?*

When I was stuck in the people-pleasing pattern, I claimed to value compassion, but in truth, I only embodied it in my interactions with others. With myself, I was judgmental and impatient. I would criticize myself after making mistakes, push myself to work harder when I was already burned-out, and berate myself for not being calmer, happier, or more present.

When I asked myself how I could show myself greater compassion, I decided that when I made a mistake, I would try to speak to myself with the same grace and gentleness I'd offer a loved one. Shortly after, I was invited to be a guest on a friend's podcast. The day we recorded it, I hadn't slept well and my brain was foggy. I struggled to find my words and I botched my explanation of a few important ideas. Overall, it was a mediocre showing. When I shut my laptop, the habitual self-judgment kicked in: "You were so sluggish on that podcast! You should have done better. Nobody will want to work with you after listening to that!"

During that *very* recording, my friend and I had discussed the importance of embodying our values. I recalled my intention to show myself compassion, and instead of beating myself up, I spoke to myself the way I'd speak to a friend. I said aloud: "You're usually sharp and lively for podcast appearances. This one was an outlier; you didn't sleep well and you were tired. It's okay. Nobody shows up perfectly all the time."

This was such a departure from how I usually spoke to myself that it took me by surprise. It didn't completely eliminate my self-judgment, but it significantly turned down the volume on my critical inner monologue. The more I practiced speaking to myself kindly after making mistakes, the more habitual it became, and the more I began to believe that I was worthy of my own self-compassion.

5

UPDATING OUR SELF-CONCEPT

While our values are the principles that guide our actions, our self-concept is our sense of identity: how we feel about ourselves, what we believe we're capable of, and what we believe we deserve. Sometimes, our self-concept is conscious; sometimes, it's hidden beneath the surface. We may believe we're too much or not enough; high achievers or slackers; lazy or passionate; good or bad. Importantly, our self-concept isn't necessarily *factual*; it's the compilation of messages we received about ourselves from our caretakers and other close relations in childhood. As children, we don't yet have the ability to evaluate or question these messages, so we internalize them as the truth.

Even when we're not aware of it, our self-concept is powerful because it influences our decisions and restricts our sense of what's possible. We avoid taking actions that don't align with our self-concept: someone who believes they're a slacker will avoid studying for a test, and someone who believes they're a people-pleaser will avoid setting boundaries or speaking up. For this reason, breaking the people-pleasing pattern requires us to update our self-concept as we release old identities of "too much," "over-giver," "chronic caretaker," and "peacekeeper" and adopt new identities of "authentic," "self-respecting," and "worthy of love." As we begin advocating for ourselves, we're not just learning new habits, we're learning new identities. And, in a cyclical way, those new identities make our new habits even easier.

In this chapter, we'll discuss why our self-concept matters; explore how to uncover it; and undertake a step-by-step plan for expanding our self-concept as we break the people-pleasing pattern.

WHY OUR SELF-CONCEPT MATTERS

According to psychologists Raymond Bergner and James Holmes, our self-concept affects us in three major ways:

1. **It limits our behavior.** For example: If we believe we are unlovable, we will act in ways that reflect our own perceived unlovability.
2. **It renders certain actions unthinkable as things we *would never* or *could never* do.** For example: "I could never leave this relationship" or "I'll never have the strength to stand up for myself."
3. **It's the lens through which we see the world.** For example: if we believe we're unlovable, we will interpret breakups as evidence of our unlovability or reject loving advances as "too good to be true."

A stable self-concept—in other words, a stable and consistent sense of who we are—is critical to our functioning in the world. In fact, we subconsciously resist changes to our self-concept because of our psychological need for consistency. Due to this inner need for consistency, we tend to prefer others to see us as we see ourselves, *even in areas where we see ourselves negatively*. To illustrate the point: if you believe that you are unlovable, you may—consciously or not—seek a partner who feels similarly toward you and reinforces your self-concept. This phenomenon is called the self-verification theory: we structure our reality to align with our beliefs about who we are and how the world operates.

Developing a more positive self-concept has a host of benefits. It enhances our relationships with ourselves, expands the actions available to us, and offers a more self-loving lens through which to view the world. When we feel more positively toward ourselves, we're also able to receive *others'* care, love, and respect.

FIVE STEPS TO UPDATE OUR SELF-CONCEPT

As we break the people-pleasing pattern, we update our self-concept. We're no longer "the over-giver" or "the pushover." We are boundary-setters. We are self-respecting. We are assertive, confident, and strong.

Luckily, our self-concepts are malleable; we can update them over time with intention and incremental shifts to our behavior. We update our self-concept by:

1. Collecting evidence of change
2. Identifying our existing negative stories
3. Illuminating alternative stories
4. Finding data to support those alternative stories
5. Taking action to *live into* our new self-concept

To illustrate these steps, we'll use the case of Chelsea, forty-five, who has been a people-pleaser for as long as she can remember. Growing up in a volatile household with an angry father, she learned that being quiet and passive was the ticket to staying safe. She spent most of her adulthood married to a manipulative man named Brian, whom she left six months ago. Chelsea feels shame that she stayed in her marriage for as long as she did. She wants desperately to become her own best advocate, but worries that she's destined to be a people-pleaser forever.

STEP 1: COLLECT EVIDENCE OF CHANGE

Research shows that the most important prerequisite for changing our self-concept is being willing to believe that we can change. If we've played the role of caregiver or pushover for decades, it can be challenging to believe that we're capable of acting in new ways; becoming more assertive may feel light-years away from where we are now. The good news is, when we're struggling to believe that we can change, we don't need to magically manifest that belief into being: we can trust the evidence of our lived experience.

If you're reading this book, there's no doubt that you've experienced major changes in your life. You've soldiered through hardships; made difficult but important decisions; weathered challenging losses; changed your lifestyle; or broken old habits. And despite those challenges, you're still here, reading these words, moving forward.

Bottom line? You already have evidence that you are capable of important changes.

Cull your past and write down ways that you have positively changed over time. These changes don't have to be related to people-pleasing specifically. You might note if you've broken an old habit; released an old addiction or compulsion; left a toxic relationship; changed your lifestyle (e.g., how you eat or how you spend money); gotten through a transition like relocating to a new city, integrating into a new community, or starting at a new job; taken on a new role in a family or a company; or adjusted how you show up in the world (e.g., became more generous, assertive, confident, or authentic).

Chelsea considers the ways she's changed throughout her life. Most obviously, she left her husband six months ago, something that, years ago, she was certain she'd never have the strength to do. She's also experienced professional changes: at her company, she worked her way up from assistant to project manager, and then from project manager to assistant director. The more she reflects, the more changes come to mind: she stopped biting her nails when she was twenty-one, a habit she'd had since childhood, and she moved to a new city after graduating college, too.

Chelsea doesn't usually think about her life from this zoomed-out perspective, but as she reviews the changes she wrote down, she feels an unfamiliar sense of pride. In truth, she *has* been through a lot; she's weathered difficult changes before.

Like Chelsea, you can reference these memories when you feel pessimistic about your potential for change. Remember what your life looked like before and after you made these changes. Remember the false starts and stops; remember that it took time; remember that, eventually, you made it through. When the critical voice says, "You could never change!" rebut it confidently with this evidence.

STEP 2: IDENTIFY NEGATIVE STORIES

We can't update our self-concept without first becoming aware of the negative stories we currently hold about ourselves. When you think about breaking the people-pleasing pattern, what cynical attitudes toward yourself could get in the way? These might include judgments of your character, doubts about your ability to change, or concerns about your work ethic.

Write down any self-doubting or judgmental beliefs you uncover. These prompts might help you fill in the blanks: "I'm too ________ to break the people-pleasing pattern," "I'm not ________ enough to break the people-pleasing pattern," "I could never ________," or "I'm too ________ to change."

Once we've identified these attitudes, we can begin rewriting them in our favor.

Chelsea considers the judgments she holds toward herself and writes down: *I'm a pushover. I could never speak up for myself. I care too much about others' opinions to put myself first.*

STEPS 3 AND 4: ILLUMINATE POSITIVE ALTERNATIVES AND FIND DATA TO SUPPORT THEM

For each negative story you listed in the prior section, identify the positive alternative. For example, "I am uninteresting" becomes "I am interesting." You don't need to believe these positive alternatives right away; just write them down so you can see them clearly.

For example:

NEGATIVE STORY	POSITIVE STORY
I'm a bad friend.	I'm a good friend.
Deep down, I'm a bad person.	Deep down, I'm a good person.
I am ruled by my trauma.	I'm capable of self-soothing and helping myself to feel safe.
I'm not strong enough to change.	I'm strong enough to change.
I'm not confident enough to stand up for myself.	I am confident enough to stand up for myself.

Chelsea considers her stories and comes up with these positive alternatives:

NEGATIVE STORY	POSITIVE STORY
I'm a pushover.	I am assertive.
I could never speak up for myself.	I can, and do, speak up for myself.
I care too much about others' opinions to put myself first.	Others' opinions do not rule my life or my decisions.

For Chelsea, these positive stories feel difficult to name. They feel so distant, so *untrue*, that she resists writing them in her journal.

Though this resistance is common for many of us, it's likely that there have been many moments we've embodied these positive stories; we just don't remember them. This is because our minds use three methods—selective attention, selective memory, and selective interpretation—to disregard evidence that would challenge our self-concepts. For example:

If I believe that I'm a bad student, I will pay attention when my teacher scolds me for talking in class, but ignore my teacher's praise for answering a question correctly (selective attention). I'll remember the two times I failed assignments instead of the fact that I got an A in the course overall (selective memory). I might also assume my professor is "just being nice" when she compliments my performance in class (selective interpretation).

To counteract our habit to recall only one side of the story, social psychologists Hazel Markus and Elissa Wurf recommend gathering empirical evidence: specific memories of times we've embodied our positive stories in the past.

Compiling Your Evidence

As Chelsea works on believing the new story that she "can, and does, speak up for herself," she tries to remember times she spoke up in different contexts: at work, with friends, with family, on the subway, with the mailman. No memory is too small.

Chelsea's evidence might include the time that she told the barista her order was wrong, or the time she corrected someone who mispronounced her name. Perhaps she has a distant memory of standing up for herself on the playground when she was five years old. It doesn't matter if it's an old memory; it goes into the evidence pile, too.

At this stage, some of us may feel like we have *no* memories of embodying our positive alternatives. Often, this is due to the selective memory defense described above: we tend not to recall instances that don't align with our old self-concept. For this reason, it can help to elicit feedback from trusted loved ones who have a more objective view. We might text our best friends or family members and ask: "Hey, can you recall a time—no matter how small—that I acted confidently or stood up for myself in some way?"

We might also identify a few positive memories, but feel tempted to write them off as "flukes," "accidents," or owing to circumstances outside of our control. But it doesn't matter if it was a fluke; it doesn't matter if it only happened once; it doesn't matter if we did it then, but struggle to believe we could do it now. This evidence proves that these new ways of being aren't "something we could never do," but something we've *already done.*

Chelsea sits with her journal as her mind wanders through her past, looking for any memories of self-advocacy she can find. It takes a while, but eventually, she comes up with the following list: *It took me a while, but I eventually did leave Brian. In third grade, I told the class bully that she was being mean to my best friend. Last year, I asked for a refund when the jewelry I'd ordered fell apart a week later. And earlier this year, I said yes when my boss asked if my workload was too heavy.*

Chelsea reviews her list. It's satisfying, but she wishes it were longer, so she texts her sister, Annalise, and asks if she has any memories to add. Annalise replies, **"Yeah, I've got a few. . . . What about that time in high school when you stood up for me with Dad when I came home after curfew? He was scary that night, but you protected me. . . . You've also said no to people who have asked you on dates since you and Brian split. I'll think of more."**

Chelsea had completely forgotten the night Annalise is referring to; she adds it to her list. Saying no to dates hadn't crossed her mind as a form of speaking up for herself, but she realizes Annalise is right; she could have just as easily said yes to please the men who asked. She adds that to her list as well.

Like Chelsea, we should take note of every recollection we can. By referencing these data points, *no matter how few,* we give ourselves the evidence we need to believe that we are capable of these positive behaviors. We can do them again because we've done them before.

STEP 5: TAKE OPPOSITE ACTION

Now that we've identified our positive stories and affirmed for ourselves that they're possible, it's time to live into this new way of being. In dialectical behavioral therapy (DBT), a key coping skill is *taking opposite action*: choosing to do the opposite of what our difficult emotions tell us to do. When we feel shame, for example, we might typically self-isolate or treat ourselves cruelly—so taking opposite action might look like connecting with friends, taking a bubble bath, or cooking ourselves a nice meal. Opposite action is a tool that we can use to step into our new, positive stories.

First, Identify Negative Action

First, we can reflect on how we act when we believe that our negative stories are true. For example: *When I believe I am uninteresting, I don't speak up at gatherings or parties. When I believe I'm a bad friend, I don't return my friends texts or calls. When I believe that, deep down, I am bad, I constantly work harder to prove that I'm good enough.* It's easy to see how our negative actions simply reinforce our existing negative beliefs.

Chelsea assesses her own negative stories and corresponding actions. She writes, *When I believe I'm a pushover, I don't bother making suggestions or speaking up when I'm with other people; I let them take the lead. When I believe I could never speak up for myself, I don't express my opinions about even the simplest things, like whether I like certain music, decor, or food. When I believe I care too much about others' opinions to put myself first, I don't even take the time to imagine what I would do, say, or pursue if I were putting myself first.*

Then, Identify Opposite Action

Next, we can consider what taking opposite action would look like: doing the opposite of what our negative beliefs and emotions are telling us to do. For example: *When I believe that I am uninteresting, I don't speak up at gatherings or parties, so taking opposite action looks like sharing a story at a dinner party.* Regularly taking opposite action helps us live into our new, positive self-concept.

Chelsea determines what opposite action would look like for each of her negative stories:

NEGATIVE STORY	CORRESPONDING ACTION	OPPOSITE ACTION	POSITIVE STORY
I'm a pushover.	I don't bother making suggestions when I spend time with other people; I let them take the lead.	When I'm planning to spend time with others, I make a suggestion of what we could do or where we could go together.	I am assertive.
I could never speak up for myself.	I don't express my opinions about even the simplest things, like whether I like certain music, decor, or food.	When a conversation about music, decor, or food arises, I express my honest opinion.	I can, and do, speak up for myself.
I care too much about others' opinions to put myself first.	I don't even take the time to imagine what I would do, say, or pursue if I were putting myself first.	I carve out time to journal about my own wants and dreams.	Others' opinions do not rule my life or my decisions.

As we explored in chapter 2, many of us make the mistake of trying to feel into a new way of acting instead of acting into a new way of feeling. Psychologist and philosopher William James wrote that "action seems to follow feeling, but really action and feeling go together; and by regulating the action, which is under the more direct control of the will, we can indirectly regulate the feeling, which is not."

We don't need to wait to feel perfectly confident in our positive stories before taking actions to support them. The items on our list of opposite actions are simple, clear steps we can take regardless of how we're feeling in the moment. With time, building a repertoire of small, self-loving actions will make identifying with our positive stories easier.

Notice when you act in accordance with your positive stories. Take note of it somewhere accessible, like in your journal or on your phone.

When you feel discouraged, review this list of actions for evidence that change is, indeed, possible.

EXERCISES TO LIVE INTO OUR UPDATED SELF-CONCEPT

As you slowly begin to shift your self-concept, these practices can help you stay grounded and motivated:

Shift How You Describe Yourself

Pay attention to how you talk about yourself with others. Notice self-deprecating comments like "Well, you know what a pushover I am," or "Gosh, I could never speak up that way!" and consider swapping out your typical description with your new, positive story. It could be as simple as replacing "You know how bad I am at assertiveness!" with "I'm really working on speaking up for myself these days."

Seek Feedback from Trusted Friends

Sometimes the people closest to us see us more clearly than we see ourselves. This includes seeing our most beautiful qualities when we cannot. Invite a small group of trusted friends to send you a list of five adjectives that describe you. Take note of which descriptors reflect your positive stories—and which descriptors surprise or delight you—and ask your friends which of your actions lead them to see you this way.

Celebrate Your Efforts

Before bed, make a list of the ways you embodied your positive stories that day. Remember: no action is too small. Continue this practice for one month, keeping all your lists in the same notebook or document. Then schedule some time to read through them. Note all the evidence that you are slowly living into your new self-concept.

Chelsea creates a note on her phone where she jots down all the moments she embodies her positive stories. At first, she feels silly documenting things like "Suggested to Annalise that we try a new restaurant" and "Negotiated a lower price for the tomatoes at the farmers' market." But as the days pass, the list grows longer. Some days, she can't think of anything to add; some days, she adds significant items like "Told Brian's lawyer I wouldn't settle for such a low alimony payment."

At the end of the month, Chelsea sets aside a Sunday morning to review her list over coffee. When she opens the note, she feels a twinge of pride at how long it has grown. Her positive story that she is someone who speaks up for herself no longer feels like a distant possibility; now it feels closer to the truth.

Channel a Role Model

Identify a role model who fully embodies one of your positive stories. Perhaps you're trying to embody more peace, so you consider Gandhi; perhaps you're trying to channel fearlessness, so you pick Beyoncé or Malala. Throughout the course of your day, channel your role model through your actions. You might ask yourself: *How would they act in this situation? How would they spend their time? How would they handle this conflict?* Let your answers show you unexpected paths forward.

6

ALLOWING OUR WANTS

As we acknowledge our feelings, tend to our needs, unearth our values, and update our self-concept, our self-esteem gradually increases. We are learning to value ourselves as whole beings, which includes allowing ourselves not only to need, but also to *want*: allowing ourselves to believe we are worthy of more than just the bare minimum from life.

Many of us don't take our wants seriously because they're not as urgent as our needs, but for the recovering people-pleaser, wants are incredibly important. Our desires are a manifestation of our unique identities; they're a way to reconnect with ourselves after years spent overidentifying with other people. While we all share the same basic needs, our wants are colored by our own passions, tastes, hobbies, and pleasures. For the recovering people-pleaser, wants aren't superfluous whims; they're steppingstones to an independent sense of self.

When we identify and pursue our desires, our lives become richer, broader, and more pleasurable. In this chapter, we'll explore how to discover our own wants after years of prioritizing others'; how to change our relationship with the very idea of wanting; and how to begin incorporating our wants into our daily lives.

SKIMMING THE SURFACE OF WANT

There are as many types of wants as there are grains of sand; it would be impossible to name them all. Our wants may be material (for objects or possessions); interpersonal (for qualities we want in our relationships); temporal (for how we wish to spend our time); physical (for how we want our bodies to feel—our desires for food, drink, touch, massage, sex); emotional (for how we want to feel); aesthetic (for how we want things to look); spiritual (for a sense of connection with a faith, the universe, or a deity); or purpose-related (for how we wish to contribute to the world or attain a sense of meaning), to name a few.

It's normal to have different relationships with different types of desires. Some of us are comfortable naming our physical wants, but struggle to identify our emotional wants. Some of us can name all of our wants rather easily, but feel ashamed to admit them to others.

In childhood, many of us expressed our desires to caregivers only to be ignored, judged, or shamed. As a result, many of us learned that wanting made us selfish or unlovable, and we learned to disavow our desires as a means of staying safe. Now, as adults, some of us know our wants, but are afraid to admit them; some of us don't know what we want at all. Instead of pursuing our own desires, we often pursue others' desires because we know in advance that they will approve.

Perhaps our colleagues like going out for Thai food, so we go out for Thai food. Perhaps our lovers enjoy sports, so we learn the names of all the teams. Adopting others' wants isn't necessarily a bad thing—healthy relationships involve expressing interest in each other's passions—but sometimes we lose sight of our own wants in the process. When our lives are built entirely around others' hobbies and interests, we begin to feel disconnected from our own desires, and subsequently, from ourselves.

Perhaps you enjoy Thai food, but you *really* want Mexican food. Perhaps you enjoy sports, but you *most* enjoy spending time in the garden. As we break the people-pleasing pattern, we begin to understand that having differing wants from the people in our life isn't a bad thing; in fact, it adds diversity and color to our interactions with friends and loved ones. Naming and allowing these small wants is a way to honor ourselves and teach ourselves that we matter.

THREE PRACTICES TO UNEARTH OUR WANTS

At first, trying to identify our wants can feel like looking into a void; we have no idea where to begin. The following exercises are designed to help us circumvent fear, look within, and unearth the desires that await us there. In the next section, we'll explore how to take the wants we uncover and actualize them in our daily lives.

To illustrate these practices, we'll use the case of Sarah. Sarah, thirty-nine, is a stay-at-home mother of three and an active member of her church. She and her husband, Gregory, were childhood friends; they grew up in the same town and decided to raise their family there. As much as Sarah enjoys being deeply rooted in her community, she feels stifled by the way her days feel predetermined as a mother, churchgoer, and member of her community. She spends so much time caring for others that she doesn't actually know what she, herself, wants.

Imagine a World of Complete Acceptance

Many of us learned to assimilate others' interests as our own in order to find acceptance and belonging. We may fear that admitting our own wants will result in being judged or ostracized. This fear can shield our desires from view and make them hard to identify. We can outmaneuver our fear with a visioning exercise designed to temporarily disable the people-pleasing pattern.

Imagine that you wake up tomorrow and the world is exactly the same, but for one key difference: every person in your life greets *every single thing* you say, do, decide, and suggest with complete and sincere enthusiasm. The rule of law still applies, and illegal or violent activities aren't allowed, but otherwise, the world is your oyster. In this world, you could suggest to your seafood-hating partner that you go out for fish and chips, and his response would be an enthusiastic "Sounds great!" In this world, you could invite ten friends to a potluck movie night, and all ten would be thrilled by whatever dish you cooked and whatever movie you selected.

This is a world where your wants can roam free, unshackled from the chains of people-pleasing, because everyone here is guaranteed to be thrilled by your choices.

If you woke up tomorrow in this world, what wants would you pursue? How would you spend your free time? What activities would you suggest to others? Notice how certain wants peek out from beneath the veil of fear when they're protected from the threat of others' judgment.

Sarah sits down with her journal. At first, she draws a blank, but she encourages herself to sit with the exercise and see what arises. Eventually, she writes: *Go hiking.* Her husband, Gregory, doesn't enjoy outdoor activities, and it would be difficult to wrangle all three kids for a Saturday hike. However, Sarah misses nature; she spent a lot of time hiking as a teenager and craves that connection with the earth.

Quickly, other wants begin pouring in. Sarah sheepishly writes: *Quit the church choir.* Her father is the director of the choir, and she would feel terribly guilty about quitting—but in this daydream of total approval, she can admit that she no longer finds this commitment enjoyable.

Finally, she writes: *Take a trip to Italy.* Ever since she was a young girl, she daydreamed about the canals of Venice and overflowing plates of Sicilian pasta.

Like Sarah, take note of whatever wants you uncover here, big or small.

Use Envy as a Guide

We experience envy when we want what someone else has, be it their qualities, achievements, possessions, or lifestyle. Envy can offer us a glimpse of our unacknowledged desires; we may not even be aware that we want something until envy rears its head. In this way, envy can be an illuminating teacher, helping us voice wants we've never named. (Research shows that envy can also be a powerful propeller for change, motivating us to improve our circumstances and attain our deeply held desires.)

Take a moment to assess your life. Are there any people you envy? What do they have that you want? Do you want their personality traits? Possessions? Intimate relationships? Career? Hobbies? Social circle? Lifestyle?

Write down what what you envy, being as specific as you can. Your answers are arrows pointing toward your own desires.

Continuing with her journaling, the first person who comes to Sarah's mind is a woman from church, Maggie. Maggie leads a fascinating life: she is unmarried, with no children, and regularly misses church because she's traveling somewhere for work. When she's in town, she attends plays and concerts and even goes square dancing at the community center. Maggie speaks with a confidence that Sarah can only imagine, and sometimes, she finds herself wishing that she could be more like her.

Sarah wouldn't trade her husband and kids for anything—she loves them immensely—but this exercise helps her realize that she craves more freedom, adventure, and novelty in her daily life.

Let Yourself Daydream

Giving ourselves permission to daydream is a low-stakes way to get familiar with wanting, even if we don't end up pursuing what we've dreamed of. When we daydream, the constrictions of normal life don't apply, and this offers us fertile ground for inner exploration. Use the following prompts as kindling to ignite a daydream and write down the wants you unearth:

- Imagine that you wake up tomorrow and find yourself in a brand-new world. In this world, your wants are flourishing; your entire day is organized not by your work and obligations, but by your desires and joys. What would this world be like? How would you spend your time? Be specific.

- Imagine that you wake up tomorrow and discover you won the lottery. You have $10 million to spend however you please, with one simple caveat: you're not allowed to spend the money on anyone else. How would you spend your winnings?
- Imagine that you wake up tomorrow and find yourself in the body of a person you've always envied. For one day, you get to live their life as them. What parts of the day do you find most enjoyable? What parts of the day do you wish you could relive again and again?

Sarah completes her journaling by imagining she won the lottery. She and her husband are in good financial shape—Gregory's job affords them a comfortable lifestyle—but having $10 million in the bank would open so many possibilities. Right away, Sarah writes: *Travel. Hire a sitter more often so Gregory and I can go out and have fun without the kids. Go out to dinner at new restaurants.*

As Sarah reflects on her responses to the three practices, she identifies some common threads. She truly craves adventure and novelty; she wants to occasionally break free from the confines of her daily life and go hiking, try new restaurants, and have date nights with Gregory. As much as she loves her church community, she also wants to decrease her involvement there so that she has more time for local arts and cultural events.

Before, Sarah hadn't even admitted these wants to herself. It was far easier to become involved in the church's wants, Gregory's wants, and her children's wants. But now she realizes that a world of her own is demanding her attention.

BRINGING OUR WANTS TO LIFE

Once we've acknowledged our desires, we're halfway there. Now it's time to pursue them. Some wants we can meet on our own; we just need to give ourselves permission to do so. Some are interpersonal and require others' participation; we just need to ask. For now, we'll focus on the wants that we can meet ourselves. In chapter 8, we'll explore how to make requests around our interpersonal wants.

Gather the many desires—big and small, life-changing and lighthearted—you've written down throughout this chapter. From here, our work is to begin bringing them to life.

Scaling the Wants Ladder

We can prepare to pursue our wants by creating a Wants Ladder: a tool that organizes our desires from easiest to hardest to attain. The bottom of the ladder contains our low-hanging fruit: the wants that we can meet simply, with just a tiny bit of intention. The top of the ladder is reserved for wants that are logistically or emotionally difficult to attain. For example:

WANTS LADDER						
I want to take a hot bath.	I want to buy a new book.	I want to feel more connected to my spirituality on a daily basis.	I want to get a massage.	I want more social connection in my life.	I want to travel to Europe for a few weeks.	I want to quit my job and get a new one.

Break down every item on your ladder into the specific steps required to bring it to life. To get a massage, for example, you may need to research local massage therapists online, select the one you'd like, check your calendar, call to schedule an appointment, set up childcare, and arrange transportation to get there.

Research shows that breaking down our larger goals into subgoals gives us a sense that our goal is attainable and increases our motivation. Having a step-by-step road map transforms our desires from vague, fuzzy ideas into clear, concrete plans.

From here, we can hold ourselves accountable by setting an intention based on our Wants Ladder. We might ask ourselves: *Today, can I commit to climbing the lowest rung of my ladder? If not today, can I do it this week? How many wants on my ladder can I commit to attaining before the end of the year? Can I devote fifteen minutes each day to prioritizing the next want on my ladder?*

The best goals will push us to the edge of our comfort zone while acknowledging that we can't rewrite our relationship to wanting all at once. At first, it might feel silly to apply discipline and organization to our desires for a new book or hot bath. But by investing this effort into our wants, we show ourselves that they—and by extension, that *we*—matter.

Sarah's Wants Ladder looks like this:

WANTS LADDER						
I want to go for a hike.	I want to attend a local concert.	I want to hire a sitter and plan a date night with Gregory.	I want to go on a kid-free weekend trip with my girlfriends.	I want to hire a life coach who can help me practice building confidence.	I want to quit the church choir.	I want to travel to Italy.

To hold herself accountable, Sarah sets the goals of fitting in a hike before the end of the month and attaining the first four wants on her ladder by the end of the year.

UNCOVERING HIDDEN BELIEFS ABOUT WANTING

Some of us just can't seem to shake the feeling that wanting is shameful, selfish, or superfluous. Understanding what we were taught about wanting as children can help us understand, and have compassion for, our difficulty honoring our wants today.

To uncover your hidden beliefs about wanting, you might explore the following in your journal:

- How did your caregivers relate to wanting? Did they express their wants? If so, how did they express them?

- Did your caregivers honor their own wants as valid, or discount them as "unnecessary," "silly," or otherwise unreasonable?
- How did your caregivers respond to one another's wants? Were they supported and encouraged? Or were they dismissed?
- Did limited financial or material resources prevent those in your household from acknowledging or attaining their wants?
- When you expressed a want as a child, how did your caregivers respond?

Your answers to these questions illuminate the origins of your own relationship with wanting. We may look back and realize that we internalized beliefs like: *My wants don't matter as much as others' wants. When two people's wants are in conflict, it's my responsibility to table my own wants and put the others' first. If I express a want, it will be ridiculed, so it's safer not to have any wants at all. If I express a want, it means I'm not grateful for what I already have. My basic needs matter, but my wants don't.* And so on.

Sarah remembers that when she was a child, her mother didn't have any interests or hobbies outside the home; she made her children and the church her entire world. Now part of Sarah believes that it's selfish, as a mother and a wife, to want things that have nothing to do with her children or spouse. The messages she's heard in church have reinforced the idea that she should be satisfied to have happy children and a happy husband, and that anything else is an unnecessary luxury. Sarah can see how she's followed in her mother's footsteps, and while she's generally happy with her life, she's beginning to recognize that she isn't completely satisfied.

Writing a New Story of Want

As we break the people-pleasing pattern, we can write a new story that normalizes our wants and celebrates us for doing the hard work of prioritizing them. Our new stories might include things like *I am allowed to want more than just the bare minimum from life. My desires are a manifestation of my unique identity, and by making time for them, I become more connected to myself.* Or, *I'm allowed to have wants that are different from others' wants.*

Sarah considers her new story and writes the following: *Mothers and wives are allowed to want things, too. In fact, allowing myself to pursue my desires might make me a better role model to my children and a better spouse to Gregory. By making more time to honor my wants, I'll become more connected to my own sense of self and sense of adventure.*

Consider the new story that most resonates with you. The more time you carve out for your wants, the more genuine—and more motivating—your story will feel.

THE FEAR OF WANTING

Some of us learned not to want because, somehow, what we wanted always evaded us. To protect ourselves from the heartache of disappointment, many of us disconnected entirely from our desires, believing it was safer not to want at all.

As we access our desires using the practices in this chapter, we may notice that we begin to feel grief for the many years we spent disconnected from the life force of our own wanting; for our younger selves who learned it wasn't safe to want; and for the years we spent believing that we weren't worthy of wanting anything at all. This grief, though painful, is a sign of healing. It's a sign that we're beginning to see ourselves as worthy of more than just the bare minimum.

We may also notice fear, because when we finally give ourselves permission to want, we become vulnerable to the possibility of not getting it. For this reason, acknowledging our wants is a deeply courageous act. As we break the people-pleasing pattern, we become willing to risk that disappointment because we crave the joy of an embodied, hungry, and desiring life.

EXERCISES FOR ALLOWING OUR WANTS

As you practice discovering and allowing your wants, consider exploring these exercises:

Challenge Yourself to Want Something Unfamiliar

Earlier in this chapter, we observed several categories of want: material, interpersonal, temporal, physical, emotional, aesthetic, spiritual, and purpose. Certain categories may feel easier for you to acknowledge than others. Identify the category that feels most difficult to access, and try your best to discern three small wants you have within that category. If you can, commit to attaining at least one of those wants by week's end.

For me, material wants had always been the hardest to access. When I was on a strict budget in college, not wanting wasn't a problem—it was an asset!—but once I got a job with a stable income, I had more resources to spare. The problem was, I had no idea what material things I wanted.

When my friends came over for dinner, I invited them to bring their own silverware because I only had two forks. ("But I live alone! I only need one!") I'd worn the same thrift store clothes for years. I regularly washed and reused the same, single bathroom hand towel instead of buying extras. I could afford new things; I just struggled to believe I was worthy of them.

When I became aware of this tendency, I challenged myself to identify three small material wants in my journal. Remembering my dinners with friends, I added a full silverware set to my list. Truthfully, it would be nice if I didn't have to invite my guests to bring their own.

I sat for a while, staring down at the blank page. I looked around my apartment for inspiration and saw my Kindle sitting on the counter. I had just read a great e-book, and enjoyed it so much that I wanted to get a hard copy. Usually, I struggled to justify the expense—e-books are so much cheaper!—but I loved the heft of a real book in my hands, and added the hardcover to my list.

For my final item, I added new earbuds. Mine had been acting up lately; their volume increased and decreased at random intervals. I'd been making do despite the glitch, but I enjoyed listening to podcasts on my daily runs, and I knew that a new set would make exercising more enjoyable.

As I assessed my list—full silverware set, hardcover book, new headphones—I decided that the silverware felt doable and practical. I promptly went online and ordered a full, twenty-four-piece set to be delivered the next day. When it arrived, I unboxed each piece and placed them proudly in my drawer. I felt an unfamiliar sense of abundance. Inspired, I committed to prioritize at least one material want every week—no matter how small—to embrace the pleasures of wanting.

Attune to Your Own Wants in a Group

Pay attention the next time you're with a group of people and you're trying to decide how to spend your time. Maybe you're deciding where to eat, what to do that afternoon, or what to read next in your book club. When someone else expresses a preference, take a moment to pause and ask yourself: *What do* I *want?* Even if you don't voice this desire, the practice of asking will help you strengthen your muscle of inner listening.

Vera has been dating her partner, Amber, for two years. Vera's begun to feel like she's losing herself in her relationship, so she decides to pay better attention to her own wants when they're together. When Amber comes over to spend the night, the two scroll through Netflix. Amber suggests a horror movie, and Vera pauses. She would normally agree, happy to just go with the flow, but now she asks to herself: *What do* I *want?*

Vera realizes that, while she'd be okay with a horror movie, she would really prefer to watch a comedy. She feels apprehensive about suggesting this to Amber; she has so little history expressing her preferences in the relationship that she's not sure how Amber will respond. She encourages herself: *Vera, just tell her you'd prefer a comedy. The worst that could happen is she says no. You've been together two years now; you deserve to speak up.*

When Vera nervously reveals to Amber that she'd rather watch a comedy, Amber seems taken aback—she isn't used to Vera making suggestions—but she's happy to oblige. An hour later finds the two giggling, immersed in the film, and Vera notices how good it feels to have influenced the trajectory of the evening.

Celebrate Your Attained Wants

After putting in the energy to finally attain one of your wants, don't just move on to the next thing—take the time to pause and celebrate! For the person who has spent decades repressing their desires, actively pursuing them is a feat. Consider talking with a friend about how it feels in your heart, body, and mind to have intentionally attained this desire.

LIVING FROM OUR FOUNDATIONS

When we regularly prioritize our feelings, needs, values, and wants, we stop living in a state of chronic disembodiment, detached from ourselves for hours, days, or years at a time. Finally, we begin to live within ourselves.

Attuning inward is a practice, not a destination. There will be days when we feel acutely aware of ourselves, living fully within our own needs and desires. Other days—harder days—we might be tugged away from ourselves by our old patterns or others' judgments. This, too, is part of the process. We're breaking a years- or generations-old pattern of other-focus. Every single time we mindfully redirect our attention to how *we* feel or what *we* want, we undermine the cycle of self-abandonment and lay the groundwork required to stop people-pleasing.

It is only from this place—from this sense of self—that we can begin the work of genuine self-advocacy. We can't protect ourselves if we don't know what we're protecting. With our five foundations firmly in place, we're now ready to make clear requests, set firm boundaries, and do the important work that we'll explore together in the chapters to come.

2

STAND UP FOR YOURSELF

7

NEEDING BEYOND THE BARE MINIMUM

Now that we've developed a stronger relationship with ourselves, we can begin asserting and protecting ourselves in our relationships with others.

The first step in this process is determining our relational needs: what, specifically, we need from our bonds with family, friends, partners, and colleagues. As we explored in chapter 1, many people-pleasers have a history of neglect or abuse; some simply had caregivers who didn't meet their emotional needs. Through these formative experiences, we learned that requiring nothing of others—while being as accommodating and likable as possible—was how we ensured our safety. In many relationships, we learned to live with the bare minimum.

But now that we're giving our own feelings, needs, wants, and values attention and respect, we begin to crave the same from our relationships. We begin to notice a simmering dissatisfaction in relationships that are all give and no take; that are imbalanced; that fill others' cups while leaving us empty. This dissatisfaction is a sign that we're starting to believe we're worthy of more. Slowly, we acknowledge that, yes—we *do* actually need affection, respect, and kindness. Yes, we *do* actually need fairness, contribution, and reciprocity. Affirming these needs for ourselves is the first step in being able to express them to others.

In this chapter, we'll explore how to identify our relational needs and silence the old voices insisting that they're "unreasonable" or "too much." In the coming chapters, we'll explore how to express and advocate for these needs in our relationships.

NEED SIGNPOSTS IN OUR RELATIONSHIPS

Identifying our relational needs after years of settling for the bare minimum can be challenging. As we saw in chapter 3, we benefit from understanding our signposts: the specific feelings and behaviors that indicate we have an unmet need. Our signposts are like flashing red lights, inviting us to consider, "What needs to change here?"

Resentment, hurt, anger, overwhelm, and feeling taken advantage of in our relationships can all signal unmet needs. Resentment arises when we feel we've been wronged, exploited, or treated unfairly in some way. Sometimes we feel resentful because we've given more than we're comfortable giving; sometimes we feel resentful when a person makes false promises or reneges on an agreement. Resentment tends to signal unmet needs for *respect, reciprocity, fairness, kindness, or equality*.

Hurt is a common reaction to being mistreated, neglected, or dismissed. It often indicates unmet needs for *attention, acknowledgment, kindness, consideration, or support*. Meanwhile, anger emerges when we feel a sense of injustice at having been mistreated. It is a fiercely self-protective feeling: a clear cry from our innermost self that what occurred offended our inner sense of right and wrong. Anger may flag unmet needs for *respect, contribution, independence, fairness, or consideration*.

Overwhelm and burnout arise when we have too many obligations and not enough rest. We might also feel emotionally overwhelmed when we've taken excessive responsibility for others' feelings. Overwhelm and burnout tend to signal unmet needs for *rest, relaxation, balance, fairness, or support*. When we feel that others are exploiting our kindness or generosity, it's a clear sign that we've given more than we're comfortable giving. Feeling taken advantage of suggests unmet needs of *equality, fairness, reciprocity, consideration, or support.*

Certain behaviors can also be signposts. Chronically venting about the same situation, repeatedly rehearsing what you wish you'd said in the past, avoiding a person or community, or ghosting on a connection altogether may indicate that this relationship—in its current form—isn't meeting your needs.

If we're chronically venting about the same situation, it's clearly causing us ongoing distress. One or more of our needs is going unmet and something needs to change. When we repeatedly rehearse what we wish we'd said in the past, it's an indicator that we didn't express a crucial feeling or need in the appropriate moment. It's likely that this unmet need is still alive within us and requires addressing.

Avoiding a person or community can be a sign that we don't feel comfortable asserting our feelings and needs with them directly. Though choosing to disengage from a relationship *can* be a valuable boundary (we'll discuss this more in chapter 11), chronic avoidance that leaves us feeling unsettled is a sign that an unmet need requires our attention. At the extreme, we may ghost on a relationship altogether—disappearing without a warning or explanation—when we feel we don't have the emotional resources to engage honestly. When we notice ourselves ghosting, it can be an invitation to consider what unmet needs were present there.

Bethany's Story

Bethany, twenty-nine, feels frustrated with her boyfriend, Rob. They live in separate apartments, but over the past six months, Rob's spent nearly every night at Bethany's place. He showers there, drinks coffee there, and eats most of his meals there, but he hasn't offered to contribute to her grocery or rent bill.

Bethany has been venting to her friends about Rob for weeks. One day, she's on the way home from the grocery store after footing another expensive bill. She feels resentful and taken advantage of and calls up her friend Vince.

"I just spent over a hundred and fifty dollars at the grocery store again," she complains. "I can't believe Rob hasn't offered to contribute to the bills! He's over at my place all the time. If I were spending that much time at his apartment, I'd have offered to contribute months ago."

Vince is a good listener, but he's heard this vent countless times before. He offers a few compassionate *uh-huhs,* and when they hang up, she feels embarrassed for subjecting her friends to the same complaints over and over again. She remembers that chronically venting about the same situation signifies an unmet need. Clearly, something needs to change with Rob.

DETERMINING OUR UNMET NEEDS

Once we recognize a signpost, it's time to pause, look within, and ask: *What is my unmet need in this situation?*

If we're struggling to find an answer, we might gain clarity by asking the question a little differently: *What would need to change in order to resolve this emotion or behavior? What needs to stop in order for me to feel a sense of well-being? What do I need more of in order to feel secure?*

As we discussed in chapter 2, our unmet need might be *personal* and include things like rest, alone time, financial security, or play. Especially when we're in a habit of over-giving, these needs are likely to be neglected. Alternatively, our unmet need may be *relational*: a need that can only be satisfied in connection with another person. Relational needs can include things like respect, love, reassurance, fairness, understanding, and empathy.

Finding Our Needs beneath Our Fears

We may struggle to name our needs out of fear that they are unreasonable; that others will mock or dismiss us; or that even if we identify our needs, they will ultimately go unfulfilled. Sometimes, these worries can be so deeply ingrained that we don't even realize them: we just feel incapable of naming what we need.

We'll explore how to confront these fears shortly. For now, as we practice simply uncovering our needs, it's important that our concern about possible outcomes doesn't prevent us from being honest with ourselves. To dig beneath our fears, we can use the exercise from chapter 6, "Imagine a World of Complete Acceptance":

> Imagine that you wake up tomorrow and the world is exactly the same, but for one key difference: everyone in your life greets *every single need* you express with sincere enthusiasm and meets your needs without complaint. The rule of law still applies, and illegal or violent activities aren't allowed, but otherwise, the world is your oyster.
>
> In this world, you can express your needs for care, affection, balance, reciprocity, understanding, kindness, respect, and more, and they will be *immediately* met with eagerness. In this world, what would you identify as the unmet need beneath your signpost?

To determine her unmet need, Bethany asks herself: *What would need to change in order to resolve my resentment?* Her response is immediate: *I need Rob to contribute financially if he's going to spend this much time at my apartment.* But even as she admits this to herself, she notices fear and self-doubt. Her mind spins: *I love Rob and I'm glad he spends time at my apartment. . . . Needing money from him makes me feel like a nag. Plus, talking about money is so hard. What if I ask him and he says no? Am I being too demanding?*

"BUT ARE MY NEEDS REASONABLE?"

For many recovering people-pleasers like Bethany, the greatest obstacle to identifying our needs is the fear that they're unreasonable or too much. As we discussed in chapter 3, how our needs were received in childhood and our previous adult relationships affects our willingness to name and prioritize them now. If our needs were historically met with criticism, disdain, or disinterest, we may avoid naming them at all in anticipation of others' judgment.

As we'll explore in the following chapters, it's very difficult to make requests and set boundaries around our needs if we don't trust that they are valid. To increase that trust, we can keep in mind the following:

The Big List of Reasonable Needs

When we've spent a lifetime putting everyone else first, having any need—no matter how basic—tends to feel like too much. It's important for the recovering people-pleaser to remember that our "too much" barometer is skewed; compared to the bare minimum, anything more feels like a luxury. The "Big List of Reasonable Needs" below offers examples of relational needs that people-pleasers often believe are too much that are, in fact, entirely reasonable. (Please keep in mind that this list is not exhaustive.)

- I need to feel safe.
- I need to be free from physical harm and violence.
- I need to be treated with respect, which includes not being humiliated or degraded.
- I need to be free from critical comments about my body and physical appearance.
- I need to be shown kindness.
- I need to be shown affection and appreciation.
- I need others to communicate their care for me using words such as "I care about you," "I love you," or "You are important to me."
- I need others to initiate spending time together and initiate communication with me, not just respond to my requests.
- I need others to show interest in me and my life.
- I need consistency, and if someone close to me is unable to

communicate or spend time with me in a consistent way, I need them to be able to explain why.
- I need others to listen when I'm speaking, which includes not constantly interrupting me or speaking over me.
- I need others to respect my concerns and passions.
- I need others to respect my right to my own beliefs even if they disagree.
- I need others to keep their word.
- I need alone time.
- I need others to respect my autonomy, which includes not trying to change me or control my actions.
- I need to trust others to say no when they don't want to do something in our relationship.
- I need others to communicate their needs clearly, not through passive aggression or sarcasm.
- I need others to respect my boundaries, which includes not throwing a tantrum or making me out to be the bad guy every time I set one.
- I need others to apologize and admit their mistakes.
- I need others to be willing to repair after a disagreement, not punish me by giving me the silent treatment, avoiding me, or pretending it never happened.
- I need a fair and equitable division of financial responsibility, household labor, and childcare in our relationship.
- I need others to respect my sexual boundaries, which include not coercing, pressuring, or guilt-tripping me in any way.
- I need others to operate within the bounds of our relational agreement (e.g., if we've agreed to be monogamous, they don't sleep with other people).

As we review this list, we may intellectually agree that these are reasonable needs, but notice an internal resistance to them. We may feel they're reasonable for others, but not for us. We may question whether we deserve this sort of treatment, especially if we've experienced it so rarely before.

Believing we deserve more doesn't happen overnight. It's an incremental process, and the more we prioritize our own needs and feelings independently, the more we believe we are worthy of prioritizing them in our relationships. Ultimately, there is no hero or authority coming to make us believe that we deserve more. Sometimes, the only way is to take a leap of faith: to be our own hero and teach ourselves, *through our actions*, that we deserve more by not settling for less.

Others' Limitations Do Not Make *Your* Needs Unreasonable

If we've spent our lives surrounded by people who were neglectful, distant, avoidant, or emotionally unavailable, we may believe that basic needs for fairness, affection, intimacy, and support are unreasonable simply because those closest to us have been unable to meet them.

After dating a series of emotionally unavailable partners, I began to believe that words of affirmation—like "I love you," "I care about you," or "You're important to me"—were an unreasonable thing to need. In one relationship, I had to beg my partner for verbal affection. He frequently said kind things about his friends, but seemed incapable of doing the same for me. I vulnerably asked if he could, every so often, offer a compliment about my personality, my outfit, my smile—anything. He didn't oblige. Then, a few months after professing he loved me, he stopped saying the words altogether. When I explained how important it was to me that we said "I love you" to each other, he agreed—but never again uttered the words.

For a while, I wondered if something was wrong with me for needing these reassurances to feel loved and secure. I questioned if needing verbal kindness from a partner was expecting too much.

But others' inability or unwillingness to meet our needs doesn't mean that our needs are too much. It's important that we don't internalize others' limitations as objective truths about who *we* are and what *we* need. There are some people who, for whatever reason, will not meet our needs. There are other people who will happily, eagerly, and without hesitation meet our needs. One person's too much is another person's just right.

Our Needs Will Not Be Others' Needs, and That Doesn't Make Them Wrong

We all have different families of origin, trauma histories, sensitivities, personalities, desires, communication styles, and more. Each of these factors contributes to our unique relational needs.

Someone who is introverted may need more time alone than someone who is extroverted. Someone who had emotionally unavailable caregivers may need more reassurance from their partner than someone who had attentive caregivers. Someone who is very verbal may need more communication than someone who is not. We have needs that others don't have; others have needs that *we* don't have. That doesn't make us "wrong"—it just makes us different.

NEEDS VS. STRATEGIES

Once we've identified our need, we can consider which strategies will meet it. Needs are generally broad and intangible (e.g., love or respect), while strategies are specific actions and behaviors (e.g., offering someone a compliment, telling someone you appreciate them). Sometimes, multiple strategies could meet an underlying need; occasionally, only one will work.

In some cases, we can meet our needs through our own actions. If I need *rest* after a busy week, my strategies may include going to bed early, canceling my evening plans, or taking a day off. If I've been preoccupied with work and need more *balance*, strategies could include spending more time with friends, carving out time for art and creativity, or taking a short vacation.

On the other hand, our relational needs—like love, compassion, support, or respect—require others' participation. If I'm going through a hard time and need *support* from my partner, a few strategies they could use include calling me to check in, cooking me a homemade meal, or cuddling with me on the couch. If a family member has been calling me names and I need *respect*, the only strategy that will effectively meet my need is for them to stop their hurtful behavior.

Sometimes, it's hard to sense whether a specific strategy will successfully meet our need. In these cases, you might imagine the strategy playing like a mental movie from start to finish. When the movie is over, how do you feel? Did the strategy work? Did you notice a decrease in the original feeling of resentment, overwhelm, etc.? While this exercise can help us anticipate a strategy's effectiveness, sometimes we can't be totally certain whether it works until we try it.

Sometimes, the Best Strategy Is Changing Our Own Behavior

When we're overwhelmed, burned-out, or resentful from a pattern of over-giving—committing when we don't have the time, giving when we don't have the resources, and supporting when we don't have the space—it's our behavior that needs to change in order to meet our needs.

Three months ago, Jenna's sister, Lillia, went through a painful divorce. Every day since, Jenna's called Lillia to check in, and Lillia talks for hours each time. At first Jenna had the emotional bandwidth for hours of conversation each day, but now she notices that she's beginning to feel overwhelmed. She needs some space. In this case, Jenna's own behavior—calling Lillia daily and making herself available for hours of conversation—is violating her own need for space. Two strategies that could meet Jenna's need include making these calls on a less frequent basis or limiting her time spent on each call.

When our over-giving is the problem, we need an internal boundary: a promise we make to ourselves about our own behaviors and commitments. We'll discuss this type of boundary in the next chapter.

Bethany's Story

As Bethany contemplates her situation with Rob, she considers which strategies will meet her needs for fairness and financial contribution. Ultimately, she concludes that she needs Rob to contribute half of the grocery bill and a small portion of the rent.

The self-doubting inner voices are still there—*Am I being a nag? Is this unreasonable?*—but Bethany reminds herself that Rob essentially lives at her apartment full-time; this is a fair arrangement. She isn't comfortable being in a relationship where she financially supports her partner, and she doesn't want her connection with Rob to be marred by this unspoken frustration. After so many months of simmering resentment, it's clear to Bethany that voicing this need is the only path forward.

Now that we've explored how to identify our unmet needs, we'll spend the next three chapters exploring how we can use internal boundaries, requests, and boundaries with others to advocate for them.

THREE STEPS TO UNCOVER OUR RELATIONAL NEEDS

To build the habit of uncovering your relational needs, use this three-step process:

1. Identify Your Signpost

Identify a specific situation where you're currently feeling resentment, hurt, anger, overwhelm, burnout, or taken advantage of—or where you're repeatedly venting about the same problem, repeatedly rehearsing what you wish you'd said in the past, avoiding a person or community, or ghosting on a relationship altogether.

2. Determine Your Unmet Need

With this specific situation in mind, ask yourself: *What is my unmet need?*

Refer to the "Big List of Reasonable Needs" for support. If it feels hard to name your need, use the magic question: *If I had a guarantee that the need I named would be met, what would I identify as my unmet need?*

3. Determine Specific Strategies to Meet Your Need

Once you uncover your unmet need, consider the strategies that would meet it. Answer the prompt: *What specific actions could meet my need for ____________________?*

If you're struggling to determine whether a specific strategy will work, imagine it playing out like a mental movie from start to finish. Take note of all strategies that arise. Remember that if only one strategy will do, that's perfectly okay.

8

SETTING BOUNDARIES WITH OURSELVES

Sometimes others' behavior must change in order to meet our needs. Sometimes, however—like in Jenna's case—our own over-giving is the source of our resentment, exhaustion, fatigue, and overwhelm. In these cases, we can meet our needs ourselves with firmer *internal boundaries*: promises we make to ourselves about our own behaviors and commitments.

We neglect our own needs for rest, relaxation, balance, and emotional well-being when we accept new commitments when we're already burned-out; spend more time with others than we want to; hold more space for others' emotions than we're comfortable holding; have conversations about topics that make us uncomfortable; or agree to things we don't actually want to do, like second dates, plans with friends, or physical intimacy. When we give past our limits in this manner, other people aren't mistreating us; *we're* mistreating us. The call is coming from inside the house.

In situations like this, meeting our needs is an inside job. In this chapter, we'll explore how we can honor our limits with internal boundaries; resolve resentments by breaking our own patterns of over-giving; and use our internal boundaries to prepare to set boundaries with others.

NEGLECTED NEEDS AND BROKEN PROMISES

If we chronically ignore our needs—or repeatedly involve ourselves in interactions that don't meet them—this is a sign that we need firmer internal boundaries.

Carla

Carla, a social media influencer, earns a living posting videos on Instagram and TikTok. Long after her daily videos are posted, she scrolls on the apps for hours, mindlessly absorbing hundreds of videos that, in seconds, she doesn't remember. The screen time is taking a toll on her mental health, and she needs more time away from social media. Her internal boundary might be: *I will only spend two hours each day on social media.*

Luis

Luis has been using dating apps for months, hoping to meet his life partner. He wants a serious relationship, but he's also lonely, so he swipes right on women who say they're only interested in casual flings. The story always ends the same way: after a date or two, the women disappear, and he's left to start from scratch, lonelier than he was before. To avoid these disappointments and prioritize his desire for a serious relationship, Luis's internal boundary might be: *I will only go on dates with people who are looking for the same thing I am.*

As these examples demonstrate, setting internal boundaries requires us to be aware of, and act in accordance with, our own needs. Without internal boundaries, we feel like we're constantly breaking promises to ourselves, which erodes our sense of self-trust over time. Honoring our own limits is our responsibility; it's up to us to make healthy decisions to prioritize our needs, even if that means not over-giving in the ways we're accustomed to.

SOMETIMES, IT'S ON US

When we feel like others are taking advantage of our time, kindness, or generosity, it's generally a sign that we have crossed our own internal boundaries and given past our limits. However, instead of taking responsibility for the fact that we've been people-pleasing, we might blame others for taking advantage of us and not mind-reading our unspoken needs.

Jill

Jill, a single mother, has twins in the fifth grade. She has a busy schedule: she runs her own business from home and constantly chauffeurs her kids to soccer practice and friends' houses. One day, Becca, the twins' teacher, asks Jill to join the PTA.

Jill is already overbooked, but she says yes because she wants Becca to approve of her parenting and involvement in the school. Later that day, Jill complains to a friend that Becca "took advantage of her kindness" by asking her to join the PTA when she's already so busy. But in fact, Jill violated her *own* need for rest by agreeing to the new commitment when she didn't have the space.

Jill's internal boundary might be: *I will not commit to new obligations when I'm already overbooked.*

Foster and Emily

Foster and Emily have a twenty-four-year old son, Jeremy. Three years ago, Jeremy graduated college and decided to pursue a career as a guitarist. He gets a few performance opportunities here and there, but he doesn't earn nearly enough to afford his rent.

Foster and Emily agreed to subsidize Jeremy's expenses while he pursued his dream, but now, three years later, they're beginning to feel the strain on their finances. They feel guilty removing their support from Jeremy, so they haven't—but during phone calls with extended family members, they complain that Jeremy is taking advantage of their support.

By blaming their son for their discomfort, Foster and Emily aren't acknowledging that they're over-giving past their own limits. They are the ones violating their own needs. Their internal boundary might be: *We will not financially support Jeremy when we can't afford to do so.*

As the cases above make clear, once we've set an internal boundary with ourselves, we often need to communicate a boundary to others. We may find ourselves needing to say no, turn down commitments, or tell our loved ones that we're no longer available in the ways we've been before. We'll discuss how to set these boundaries with others in chapter 10.

Sometimes, we may think to ourselves: *But they* are *taking advantage of me! They know I'm a giver and they know I have trouble saying no. That's why they ask me for favors.*

People-pleasers regularly resent that others put us in the position of having to set boundaries. In these cases, the old quote rings true: givers have to set limits because takers rarely do. Even if other people ask us favors because they know we tend to over-give, it's still our *own* responsibility to protect our needs and say no.

DISCOVERING OUR INTERNAL BOUNDARIES

As we saw in chapter 7, signposts like resentment, overwhelm, and burnout signal that we're over-giving or overcommitting in our relationships. To discover your internal boundaries, take stock of your current situation. Are there any areas of your life where you're currently:

- Consciously neglecting your own needs for time, space, or rest?
- Taking on more than you have the space for?
- Saying yes to something when you really feel a no?

- Supporting others to the point of fatigue, exhaustion, or burnout?
- Giving support that you don't feel comfortable giving?
- Doing something for someone in order to be liked, but resenting the other person afterward?

For every situation you uncover, determine an internal boundary—a promise to yourself about your own behavior—that will honor your limitations.

For example: *I will go to bed by 10:00 p.m. I will say no to new plans if I don't have time. I will tell my friends when I don't have the emotional bandwidth to speak on the phone. I will tell my manager when I feel overwhelmed at work. I will be honest when I don't have the space to offer another person support.*

Once we've affirmed our internal boundaries, our task is putting them into action. Sometimes, this simply means tending to our personal needs as we explored in chapter 3. Sometimes, this involves verbalizing our needs using requests or boundaries with others, which we'll explore in the coming chapters.

Our internal boundaries are only effective if we embody them with our actions. This requires us to prioritize them even when it's hard. These strategies can help you strengthen your commitment:

Make Your Commitment Visible

Write down your internal boundary and place it somewhere visible as a reminder of your commitment. You might write it on a piece of paper and place it on your refrigerator, bathroom mirror, or car's dashboard; set it as your phone wallpaper; or repeat it as a mantra each morning or night.

Share Your Commitment

Research suggests that sharing your goal with a person whose opinion you value increases the likelihood that you'll attain it. To hold yourself accountable to your internal boundary, share it with a friend, loved one, or therapist. From time to time, share with them how you've upheld your boundary to celebrate your success.

Imagine the Long-Term Benefits

In your journal, imagine what your life would look like in one year if you spent that year maintaining your internal boundary. How will your physical and mental health improve? How will resentment decrease in your relationships? How will your relationship with yourself change? What other benefits might you experience?

ALL BOUNDARIES BEGIN WITHIN

Understanding our internal boundaries is a prerequisite to communicating our needs and boundaries in our relationships. After all: If we don't feel comfortable protecting our time when we're alone, how will we possibly set limits around our time with others? If we're not making rest a priority in our own lives, how will we possibly advocate for rest effectively in our families, friendships, and workplaces? Now that we've clarified our needs and limits, we'll explore how to put them into action using requests and boundaries with others.

9

MAKING THE ASK

Once we determine what we need in our relationships, we may conclude that fulfilling our needs would require others to change. We may need more communication, more affection, or more balance; we may need less disrespect, less passive aggression, or less time together.

Now it's time to make a request: to ask others to change their behavior to meet our needs. Requests can look like:

- "Could you please lower your voice when you speak to me?"
- "Would you initiate plans more often?"
- "I'm feeling tired—can I have some time alone?"
- "Can you share with me how you're feeling?"
- "Could you please stop making jokes about that?"

Giving voice to our needs with requests is how we show ourselves—and others—that our needs matter. In this chapter, we'll debunk the myth that other people "should just know what we need" without being asked; explore scripts for putting our requests into words; discuss five common outcomes of how requests unfold in our relationships; and explore what to do when someone can't meet our requests.

"I SHOULDN'T HAVE TO ASK—THEY SHOULD JUST KNOW"

One of the greatest barriers to making requests is the idea that other people "should just know" what we need, how to care for us, and how to love us without being told. Our spouses "should just know" that we need more affection; our bosses "should just know" that we're overwhelmed with tasks; our friends "should just know" that we can't host them in our home for weeks at a time.

But not all people express interest, care, or love in the same manner—and not all people have the same needs for affection, space, or rest. How we were raised, our cultural heritage, our distinct personalities, and our unique sensitives all impact our template for interacting with others. Expecting people to relate to us the precise way we prefer—without ever being told—is not only unrealistic but also a recipe for resentment. Only when we've been verbal about our needs can we say that others should just know: because we've told them already.

Though making requests can feel vulnerable, it gives others the information they need to take care of us properly. We can't guarantee that they'll act on that information in the way we want, but by making a request, we can rest assured that we've done our part to give others the chance to meet our needs.

Devlin's Story

Devlin and his partner, JD, just moved in together after dating for two years. Devlin works full-time as a construction foreman, and JD is a freelance writer who works from his home office. When Devlin gets home at the end of his nine-hour shifts, he's exhausted; he would prefer to shower and relax a bit before having a long conversation. Meanwhile, JD has been working alone all day, and Devlin's return gives him someone to talk to.

Each day when Devlin walks through the door, JD greets him with a slew of questions: "How was your day? How's the project going? When do you think it will be finished?"

Devlin has tried to be receptive, but he notices that he's beginning to feel frustrated. *Why is JD hammering me with questions the moment I walk through the door?* he thinks. *He should know that I'm exhausted after a long day.*

However, this chatty enthusiasm is how JD has always greeted Devlin; when they were dating, they would meet for dinner or drinks, and Devlin always found JD's liveliness and curiosity endearing. Now their circumstances have changed: they live together, and quiet moments alone to recharge have become moments shared. Devlin acknowledges that they've never been in this particular situation before, and the only way he can be certain that JD knows his need for time alone is to tell him.

PUTTING REQUESTS INTO WORDS

Requests are relatively straightforward. Generally, they take five forms: asking others to start doing something, do more of something, stop doing something, do less of something, or do something differently.

At first, we may feel tempted to be verbose in our requests, offering lengthy explanations or irrelevant details. This often stems from nervousness and our belief that we need to "make a good case" for our needs. But in fact, the most effective requests are clear, precise, and simple. Here are three approaches you might use:

The Short and Sweet Approach

If you're asking for more of something, you might say:

- "Could you please ______________________?"
- "I need ______________________. Can you help?"
- "Are you open to ______________________?"

If you're asking for less of something, you might say:

- "Can you stop ____________________?"
- "Would you mind not ____________________?"
- "Moving forward, could you not ____________________?"

If you want to give your request more context, you can accompany the ask with your core need. You might say, "I want to feel more *connected*. Would you mind using your phone less during our one-on-one time together?" or "I want to be *honest* with you: I feel overwhelmed by how often you ask me to babysit. Could you limit your asks to once a month?"

The I-Statement Approach

Developed by psychologist Thomas Gordon in 1970, the I-statement is a four-part communication tool that helps us be clear and direct about our feelings and needs.

An I-statement includes four parts: I feel ____________ when you ____________ because ____________. I need ____________.

I recommend ending your I-statement with a clear and direct request: Can you ____________?

In practice, this approach looks like: "*I feel* sad *when you're* on your phone so often *because* it prevents us from being present with each other. *I need* to feel more connected. *Would you mind* spending less time on your phone when we're together?" or "*I feel* overwhelmed *when you* ask me to babysit so often *because* I already have a very busy schedule. *I need* to feel more considered in our connection. *Could you* please ask me to babysit no more than once a week?"

The Radical Transparency Approach

Sometimes, our requests pose changes to a long-standing pattern in a relationship. Sometimes, what we need now is not what we needed before. Sometimes, our requests may be hard for others to hear.

The radical transparency approach is based on the belief that we don't need to pretend to be cold, stoic, or flawlessly confident when advocating for ourselves. In fact, by acknowledging that this request is new, unexpected, or even scary to make—or by acknowledging that it may be difficult to hear—we can invite the recipient in for a vulnerable and compassionate conversation.

Radically transparent requests might sound like:

- "It's hard for me to say this, but I want to be honest with you: ________ isn't working for me anymore. Could you ________ instead?"
- "I know that in the past I've needed ________, but I'm realizing that my needs have shifted, and what I need now is ________. Can you help?"
- "I know that in the past I was okay with ________, but I'm trying to take better care of myself now, and I'm realizing that ________ no longer works for me. Could you please stop ________?"
- "I'm afraid of hurting you, but it's important to me that we can be honest with each other. I want you to know that when you ________, I feel ________. Moving forward, would you please ________?"
- "I'm nervous to say this, but I'm trying to be more honest with the people I love, so I need to tell you that ________."

The radical transparency approach works best with people you trust: people who care for your well-being and are unlikely to weaponize the vulnerability of this approach against you.

Devlin's Story

Devlin is worried about making a request because he doesn't want to hurt JD's feelings. They just moved in together and things have been going so well; he doesn't want to dampen the mood. Given the delicacy of their situation, Devlin decides to use the radical transparency approach. One night over dinner, Devlin asks JD if he can talk about something.

"Of course," responds JD. "What's up?"

Devlin says, haltingly at first, "Okay. It's . . . It's hard for me to say this, but I want to be honest. Um . . . When I get home from work, I'm usually really tired. I know you've been here alone all day and want to chat, but I need to take a shower and relax a bit before I'm ready for a long conversation."

More confidently now, he concludes, "Would you mind saving your questions about my day and my projects until then? I'll have more bandwidth to talk, and then I can ask you about your day, too."

JD listens, poking at his food with his fork. "Oh," he responds, "I'd been wondering why you seemed short with me after work."

Devlin nods. "It's just hard for me to feel present before I've had some time to myself after a long shift."

JD frowns. He's quiet for a few moments. "Okay," he eventually says, "I get it. I guess I just feel insecure, like . . . I don't know. Like us living together is a burden to you or something."

Devlin reaches across the table for JD's hand. "JD," he says, "I *love* living with you. I promise. Moving in together comes with a learning curve, you know? We've never done this before, and we both have to learn what the other needs."

Devlin squeezes JD's hand. "I hope that me telling you what I need makes *you* feel more comfortable telling me what *you* need, too."

Finally, JD offers a smile. "Okay. Yeah, I'm glad you told me. And yes—I can definitely wait a bit before asking you questions about your day."

HOW REQUESTS PLAY OUT

Making requests is, at its core, an attempt at collaboration. Requests give others a chance to know us better, to understand what we need, and to meet us there. After we make a request, we typically experience one of these outcomes:

They Agree to Meet Our Need

In the simplest cases, our requests fall on receptive ears. As with Devlin and JD, the other person is open to meeting our needs in the way we'd like, and all is well.

They're Receptive and Demonstrate Change, but Need an Occasional Reminder

Sometimes, especially if our request alters an existing pattern in a relationship, the other person may be receptive but require reminders from time to time.

After working at a tech start-up for three months, Nipun finally gathers the courage to tell his boss that she's been mispronouncing his name. His boss apologizes and corrects herself, but in the weeks that follow, she accidentally uses the incorrect pronunciation from time to time.

Lina, a stay-at-home parent, asks her partner, Koa, to contribute to the household by doing the dishes more often. Koa is receptive, and does the dishes most nights, but occasionally becomes preoccupied with work and forgets.

People aren't perfect, and it's normal to occasionally forget, slip up, and make mistakes. In these cases, Nipun and Lina might choose to restate their requests every time there's a lapse; or, they may decide that because their need is being met the majority of the time, they're comfortable letting these moments pass without comment.

They're Receptive to Our Core Need, but They're Unwilling or Unable to Use the Specific Strategy We've Asked For

Sometimes, a person wants to meet our core need—for connection, intimacy, trust, compassion, etc.—but they can't or won't do so in the specific way we've asked.

Natalie and Joseph have been dating for a year. They spend two nights per week together, and Natalie wishes it were more. She says to Joseph, "I need to feel more connected to you. Can we spend three nights a week together instead of two?"

Joseph wants Natalie to feel more connected, but the strategy she suggested doesn't work for him; he has a very busy work schedule and isn't comfortable spending more than two nights per week together right now. Still, Joseph is committed to helping Natalie feel more connected.

A mismatch like this requires some brainstorming and collaboration: What additional strategies could be used to meet this core need? Perhaps Joseph decides that he's comfortable chatting on the phone the nights that they're apart. Perhaps he decides to invite Natalie to join his weekly trivia game with his friends as a means of making her feel more connected. From here, it's up to Natalie to determine if these alternative strategies would effectively meet her need for connection.

They Claim to Be Receptive, but Don't Change Their Actions

Sometimes, the recipient of our request claims to be receptive, but over time, their actions don't reflect this change. These instances are confusing and leave us wondering: *Are they able to meet my needs or not?*

When Mona gently tells her father that his angry outbursts make her feel unsafe, he listens and promises to get a better hold of his temper. But during their interactions over the following months, he's as angry as ever.

A year ago, Penny invited Violet to move into her two-bedroom apartment. Recently, Violet's drinking has gotten out of control, and Penny isn't comfortable sharing space with someone who stumbles around drunk all hours of the night. When Penny asks Violet to cut back on her drinking, Violet agrees, but Penny sees no reduction over time.

In situations like this, others' words convey one story, but their actions convey another—and it's important to trust the information we gather from their *actions*. Empty promises do nothing to meet our core needs, and over time, these mixed messages erode trust and build resentment in the relationship.

They're Not Receptive to Our Request

Sometimes, our request is unsuccessful: the other person is unwilling or unable to adjust their behavior. Sometimes, this takes the form of a simple no: "I can't do that." Other times, it takes the form of mockery, judgment, or criticism.

At their core, requests are fundamentally unenforceable. Just because we ask doesn't mean that they'll accommodate. Regardless of the outcome, we can move forward knowing that we've done our part to communicate our needs. Whether they choose to meet us there is out of our control.

When our request is unsuccessful, we may wonder: *What now?*

THE CYCLE OF ENDLESS REQUESTS

Unfortunately, many of us continue making the same requests long after others have shown us they can't or won't meet our needs. Often, we do so out of an illusion that we can somehow control others' willingness merely by asking. This is how we get stuck in the Cycle of Endless Requests.

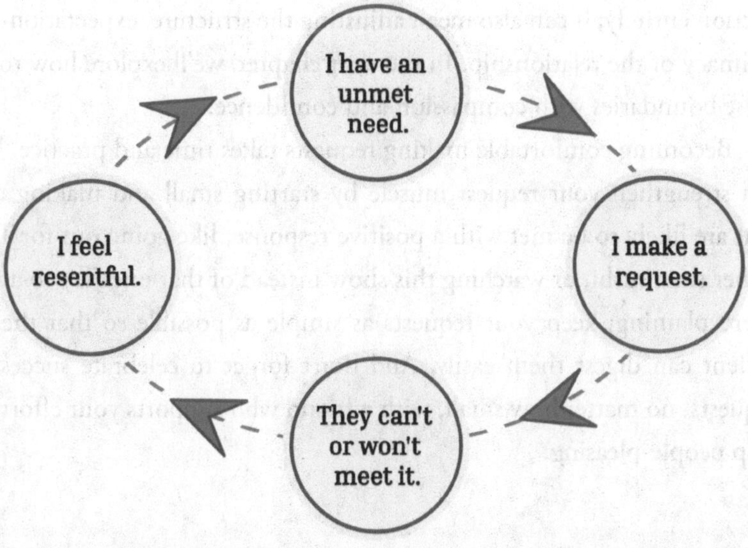

In this cycle, our needs stay unmet indefinitely as we ask, over and over again, for others to change. When they don't, we feel helpless; we feel like the victim of their actions and choices. We become resentful that our needs aren't met, but we don't take meaningful action to alter our circumstances; we just ask again, and again, and again.

We might get stuck in this cycle when we repeatedly ask others to show us more affection, respect, or kindness; to stop engaging in addictive or destructive behaviors; to stop making the same old hurtful comments; or to contribute fairly to childcare, the finances, or household labor. The Cycle of Endless Requests is driven by a deep, wrenching desire that others will finally care for us in the ways that we need. This yearning is so potent that it blinds us to the reality before us: that they are not, in fact, changing. For this reason, the Cycle of Endless Requests is a one-way ticket to frustration and heartbreak. It leaves us feeling entirely disconnected from our agency.

We can regain our power and break the cycle by radically accepting that their behavior isn't changing. From here, we can either make the conscious choice to stay in the situation *as it is*, or set a boundary that acknowledges that this relationship, in its current form, is unable to meet our needs. Setting a boundary doesn't necessarily mean ending the connection entirely; it can also mean adjusting the structure, expectations, or intimacy of the relationship. In the next chapter, we'll explore how to set these boundaries with compassion and confidence.

Becoming comfortable making requests takes time and practice. You can strengthen your request muscle by starting small and making asks that are likely to be met with a positive response, like going out for Thai rather than sushi, or watching this show instead of that one. Try to avoid overexplaining; keep your requests as simple as possible so that the recipient can digest them easily. And don't forget to celebrate successful requests, no matter how small, with a friend who supports your efforts to stop people-pleasing.

10

SETTING BOUNDARIES WITH OTHERS

In the simplest sense, a boundary separates one thing from another. A fence is a boundary between two properties; our skin is the boundary between our organs and the outside world. A boundary is the line where one thing ends, and another begins.

When we set a boundary with another person, we create some sort of separation between us. We might imagine our boundaries as shields that protect us from things that would threaten our well-being, such as others' rudeness, others' emotional dumping, unwanted touch, or commitments we don't have the time and space for. Boundaries enable us to honor our limits—what works for us and what doesn't—and design our lives and relationships around those limits.

Ultimately, boundaries are a recognition that we can't control what others say or do, but we *can* control how *we* respond and what *we* allow into our environment. That's what boundaries are all about. Although boundaries create separation in the short term, they are actually necessary and healthy in all relationships. In this chapter, we'll clarify the difference between boundaries and requests; explore how to effectively set and enforce boundaries; discuss how to disengage from unwanted interactions as a form of boundary-setting; and explore how to proceed when others don't like our boundaries or push back against them.

NAOMI'S STORY

Naomi, thirty-three, and her sister, Aria, thirty-one, are very different, but very close. Naomi is quiet and reserved, while Aria is boisterous, irreverent, and risk-taking. The sisters live in the same city, and though they don't see eye to eye on many things, they still get together once a week for coffee or dinner.

Last year, Aria married a man named Ken. Like Aria, Ken has a big personality: he's fiery, opinionated, and bold. But Ken's opinionated nature veers headlong into disrespect, and his frequent sexist comments make Naomi deeply uncomfortable. When Aria got a promotion at her job—one she'd been diligently working toward for years—Ken joked that her hourglass figure had something to do with it. Over family dinners, he's joked that women belong in the kitchen, not the workplace. When Naomi's dog died, she visited Aria and Ken distraught, and his first comment was: "It's sad, but not *that* sad. Are you on your period or something?"

Naomi loves her sister, but she dreads interacting with Ken. When she addresses Ken's behavior with her sister, Aria shrugs. "Look, he's just joking. He doesn't mean anything by it, okay?"

Naomi doesn't know what to do. She doesn't want to jeopardize her relationship with Aria, but spending time with Ken pushes her to the edge. A few times, Naomi has pulled Ken aside to speak with him privately. She's tried gently explaining why his comments are offensive. She's told him that his "jokes" make her uncomfortable and asked him to stop. Every time, Ken laughs and brushes her off, saying that she's being "too sensitive" and "should lighten up once in a while."

Naomi feels stuck. She's no longer willing to sit idly by in the face of Ken's blatant sexism. Her requests have been unsuccessful, so now it's time for a boundary.

BOUNDARIES VS. REQUESTS

When we make requests of others, we ask them to change their behavior. But when we set a boundary, we change *our own behavior* to protect ourselves, our needs, and our limits. As we discussed in the previous chapter, requests are, at their core, collaborative: a successful request requires another person to change their actions. Boundaries, on the other hand, don't require others' participation. When we set a boundary, we are assessing what doesn't work for us and acting accordingly. These examples demonstrate the difference between requests and boundaries:

SCENARIO	REQUEST	BOUNDARY
Your father always calls you when he's drunk, and it makes you uncomfortable.	"Would you mind only calling me when you're sober?"	Words: "I can't have a phone conversation with you when you're drunk. I'll call you tomorrow." Action: Hang up the phone.
Your spouse is raising their voice at you during an argument.	"Can you please lower your voice when you speak to me?"	Words: "I won't have a conversation when you're yelling at me." Action: Exit the conversation when yelling arises.
Your mother-in-law regularly gives you unsolicited parenting advice.	"I'm raising my children in the way that feels best to me, so could you please stop offering unsolicited advice?"	Words: "I'm not willing to talk about this if you're going to keep giving me unsolicited advice." Action: When unsolicited advice arises, either end the conversation or don't respond.

As you can see in these examples, our boundaries aren't about changing other people: they're about setting clear limits for what we will and will not tolerate from other people. For this reason, boundaries aren't tools to get *more* of something from someone. We can't "boundary" a person into giving us more affection, attention, kindness, or collaboration. We can *ask* them for more—that's what requests are all about—but ultimately, boundaries are about separating ourselves from situations that don't meet our needs, or interactions that make us feel unsafe, unseen, or harmed in some way.

Naomi has already made multiple requests of Ken. She asked, "Would you mind not making those jokes around me?" and "Could you stop making comments like that when I'm around?" Ken hasn't responded favorably, and he hasn't adjusted his behavior at all. Naomi acknowledges that she can't control Ken; she can't *make him* become willing to accommodate her requests. Instead, Naomi recognizes that she needs a boundary: she needs separation from Ken and the behavior she finds intolerable.

TYPES OF BOUNDARIES

Our boundaries can be physical, material, emotional, time-related, financial, or mental.

TYPE	EXPLANATION	EXAMPLE
Physical	Physical boundaries pertain to our bodies.	"I don't kiss on the first date. We can hug instead."
Material	Material boundaries pertain to our possessions and belongings.	"I'm not comfortable lending you my car for the weekend."
Emotional	Emotional boundaries help us take responsibility for our own emotions without taking responsibility for others' emotions. They help us differentiate where we end and another person begins. (We'll explore emotional boundaries more in the next chapter.)	"I can't be the person you vent to about your marriage anymore."
Time	Time boundaries pertain to our schedules and commitments.	"I have to get off the phone now. Let's resume this conversation tomorrow."
Financial	Financial boundaries are all about money: how much we spend, on what, for whom, and why.	"I can't live in shared housing unless we're all splitting rent equally."

TYPE	EXPLANATION	EXAMPLE
Mental	Our mental boundaries pertain to our beliefs, opinions, and values. Healthy mental boundaries enable us to hold on to our opinions even in the face of disagreement—but also leave us open to learning, curiosity, and growth.	"Let's agree to disagree on this."

Naomi concludes that she can set a physical boundary by leaving the room when Ken makes sexist jokes; a time boundary by spending less time around him; or a mental boundary by making it clear that she does not agree with his opinions instead of staying silent.

COMMUNICATING OUR BOUNDARIES

How we communicate our boundaries depends on our situation. We might use:

The Short and Sweet Approach

The short and sweet approach tends to work best when others make requests of us that we can't or don't wish to fulfill. Perhaps our sister asks if she can borrow our car; perhaps our date asks if we'd like to go back to their apartment; perhaps a community member asks if we can volunteer at the neighborhood bake sale.

In these cases, a clear, straightforward boundary will do:

- "No."
- "No thank you."
- "I can't."
- "I don't have time."
- "Not today."
- "That's not going to work for me."

- "I don't have time for that right now."
- "Now's not a good time."
- "Maybe some other time."

The I-Statement Approach

Like we discussed in the prior chapter, the I-statement is a four-part communication tool that helps us be direct about our feelings and needs: "I feel ____________ when you ____________ because ____________. I need ____________."

When setting boundaries, the I-statement looks like: "*I feel* overwhelmed *when you* try to talk things out moments after an argument *because* I haven't had time to process on my own. *I need* to wait at least an hour to cool down before discussing it with you" or "*I feel* upset *when you* discuss my mental health issues with the family *because* it violates my privacy. *I need* privacy, so I will keep information about my mental health to myself from now on."

For Naomi, this approach might look like: "Ken, *I feel* uncomfortable *when you* make jokes about women *because* they are sexist and offensive. *I need* space from this behavior, so I will leave if you make these jokes again."

The Radical Transparency Approach

We can also use the radical transparency approach to set boundaries. As a reminder, this approach works best with people you trust: people who care for your well-being and are unlikely to weaponize the vulnerability of this approach against you.

- "It's hard for me to say this, but I want to be honest with you: ____________."
- "I know that in the past I've ____________, but I'm trying to take better care of myself now, so I can't continue to ____________."

- "I'm afraid of hurting you, but it's important to me that we can be honest with each other. I want you to know that I'm no longer able to ________________."
- "I'm nervous to say this, but I'm trying to be more honest with the people I love, so I need to tell you that I can't ________________."

Radical transparency looks like: "Dad, I'm afraid of hurting you, but it's important to me that we can be honest with each other. I want you to know that I can't listen when you vent about Mom anymore. It puts me in the middle and I'm not comfortable playing that role" or "Gloria, I know that in the past I've joined you and your friends for the annual retreat, but I'm trying to save money this year, so I can't make it."

Given how dismissive Ken has been, Naomi doesn't feel comfortable using the radical transparency approach with him. However, she might opt for this approach when communicating her new boundaries to her sister, Aria: "Aria, it's hard for me to say this, but I want to be honest with you: I'm no longer willing to be around Ken's sexist jokes. They're too much for me. If he makes them when we're together, I'll have to leave."

The Speaking Up Approach

Sometimes, we want to speak up as a means of making our own beliefs known. Especially if someone is expressing values or ideals we don't agree with, speaking up can be a way to both honor our integrity and insert a mental boundary: separation between what they believe and what we believe.

Speaking up can look like saying, "I disagree," "I don't share your opinion," "I actually believe that ________________," or "I find what you're saying to be sexist/racist/transphobic."

For Naomi, this approach might look like "Ken, I don't share your opinion, and I actually find it extremely disrespectful to women" or "Ken, that's a sexist comment and I fully disagree."

What about White Lies?

When we're worried about hurting someone's feelings, we might consider using a white lie to smooth over the interaction. When an acquaintance asks us to coffee and we're not interested, is it okay to tell them we're busy when we're not? When a distant colleague invites us to their baby shower and we don't want to stomach the cost of a gift, is it okay to lie and say we'll be out of town?

White lies can be helpful tools to smooth over awkwardness in low-stakes situations, especially with people we don't know very well. Being 100 percent honest 100 percent of the time isn't always feasible, or even desirable; in some cases, it only hurts others' feelings unnecessarily.

However, we shouldn't use white lies to avoid hard, important conversations with the people we're close to, especially if the situation is just going to arise again later. Repeated white lies that "we're just busy" or "just overwhelmed right now" become suspect; the people close to us can sense that we're not being fully honest. Over time, these white lies slowly erode trust in a relationship. It's better to be clear about where we stand, what we need, and what we want the relationship to look like—even if it's hard for others to hear.

PUTTING BOUNDARIES INTO ACTION

If we set a boundary that a certain behavior doesn't work for us, we need to remove ourselves from that behavior when it arises. Otherwise, our boundary is a meaningless statement that offers us no protection.

If you set a boundary that you can't participate in gossip anymore, then *enacting* it looks like exiting the interaction when someone starts gossiping. If you tell your mom that you can't take her calls during work hours anymore, *enacting* that boundary means letting the phone go to voicemail when she calls you during a meeting. If you set a boundary that you won't continue a conversation when your spouse is yelling, *enacting* it looks like leaving the conversation when your spouse yells.

Other people may not like our boundaries or may push back against them—we'll discuss this soon—but ultimately, because our boundaries are about our own actions, enacting them is always within our control.

Do I Always Need to State My Boundary?

Not all boundaries need to be spoken. It can be helpful to state your boundary aloud if this is the first time the other person is hearing about your need; if you're making a change to an established pattern in your relationship, and you want the other person to be aware of it; or if it's important to you that the other person understands how their behavior is impacting your actions.

However, you might decide not to state your boundary—and simply enact it—if you've already stated your needs and made multiple requests to no avail; if you know from past experience that stating your boundaries with this person always leads to harsh pushback; or if your need is urgent, and you don't have the emotional bandwidth for a conversation about your boundary.

Since Naomi has already made her feelings and needs known, she doesn't need to state her boundary aloud. She can simply enact it: she can leave the room when Ken makes offensive jokes or be less available for family gatherings if she knows Ken will be there.

DISENGAGING AS BOUNDARY-SETTING

When we disengage, we exit an interaction that is harmful to us. By disengaging, we acknowledge that we can't control others' actions, but we *can* control the part we play in our dynamic. Instead of playing tug-of-war, we drop the rope.

For the longest time, the idea of disengaging to set boundaries felt strange to me. After all, I was trying to get better at speaking up, and this felt like the *opposite* of speaking up. I worried that disengaging was the same as avoiding conflict: something I did in my people-pleasing days. However, I quickly learned that disengaging as a form of people-pleasing is very different from disengaging as a form of boundary-setting.

For years, one of my family members had made judgmental comments about other people's weight. It bothered me to no end. I'd spent *years* struggling with my weight, as had many of my loved ones, and I found these comments callous and dehumanizing. I tried so many times to convince them to stop, but it never worked. They thought I was being "too sensitive" and taking things "too seriously." No matter how much I argued and cajoled, they wouldn't change.

These frequent debates took a toll on me. After every single one, I felt frustration and rage, and it took hours for me to feel calm again. Eventually, I realized that I was trying to change someone who wouldn't change and harming myself in the process. So instead of continuing to speak up, I disengaged. When they made comments about people's weight, I didn't reply. I didn't respond to the text; I ended the phone call; I left the room. I couldn't control them, but I could control whether I dignified their comments with my participation and my presence.

Disengaging from a place of people-pleasing is *fear-based.* When we disengage out of fear, we're thinking: "I'm afraid to speak up because I want them to like me," or "I don't want to rock the boat, so I better stay quiet," or "I don't want them to know I have this need because I'm afraid they'll judge me, so I won't say anything."

Disengaging as a boundary is *power-based.* When we disengage as a boundary, we're thinking: "I can't control how they treat me, but I can control how much negative treatment I choose to endure," or "I will not spend my valuable time and energy debating this once again," or "I will not dignify this rude comment with a response."

Sometimes, a person's behavior is so hurtful that our only option is to leave the relationship entirely. Other times, we find that we can maintain a relationship if we disengage from unpleasant interactions, or decrease our degree of intimacy over time. There are six boundary strategies—three short-term strategies and three big-picture strategies—that we can use to disengage in this manner. Please note that not every method will work for every circumstance, and it's possible that not every method will feel like the right fit for you.

Short-Term Strategy: Exit the Interaction

When we exit an interaction, we remove ourselves physically or verbally from an unpleasant situation. Physically exiting might look like walking out of the room; creating physical space between us and the person engaging in the behavior; or leaving the environment altogether. Verbally exiting can look like not replying to a message or call; hanging up the phone; or choosing to stay silent instead of being goaded into an argument.

This method works well for: most interactions if you're able to physically leave the space.

For Naomi, this method looks like leaving the room or the gathering when Ken makes crude jokes, or not replying to Ken's text messages that contain offensive comments.

Short-Term Strategy: Go Gray Rock

Coined by a blogger named Skylar in 2012, the gray rock method is a strategy for dealing with unwanted behaviors when we can't exit an interaction physically, but still want to curtail our involvement in it. Going gray rock entails becoming as unresponsive and unexpressive as possible. In the face of an unwanted behavior, we don't give the other person the satisfaction of our engagement, avoiding eye contact, giving short, one-word answers, or appearing completely disengaged.

At first, going gray rock can sound a lot like people-pleasing: staying silent to avoid conflict. Again, what makes this method different is our intention and mindset. Staying silent as a form of people-pleasing is fear-driven; going gray rock as a boundary is a way of saying, "I will not dignify this interaction with my involvement."

This method works well for: interactions when you can't leave the physical space; interactions with frustrating colleagues.

For example: Vikram's family immigrated to the United States from India twenty years ago. Now twenty-five, Vikram has grown to be a free spirit; meanwhile, his parents are very traditional. They constantly ask him about his dating life and encourage him to get married, and though he's asked them hundreds of times to stop, they continue.

On the car ride home from a family dinner, Vikram's parents try to persuade him to go on a date with a family friend's daughter. He's heard this lecture before; it's frustrating, but he can't exit the interaction because he's stuck in the car. Instead of engaging, Vikram goes gray rock: he stares out the window and offers only brief *mhms* and *uh-huhs*. Eventually, his parents tire themselves out and start talking about something else.

Short-Term Strategy: Differentiate

Differentiation is the ability to know where we end and others begin: to recognize that we are fundamentally separate from others. The more differentiated we are, the more of a strong and independent sense of self we bring to our relationships. From this place of separateness, others' differing thoughts or feelings are less threatening. We're less dependent upon others' agreement or approval because we are confident within ourselves.

When we're less differentiated, we think, "They must agree with me and approve of me," but when we're more differentiated, we think, "It would be nice if they approved, but it's not necessary."

When we're less differentiated, we think, "I can't tolerate conflict or disagreement," but when we're more differentiated, we think, "We are two separate people; we don't have to agree on everything."

When we're less differentiated, we think, "I can't help but react to everything they feel, say, and do," but when we're more differentiated, we think, "I can choose whether or not to react when their behavior annoys me."

When we practice differentiation as a boundary, we observe someone's behavior without reacting to it. When someone says something we don't agree with, we can remind ourselves: "Just because they act, that doesn't mean that I need to *react*," or "I don't like that they believe this, but they are entitled to their own beliefs," or "Just because they're having this emotional experience doesn't mean I need to fix it."

This method works well for: interactions with people who have opinions and beliefs that differ from our own; interactions with difficult collaborators on a project; interactions with people who we love, but who don't share our values.

I've used this strategy many times when interacting with family members whose political beliefs differ vastly from my own. For years, I debated them fiercely, doing everything I could to change their views. No matter how many compelling statistics or heart-wrenching stories I shared, it never worked. Every time, I ended up feeling angry, fatigued, and, most of all, disconnected. The more I tried to change them, the more our relationship suffered.

I eventually came to the conclusion that maintaining these relationships was more important than seeing eye to eye, so when they expressed their views in conversation, I began to differentiate. I intentionally chose not to react as I reminded myself: *They already know how I feel. We are separate people; we don't have to agree on everything. This is not what I believe, but they are entitled to their beliefs.*

I knew I could advocate for important causes and make a difference in other areas of my life. I was gaining nothing—and losing a lot—by unsuccessfully trying to change the minds of my loved ones. By differentiating, I began to feel grounded in myself instead of forced into yet another debate I didn't want to have.

MAKING BIG-PICTURE SHIFTS

Disengaging from difficult interactions can protect us in the short term, but repeatedly needing to disengage can become exhausting over time. Sometimes, we need to do more than just take space; we need to make a big-picture shift to the relationship.

The following big-picture shifts reduce our participation in the relationship overall and give us more space, time, and distance from behavior we find difficult or unacceptable. Sometimes, reducing our participation is enough to make the discomfort of the connection feel bearable. Sometimes, we find that we need to leave a relationship altogether to truly feel safe.

Big-Picture Strategy: Decrease Intimacy

When someone is unwilling to change their behavior, we can't change them. We can only decide how close and connected we want to be with them, and make big-picture adjustments to how frequently we spend time with them; the length of time we spend with them; the methods we use to communicate with them (e.g., phone, text, email, etc.); the topics we choose to discuss with them; or the entanglements we share with them (e.g., co-owning a business, sharing pets, etc.). Interacting with a complicated relationship in smaller doses can help it feel less taxing and more sustainable over time.

This method works well for: any relationship that you wish to maintain but, in its current form, feels overwhelming, tiring, frustrating, or otherwise impairs your mental health.

For Naomi, this method looks like telling Aria she can only come for dinner once a month, not once a week; telling Aria that if she'd like to get together otherwise, she can only do so if Ken isn't involved; limiting her time spent at Ken and Aria's house to two hours maximum; and getting a hotel room when her parents host the family for the holidays so that she can have space from Ken.

Naomi understands that if she wants to maintain a relationship with Aria, she will have to see Ken, at least occasionally. However, interacting with him in smaller doses might help Naomi feel less overwhelmed. It will still be frustrating and difficult, but she prefers this option to ending the relationship altogether and managing the corresponding fallout with her sister.

Big-Picture Strategy: Adjust Expectations

If we wish to sustain a relationship, it's critical that we adjust our expectations of the other person to accurately reflect the *reality* of how they treat us and their degree of emotional maturity. We'll feel permanently disappointed and resentful if we're constantly measuring the relationship against our imagined ideal. Setting realistic expectations allows us to appreciate the connection for what it is now instead of what we wish it were. Typically, we also pair this method with another form of boundary-setting, like decreasing intimacy.

When we adjust our expectations, we might replace the belief "One day, they'll give me all the affection I crave" with "They may never show me affection in the way I'd like them to." We might swap "They will accept me and approve of my choices" with "They may never truly understand or support me." Instead of believing "One day we'll be super close, just like other families," we might accept that "We may never be close the way other families are."

This method works well for: relationships that you wish to maintain but feel chronically disappointed by; relationships with family members that are a regular source of frustration.

Sometimes, we hold out hope that others will become who we want them to be despite piles of evidence to the contrary. Suspending reality like this prevents us from setting the boundaries we need. Naomi has spent a long time trying to find a magic solution to her woes with Ken. She has made many requests and resisted setting boundaries, thinking, *This isn't fair! He should recognize just how harmful these jokes are. My sister should cut him loose.*

Unfortunately, these resentful musings haven't yielded any changes. Naomi is finally beginning to accept that the only solution is to change her reactions to Ken's behavior. To adjust her expectations, she reminds herself: *No amount of arguing will make Ken change. He may never be someone I can feel comfortable around. His marriage to my sister might mean that I need to remove myself from family interactions if I'm going to respect my own boundaries. It sucks, but it's the reality of the situation.*

Big-Picture Strategy: Leave the Relationship Altogether

The decision to end a relationship is a highly personal one. Sometimes, especially in the face of abject harm or mistreatment, leaving the relationship is the only boundary that will preserve our health and well-being. Sometimes, the decision to leave is less clear-cut. What about the friend who really bothers you, but also shows you care? What about the family member whose beliefs you find repugnant—but with whom you have a long and storied past? What about the loved one who seems incapable of holding space for you in conversations—but shows you kindness in other ways?

Unfortunately, there's no calculator into which we can plug our grievances and receive a clear instruction to stay or go. The ultimate decision lies with us. As we contemplate whether a relationship is one we need to leave entirely, these questions can help us gain clarity:

- Has this relationship consistently caused me more harm than good?
- Is this relationship having chronic, negative impacts on my mental or physical health?
- Have I already experimented with different boundaries to make this relationship feel more sustainable? Have they failed?
- Is the only reason I'm staying in this relationship external (e.g., to gain others' approval, to avoid judgment, to make others happy)?

Naomi, Revisited

Naomi begins enacting her boundaries with Ken. The next week, Aria and Ken host dinner and invite Naomi and their parents.

Over dessert, Naomi shares that she just lost some money in a bad stock investment. "I'm pretty frustrated," she admits. "It was a promising company, but it totally tanked this week. All that money down the drain."

Her parents and Aria offer consoling murmurs. Ken stretches his arms above his head and sighs lazily. "What did I tell you, Naomi? This is why you have to leave investing to the boys."

Naomi feels heat rise to her cheeks. *This is it*, she thinks. She closes her eyes for a moment, takes a deep breath, and stands from her seat.

"Thanks for the lovely dinner," she says to the table, "but I have to get going now."

As she walks into the kitchen with her plate, Ken calls out: "Jesus, come on, Naomi! Are you really going to ruin the night over a joke?"

For a moment, Naomi questions herself—*Am I being too sensitive?*—but the fire in her heart says otherwise. She doesn't respond to Ken's provocation. Instead, she simply places her dish in the sink, grabs her purse from the counter, and walks out the front door.

When Naomi gets to her car, she is shaking. On the one hand, she feels guilty for walking out mid-dinner, and she wonders if her family is upset with her. On the other hand, she also feels *strong*: she can't help but contrast the power she feels in this moment with the powerlessness she feels when she silently listens to Ken's remarks.

The next day, Aria calls Naomi. "I know you don't like his sense of humor," says Aria, frustrated, "but did you *really* have to leave? It made everyone feel kind of awkward."

"Aria," responds Naomi, "I love you, but yes, I *really* did have to leave. I'm just not comfortable being around those comments anymore."

Aria sighs.

Naomi continues. "Honestly, moving forward, I think it's best if you and I spend more time together one-on-one. I can still come by once a month or so for dinner, but right now, weekly feels like too much."

Aria is silent for a moment. "I'll think about it," she responds quietly. "It just sucks to feel like my own sister doesn't like my husband."

Naomi can sense Aria's disappointment. She knows Aria wants her to be reassuring; to affirm that she *does*, in fact, like Ken. It takes everything in her power not to fall into the old habit of being dishonest just to create harmony.

"I can understand the difficult position you're in, Aria," says Naomi.

"If Ken ever decides to stop making sexist remarks, we can talk about putting weekly dinners back on the calendar."

They hang up shortly after, Aria agreeing to meet Naomi next week for coffee one-on-one. As Naomi ends the call, she feels those two familiar feelings: the guilt alongside the strength. Aria isn't happy, that's clear—but Naomi *finally* feels like she's not betraying herself just to keep the peace. It's enough to help her feel confident moving forward with her boundaries.

NAVIGATING BOUNDARY PUSHBACK

Some people will be completely receptive to our boundaries. Others will be disappointed or hurt by them, but will ultimately respect them with their actions. Still others won't like our boundaries and will do everything they can to push back against them.

Boundary pushback can look like someone telling us why our boundary is mean or unfair; trying to start a debate about our boundary; using anger and hostility to get us to change our mind; using guilt trips to get us to change our mind (e.g., "If you don't come home for Christmas, you'll ruin the holiday for everyone"); or trying to gaslight us (e.g., "You're crazy—I never do what you're accusing me of doing!").

Faced with their resistance, we might be tempted to take back our boundary to keep the peace. But we absolutely must stay the course. Instead of changing our boundary, it's important that we limit our engagement with boundary pushback. To do so, we can use one of the following strategies:

Empathize and Hold Firm

When we empathize and hold firm, we acknowledge the recipient's frustration, hurt, or disappointment while also maintaining our boundary. This approach works best with people we trust: people who generally show that they have our best interests at heart.

We might say, "I understand that this is disappointing for you. I really need this in order to feel safe/comfortable/balanced," or "I can see that you're upset. This is important to me, and it will help me feel more comfortable in our relationship," or "I know that you are hurt by this. I care about you, and I want our relationship to last. This will help our connection feel more doable for me in the long-term."

The Broken Record Technique

The broken record technique is a form of assertive communication originally coined by Manuel J. Smith. When we use this technique, we repeat the same message over and over to avoid getting sucked into a debate or argument. For example:

NAOMI: "I can't come over for dinner every week."

ARIA: "But, Naomi, we're family. Don't you think it's a little ridiculous that you're so offended by Ken's jokes?"

NAOMI: "That may be your opinion, but I can't come over for dinner every week."

ARIA: "Can't, or won't? This seems like a trivial hill to die on, doesn't it?"

NAOMI: "I can't come over for dinner every week."

Exit the Interaction

Exiting the interaction is a completely reasonable response in the face of pushback. This may feel heavy-handed, but remember: they have shown us with their actions that they're not willing to respect our boundary. At this point, our responsibility isn't to cater to their emotions—it's to protect ourselves. Leaving the situation can look like physically walking out of the room, hanging up the phone, or not replying to a text message.

THE HARD TRUTH ABOUT BOUNDARIES

Silvy Khoucasian, a relationship coach and therapist, puts it well: "Sometimes, one person's boundaries are incompatible with another person's needs." Our new boundaries may highlight a fundamental mismatch in needs that makes a relationship unsustainable. We're allowed to set boundaries with others, and they're allowed to determine if those boundaries work for them. A friend might be so offended by our boundaries that they choose to end the friendship. A loved one might tell us that these new parameters simply don't work for them. A family member might say that they'd rather be completely disconnected than deal with us within our boundaries.

In these cases, the only way to maintain the relationship would be to revert to our old, people-pleasing ways. Like Naomi, we may feel tempted to do whatever it takes to keep the peace—but we must remember that relationships that are only sustainable when we self-neglect are unhealthy for us. We've spent a lifetime witnessing the mental and physical toll they take.

After years of silence and passivity, our boundaries are how we begin to trust ourselves to protect ourselves. At their core, they are a declaration of self-respect; they make known that we will no longer tolerate mistreatment, imbalance, or neglect. The more comfortable we become with setting boundaries, the more we recognize that we don't have to exist in relationships solely on others' terms. We, too, get a say.

11

SETTING EMOTIONAL BOUNDARIES

While the boundaries we discussed in the previous chapter create space between ourselves and others' behavior, emotional boundaries create healthy separation between ourselves and others' emotions. Without emotional boundaries, others' feelings flood into our own like ink into a pool of water. We become so engulfed by everyone else's stress, anxiety, frustration, and sadness that we struggle to access what *we* feel and what *we* need.

People-pleasers have underdeveloped emotional boundaries because many of us learned to manage others' feelings as a way to stay safe in childhood. As adults, when we lack emotional boundaries, we feel responsible for solving others' problems; offer unsolicited advice; enter conflicts that don't involve us; struggle to agree to disagree; and do whatever it takes to assuage others' anger, frustration, and anxiety. Over time, this emotional self-abandonment results in not being able to identify what *we* feel and need; altering our actions to please others in ways that harm us; and feeling like our lives are not truly our own.

When we strengthen our emotional boundaries, we gain stability, independence, and autonomy. We become capable of having compassion for others' discomfort without feeling responsible for fixing it. Free from this burden of undue responsibility, we finally have the space to prioritize ourselves.

For the recovering people-pleaser who was taught that everyone else's feelings were theirs to manage, emotional boundaries are some of the most liberating boundaries of all. In this chapter, we'll learn how to release a sense of responsibility for others' emotions; distinguish between feeling compassion for someone's emotions and feeling responsible for them; and explore the four steps to setting healthy emotional boundaries in our relationships with friends, partners, family members, and loved ones.

AMY'S STORY

Sophia has two adult children: Amy, twenty-five, and Noah, thirty. Amy is affectionate and outgoing, and she and her mother have always been close. Noah is moodier and more withdrawn, and his relationship with Sophia is loving, but strained.

Noah moved across the country when he went to college, but Amy went to a local university to stay near her family. Now she visits her parents for dinner at least once a week, and she and Sophia speak on the phone nearly every day.

Ever since Amy was a child, many of her conversations with her mother were about Sophia's frustrations with Noah. Depending on the day, Sophia would be upset by his disrespectful attitude, yearning for a deeper connection with him, or disapproving of his new job or girlfriend. For years, Amy listened compassionately to Sophia's complaints and offered advice where she could. She felt grateful to be her mother's teammate and confidante in these covert conversations.

However, as she's gotten older, Amy's begun to feel overwhelmed by her mother's frustrations. When Sophia complains about Noah, Amy feels her mother's unhappiness wrapping around her like a vice. Despite Amy's plentiful advice, Sophia never changes her behavior or addresses her complaints with Noah directly. For Amy, their conversations are beginning to feel both exasperating and purposeless; she wishes her relationship with her mother could be more about *them* and less about Noah. As these feelings of resentment build, Amy realizes that she needs some emotional boundaries; she's no longer comfortable in her old role as a sounding board.

TELLING A NEW STORY OF RESPONSIBILITY

As people-pleasers, we've spent our lives accommodating, prioritizing, tending to, and tiptoeing around others' emotions. Deep down, many of us believe that we're responsible for making everyone in our lives feel good; that we're not safe if others are uncomfortable; that managing others' emotions makes us worthy of their affection; or that we won't be lovable if we focus on our own feelings.

Perhaps we, like Amy, spent our childhoods being confidantes, therapists, or sounding boards for caregivers who over-relied on us for emotional support. This parentified relationship may have left us with the false impression that we had to take care of others' emotions at the expense of our own. Perhaps our caregivers grappled with addiction, mental health challenges, or other hardships, and to ease their suffering, we donned a permanent mask of cheerfulness, believing it was our responsibility to brighten others' moods. Or perhaps our caregivers were emotionally dysregulated, incapable of effectively handling their own stress, sadness, anxiety, or anger. Lindsay Gibson, in her book *Adult Children of Emotionally Immature Parents*, depicts how being raised in such environments results in having underdeveloped emotional boundaries:

> Emotional parents are run by their feelings, swinging between over-involvement and abrupt withdrawal. They are prone to frightening instability and unpredictability. Overwhelmed by anxiety, they rely on others to stabilize them. . . .

> It doesn't take much to upset them, and then everyone in the family scrambles to soothe them. . . . Many children of such parents learn to subjugate themselves to other people's wishes. Because they grew up anticipating their parent's stormy emotional weather, they can be overly attentive to other people's feelings and moods, often to their own detriment.

Through experiences like this, we may have learned that the only way to attain a sense of safety was to be a fire extinguisher for our caregivers' bursts of anger, anxiety, or stress.

As we break the people-pleasing pattern, we must recognize that our caregivers were wrong to make us responsible for managing their emotions. Fundamentally, children are not responsible for knowing how to make their volatile caregivers less angry or their depressed caregivers more cheerful. The pressures they imposed upon us—intentionally or not—to take care of them emotionally, dispel their difficult feelings, or create harmony in the household were not fair, realistic, or age-appropriate.

Recognizing that our sense of responsibility stems from inappropriate expectations in the past helps us reorient that sense of responsibility in the present. As adults, we are each responsible for regulating our own emotions. Though we can (and should!) offer others support, compassion, and kindness when we have the capacity, we are not the managers of their emotions. Others' emotions are fundamentally their responsibility, and our emotions are fundamentally ours.

Amy takes some time to reflect on her old beliefs and is surprised to notice a surge of unfamiliar anger toward her mother. She reflects on all the phone calls, dinners, and car rides spent problem-solving Sophia's and Noah's troubles. Amy imagines herself as a child—pigtails, strap-on sneakers, and all—listening earnestly to her mother's many adult concerns. She thinks of all the hours she spent tending to her mother's emotions that her mother could have, *should* have, spent tending to her.

For Amy, this anger feels almost sacrilegious, like she's betraying her mother by being upset with her. However, Amy's anger is an important sign of emotional separateness: a sign that Amy is beginning to honor that her relationship with her mother hasn't met her needs.

Amy thinks: *I spent my life believing that my mother's relationship with Noah was my responsibility to manage; that I could single-handedly mend their connection; and that talking with me was the only way my mother could get support on this issue. Now I'm working on trusting that my mother's relationship with Noah is her responsibility to manage; that she and Noah are the only ones who can mend their relationship; and that she has more appropriate options for getting support, like talking with my father or seeing a therapist.*

Amy notices how strange and unfamiliar these new beliefs feel. She intellectually recognizes their accuracy, but her heart still feels responsible for her mother's emotions. *As a parent, it must be hard for my mother to have such a difficult relationship with her son,* Amy thinks. *I still want to show her care and compassion.*

For Amy, like for so many of us, setting emotional boundaries will require her to distinguish between having compassion for her mother's emotions and taking responsibility for them.

COMPASSION VS. RESPONSIBILITY

Not caring about others' emotions isn't the goal of emotional boundaries. It's entirely healthy to have compassion for others' feelings: to feel a little sad when a loved one feels sad, or to be troubled by a loved one's struggles. In fact, the success of intimate relationships depends on this sort of empathy. However, problems arise when we take *responsibility* for others' emotions. Then, others' feelings begin to dominate our lives; our ability to understand what *we* feel and need becomes clouded; we feel obligated to give support that violates our own boundaries; and we find ourselves unable to participate in our relationships as independent people.

On the other hand, when we show others *compassion*, we're genuinely interested in their well-being. We may listen empathetically to their struggles; offer them kindness; and give support *within the scope of our own boundaries and limitations*. We're happy to help, while also recognizing that ultimately, they—not we—are the true captains of their own emotional experience.

When we develop healthy emotional boundaries grounded in compassion instead of responsibility, we're able to offer kindness, love, and support without feeling responsible for changing others' emotional states; witness others' emotions without letting them become ours; set limits around how much support we can offer during a difficult time; tolerate differences of emotional state in our relationships (e.g., stay calm even in the presence of a partner's anxiety); and take others' emotions into account without letting them become the sole deciding factor for our decisions.

Amy realizes that in the past, no matter what sort of day she was having—no matter how she felt—she always put her mother's emotions first. Sophia's emotions became Amy's emotions. In retrospect, Amy can see how these tendencies were more than just having compassion for her mother; they were taking responsibility for her. From here on out, Amy promises herself that she will set boundaries separating her own emotions from Sophia's.

FOUR STEPS FOR EMOTIONAL BOUNDARIES

Setting emotional boundaries requires us to recognize the urge to take responsibility for others' emotions; create a sense of emotional separateness; shift our actions with a boundary; and remember the long-term benefits.

STEP 1: RECOGNIZE THE URGE TO TAKE RESPONSIBILITY

The first step in setting any boundary is becoming aware of our need for one. At first, it may be difficult for us to recognize our urge to take responsibility for others' emotions because it dominates so many of our interactions. It is the water we swim in, and thus, invisible to us.

The following behaviors are helpful signposts that draw our attention to our need for an emotional boundary:

We're Trying to Fix Others' Problems

Like Amy, do you find yourself trying to resolve conflicts between members of your family? Are you the first to attempt to smooth things over when members of your friend group are on the outs? When someone approaches you with a personal problem, do you feel like your advice is the only thing that can save them from their distress?

Beneath our attempts to resolve others' conflicts lie our hidden beliefs about their ability to manage their own problems and withstand their own emotions. Perhaps we get involved because we don't believe that they can handle it on their own; perhaps we believe that we have the best solution.

Many of us adopt this fixer role because we feel fundamentally uncomfortable witnessing others' discomfort. Yes, we want to help—but we also want to eliminate *their* discomfort because it *feels as if it were our own*; it has trickled into our own emotional bubble. We'll go to great lengths to eliminate such discomfort, even if that means stepping on others' toes in the process.

We're Considering Changing Our Behavior in Response to a Guilt Trip, Even When We've Done Nothing Wrong

Instead of making informed decisions that prioritize our own needs, desires, and values, we may succumb to guilt trips and do what others want us to do, simply because their discomfort is so palpable, and so uncomfortable, to us.

For the first time in six months, Margot, a single mother, plans a night out with her girlfriends. She's been incredibly busy at work and desperately needs an evening to relax and enjoy her friends' company.

The night she's scheduled to go out, Margot's boyfriend, Bruce, asks if she'd like to come over. When she explains that she has plans with friends, Bruce is disappointed. "You've been so busy at work that I've only been able to see you once a week," he complains. "Come on. Can't you see your friends another time?"

Margot knows how badly she needs this rare night out, but she's so uncomfortable with Bruce's disappointment that she considers changing her plans. This is a clear sign that Margot needs an emotional boundary.

We're Struggling to Agree to Disagree

Without emotional boundaries, we struggle to discern where we end and others begin. Despite being in a two-person relationship, we may see ourselves as fundamentally one unit. This can feel pleasant when things are harmonious, but it can become deeply uncomfortable when we don't share the same feelings or beliefs. Because we see ourselves as one entity, we may feel a deep, even frantic need to reach an agreement on issues big and small, often sacrificing our own feelings and opinions in the process.

Clay and Halley have been dating for six months when Clay invites Halley to his company's annual holiday party. They get dressed up and spend a pleasant evening enjoying food and drink with Clay's colleagues. On the car ride home, they hold hands and recap some of their favorite moments. Clay asks Halley what she thought of his teammates. Halley speaks favorably about almost everyone she met, but admits that she found his colleague Rick somewhat annoying.

Clay is surprised; he doesn't share Halley's opinion. When he asks her why she feels that way, she offers a few reasons that Clay doesn't find satisfying.

"I don't agree," Clay rebuts. "He's not annoying."

Halley shrugs. "Okay, I didn't mean to be offensive," she replies. "That's just my take. We can drop it."

Clay feels tempted to continue the discussion. He's head over heels for Halley and they agree on nearly everything; he doesn't like the fact that they don't share the same opinion of Rick. However, this disagreement is relatively low-stakes; Clay and Halley don't have to feel the same way about every single person and idea. Clay's difficulty agreeing to disagree is a sign that he needs a firmer emotional boundary.

We Spend Too Much Energy Seeking Approval for Our Decisions

When we're highly reactive to others' emotions, our own enthusiasm, passion, or intuition never feel like enough; we need others' approval, too. When making decisions, we may feel the need to call every close friend in our contact list to get their advice. The tiniest hint of doubt, disapproval, or disagreement from a loved one stops us in our tracks and makes us question everything we thought we wanted. Chronic approval-seeking is a sign that we're disconnected from our own emotional center and need a firmer sense of separateness.

We Do Whatever It Takes to Assuage Others' Sadness, Frustration, or Anxiety, Even If Those Actions Aren't Aligned with Our Values

When we lack emotional boundaries, we feel the urge to dispel all discomfort in our vicinity—even if that means acting against our own best interests. This can look like saying yes to a second date with someone we're not interested in because we don't want to hurt their feelings; laughing at an offensive joke to smooth over the tension it creates; agreeing to help with a project we don't have time for; giving money to a person or cause out of a sense of guilt or obligation instead of genuine desire; agreeing to unwanted sexual intimacy because we don't want them to feel rejected (more on this in chapter 19); or redacting an important boundary because someone else is sad about it.

STEP 2: REMEMBER EMOTIONAL SEPARATENESS

A popular quote widely attributed to psychiatrist Viktor Frankl reads: "Between stimulus and response lies a space. In that space lie our freedom and power to choose a response." Once we realize that we're feeling the urge to take responsibility for others' emotions, we can insert a space between this recognition and our old, habitual actions. During this pause, we can remember our separateness and recall that, as adults, we are each responsible for feeling and managing our own emotions.

It's helpful to remember that our emotional boundaries are like a protective bubble, keeping our emotions within and others' emotions on the periphery. Taking a moment to visualize this bubble helps us internalize our emotional separateness in a concrete way. It might feel silly to imagine a bubble surrounding you in the midst of a heated discussion, but it works! Visual metaphors have been proven to help us understand our problems and imagine new solutions, and we can easily access them in moments of need.

Our boundary bubble can take various forms. Consider the imagery that most resonates with you. Do you prefer the image of a translucent bubble in which you feel safe? A shimmering force field that surrounds your entire body head to toe? A sturdy castle surrounded by a protective moat? A bold circle drawn on the ground around you?

We may find it helpful to accompany our visualization with a simple mantra, such as "We are two separate people," "I am at peace inside my bubble," "That does not belong to me," "Their emotions cannot penetrate my bubble," or "Only my bubble is my responsibility."

We can also proactively visualize our bubble to fortify us before entering situations that we know will be emotionally charged. We might do a visualization before going home for the holidays where we tend to take on our parents' stress; getting coffee with a friend who always has some sort of emotional emergency; addressing a grievance with our partner; or entering difficult workplace meetings.

The next time Sophia calls Amy to complain about Noah, Amy pauses and imagines a shimmering bubble around her. This bubble is Amy's space, and hers alone; in it, she is at peace. She can hear her mother's words, but they don't penetrate her bubble; she imagines that, like raindrops on the roof, they simply land on her bubble and fall slowly away. This visualization helps remind Amy to stay grounded within herself in the face of her mother's discomfort.

Taking a time-out can also help us remember our emotional separateness. If we find ourselves in a challenging interaction that triggers our feeling of responsibility, we should pause and step away if possible. We might take ten minutes to leave the interaction, find a quiet space alone, take a series of deep breaths, and pay attention to the sensations moving through our bodies. This brief break from others' emotions enables us to reconnect with ourselves and be present for our own emotional reality.

STEP 3. SHIFT OUR ACTIONS WITH A BOUNDARY

Once we've created emotional space, it's time to respond to the situation before us. In the past, we would have offered unsolicited advice; attempted to solve others' problems; gotten involved in others' conflicts; or done whatever we could to assuage others' anger, frustration, anxiety, or guilt. Now we're committed to responding in new ways. This new response typically takes the form of an internal or external boundary. If *we are the only ones* expecting ourselves to take responsibility for others' emotions, an internal boundary is all we need. However, if *others are expecting us* to manage, solve, or fix their emotions for them, we will need to set a boundary with them as well.

Setting an Internal Boundary

Fundamentally, emotional boundaries are internal boundaries: we're promising *ourselves* that we will no longer try to fix, solve, or manage other's feelings. Internal emotional boundaries look like this:

DEBORAH

Deborah and her daughter, Pema, are very close. Pema is away at college for her freshman year, and when she calls Deborah and shares the challenges she's facing—like deciding which sports team to join and struggling with the workload—Deborah rushes immediately into problem-solving mode. Pema tells her mom that she finds this frustrating; she wishes she would simply empathize and listen instead of immediately offering solutions. In this case, Deborah needs an *internal boundary* because she is the only one expecting herself to take responsibility for Pema's problems. She needs to resist the impulse to problem-solve.

Deborah's internal boundary might be: "I will not provide unsolicited solutions to Pema's problems. I will simply listen and empathize. If Pema asks me for my advice, I will offer it."

SIENNA

Sienna, a college student, has been dating her boyfriend Brad for six months. Sienna is preparing to leave for a semester abroad in France, and while Brad has been very supportive, he's sad that they'll be apart for so long. Witnessing his sadness has been challenging for her—so challenging that she's been considering canceling her trip.

Sienna needs an *internal boundary* because, like Deborah, she's the only one expecting herself to "solve" Brad's discomfort. She wants to get better at prioritizing her goals and dreams even when they're not perfectly aligned with those around her.

Sienna's internal boundary might be: "I will pursue my dreams, even if I know Brad will miss me" or "I will stay grounded in my own excitement about this semester abroad."

BEFORE AND AFTER

When we set an internal boundary, we're changing our *own* expectations and behavior. In practice, this might look like:

BEFORE AN INTERNAL BOUNDARY	AFTER AN INTERNAL BOUNDARY
Providing solutions to a loved one's problem	Listening compassionately as they share about their problem and affirming their ability to handle it
Laughing at an offensive joke to make the teller more comfortable	Letting the joke land on silence
Changing your behavior because you've been guilt-tripped	Staying the course and affirming your own choices internally
Arguing in circles to get somebody to understand your point of view	Allowing a conversation to end, feeling confident in your own opinion and agreeing to disagree

Setting a Boundary with Others

When *others* are expecting us to manage, solve, or fix their emotions for them, we can set an external boundary, alerting them that we're no longer willing to play that role. An external boundary may also be helpful if we're no longer offering support that we'd previously offered.

Chloe's longtime boyfriend, Ben, regularly comes home from work stressed because he and his boss don't get along. Every night over dinner, Ben asks Chloe to help him process their conversations. "How should I handle this?" he asks her. "What should I say?"

For a while Chloe was happy to help, but these sessions have become so frequent that she feels frustrated and resentful. She's no longer willing to participate in this daily problem-solving. As an external boundary, she might say to Ben: "I'm sorry you're having such a hard time at work. I want to support you, but these daily conversations about your boss are overwhelming for me. I'm happy to talk about it with you once a week, but not every day." Or, she might say: "Ben, I'm so sorry you're experiencing this at work. I can't give you any solutions, but I'm happy to listen."

HELGA

Helga, forty, regularly meets her parents for dinner downtown. Helga's father, Gene, is curmudgeonly and bad-tempered. No matter what restaurant they choose, Gene finds something to complain about—and loudly. Helga and her mother, Elly, feel responsible for Gene's rudeness and apologize to restaurant staff on his behalf.

Recently, Helga has been working on setting emotional boundaries. She finds her father's behavior embarrassing, and she's no longer willing to play peacekeeper. The next time it happens, she notices her own discomfort—imagines her own boundary bubble—and sets an external boundary: "Dad, I feel embarrassed when you criticize the waitstaff. It strikes me as rude and makes our dinners feel tense. I'm not willing to sit here with you if it continues."

If Gene doesn't stop, Helga can leave the restaurant and go home, or pause her involvement in the family dinners altogether.

Same Situation, Different Boundaries

Some situations can be resolved with either internal or external boundaries; the choice is ours. In these cases, we can decide whether (1) we find the other person's behavior so distressing that we need to remove ourselves from it, or (2) we feel capable of creating enough *emotional* distance from their behavior that being around it doesn't affect us too deeply.

These examples show how internal and external boundaries can be applied to the same situation:

AUTUMN

Autumn and her husband, Jeff, are parents to Colin, twenty-nine. Colin has been using drugs on and off for five years, and it's put an enormous strain on the family. One night, Autumn and Jeff discover Colin stealing money from their bedroom. They're at their wit's end, and they give him a choice: either they press charges, or they will pay for him to enter a six-week rehab facility for his addiction.

Colin has been in rehab for two weeks. He calls Autumn daily to offer frantic apologies, complain about his peers, and beg her to take him home. It upsets Autumn to hear his distress, but she feels strongly that he needs to stay in rehab.

For Autumn, *weak emotional boundaries* would look like removing Colin from the facility because his discomfort makes her so uncomfortable. Instead, she could set an *internal boundary* by listening to Colin's complaints compassionately; reminding him of her love; maintaining her boundaries by not agreeing to his requests for removal; and self-soothing after his calls. She could also set an *external boundary* by telling Colin she has to get off the phone because she finds these daily pleas too distressing.

In both scenarios, Autumn maintains her boundaries by refusing to remove Colin from rehab. With an internal boundary, she stays in the interaction, but creates inner emotional distance; with an external boundary, she leaves the interaction to create emotional distance.

CLEO

Cleo, twenty-four, moved away from her hometown in Kansas to begin a new career in New York City. She and her mother, Cindy, are very close, and Cindy was devastated when Cleo moved away. They speak daily on the phone, and Cindy never ends a call without trying to guilt Cleo into moving back home.

For Cleo, *weak emotional boundaries* would look like apologizing for moving away and scheduling an immediate trip home, even though it's not convenient. Instead, she could set an *internal boundary* by agreeing with Cindy that the distance is hard; reminding her mother of the importance of her move; and changing the topic when guilt trips arise. Alternatively, she could set an *external boundary* by saying, "Mom, this move has been a difficult transition for both of us. Your guilt trips make this hard decision even harder for me. I won't be able to talk as often if this is how every call with you ends."

Again, in both boundary scenarios, Cleo maintains her boundaries by not rushing in to fix her mother's emotions. With her internal boundary, she stays on the call, but doesn't participate in the aspects of it that she finds frustrating; with an external boundary, she tells her mother she'll speak with her less often if the guilt trips continue.

Amy, Revisited

One morning, Sophia calls Amy with news. Sophia had been planning a trip to visit Noah, but the day before, he called to cancel; apparently a work deadline arose. This isn't the first time that he's canceled a visit last minute, and Sophia is devastated. She vents to Amy about her disappointment that Noah doesn't seem to want a close relationship with her.

As Amy listens to her mother's frustrations, she's tempted to offer advice and involve herself in the conflict—but then she remembers that this is an emotional boundary signpost. She takes a moment to recall her boundary bubble, shimmering and self-protective around her. Then Amy says gently to her mother, "I'm sorry to hear he canceled the trip; that's so frustrating. This actually reminds me of something I've wanted to talk with you about."

"Oh, okay, sweetheart," says Sophia. "What's going on?"

Amy takes a deep breath, acknowledging the fear she feels in the pit of her stomach. Bravely, she continues:

"Okay. This is kind of hard for me to say," she begins, her voice shaky, "but I'm realizing that it's hard for me to hear your frustrations about Noah. It makes me feel like I'm being put in the middle of two people I really care about. I love you, Mom, and I want to help you, but I think that it's best if you and I talk about other things."

Amy realizes that her hands are trembling as she finishes speaking. Her heart beats loud in her ears. It's silent on the other end of the line for longer than she would like.

"Mom?" Amy finally asks. "Are you still there?"

"I'm sorry, sweetie," Sophia replies. Her voice sounds far away. "I . . . I didn't realize I was putting you in the middle like that. You've always been so helpful during our talks. I didn't realize I was hurting you."

Amy's heart aches at her mother's response. The last thing she wants is for Sophia to feel *more* pain on top of the pain she's already feeling about Noah. But Amy resists the urge to rush in and take responsibility for her mother's emotions.

Instead, Amy replies softly, "I understand, Mom. I don't think I realized it, either, until recently. I know it wasn't intentional."

Amy can tell that her mother is rattled, but is doing her best not to show it. They end the call shortly after, signing off with the usual "I love you," and Amy feels a mixture of heaviness and guilt. She's terrified that she's hurt her mother. It takes all of Amy's strength not to redial Sophia, take her boundary back, and make herself available for whatever her mother needs.

STEP 4: REMEMBER THE LONG-TERM BENEFITS

As Amy's story shows, emotional boundaries—especially those that break old patterns of over-giving—can be difficult to set. Afterward, we may worry we've hurt our loved ones and feel overcome with guilt. In these moments, we can stay the course by remembering how these emotional boundaries will benefit ourselves, others, and our relationships as a whole in the long term.

We can reflect: What have I lost by taking responsibility for their emotions in the past (emotionally, mentally, financially, energetically)? How do I neglect my responsibility to *myself* by feeling overly responsible for their emotions? If I didn't take on their emotions, how might they be able to grow or develop more independence? What might the positive outcomes be—in the short or in the long term—if I don't take on responsibility for their emotions? And how might our relationship benefit from these emotional boundaries over time?

After Amy's difficult call with her mother, she reflects on these questions and comes to a few reassuring conclusions.

First, she realizes that her new boundaries might encourage Sophia to find better, more appropriate ways to manage her frustrations. Perhaps Sophia will speak more with her husband; perhaps she'll address her frustrations with Noah directly. Amy's absence could, in fact, be the incentive Sophia needed to grow.

Amy also hopes that, in the long term, this boundary will ultimately benefit her bond with her mother. By removing Noah from their daily talks, Amy imagines that they might have more enjoyable things to discuss. Amy would love to tell Sophia more about her job and her friends, and she'd love to hear more about Sophia's many passions and projects. These conversations would build an intimacy founded not on complaints, but mutual interests and curiosity. Amy writes these reflections in her journal and reviews them when she needs to bolster her confidence about her emotional boundary.

Over the next few weeks, Amy and Sophia continue their regular calls and visits. For a while, it feels awkward. Amy can tell her mother is doing her best to honor her boundary, and even Amy has to resist the urge to ask how things are going with Noah. Sometimes, their conversations fall into unfamiliar lulls; now that Noah isn't up for discussion, Amy and her mother aren't sure what to talk about. Aware of the elephant in the room, Amy gently fills the silence, sharing stories about her friends and asking Sophia about her projects.

Call by call, visit by visit, the two build a new way of interacting with each other over the course of months. Slowly, the awkwardness fades from their conversations. Amy notices how, thanks to her new boundaries, the resentment and frustration she'd been accumulating have disappeared.

They're still mother and daughter—they still have conflicts, disagreements, and spats—but Amy no longer feels the burden of responsibility that she did before. In its absence, she feels able to connect with her mother in a more authentic and enjoyable way. Amy still hopes that her mother's relationship with Noah improves, but ultimately, she knows that either way, it's out of her hands.

IT'S A PROCESS

Remember that emotional boundaries are a process, not a destination. With time, dedication, and trial and error, our emotional boundary bubble becomes firm and clear: a protective force that keeps us safe. With time, we're no longer hobbled by others' guilt trips; we're no longer destabilized by others' conflicts. Finally, we can provide the care and attention that our *own* emotions have needed all along.

12

WHAT WE CAN AND CAN'T CONTROL

People-pleasers tend to have a backward relationship to control. As I noted in the previous chapter, we spend too much energy trying to control others' actions and emotions and too *little* energy taking responsibility for our own needs and boundaries. In this chapter, we'll examine people-pleasers' inverse relationship to control; differentiate between influencing others and controlling others; explore how to regain our power by focusing our attention inward; and discuss how to accept the hard but liberating truth that, ultimately, we cannot control other people.

JARED'S STORY

Over brunch one Sunday morning, Jared's partner of three years, William, says that he isn't happy in their relationship, and hasn't been for a while. Time stops for Jared. The sound of clinking silverware feels miles away as his heart races in his chest. "Okay," Jared says slowly. "Let's talk about how we can work on it. I've mentioned it before, but I think couples therapy could be helpful for us."

"I don't want couples therapy, and I don't want to work on it,"

William responds, shrugging. These days, apathy is William's response whenever they speak about their relationship. Throughout their three years together, they've had countless arguments lasting from midnight to sunrise. William used to engage in these conflicts and seek solutions, but over the last year, he has become painfully detached. Meanwhile, Jared has thrown his whole self into their relationship, desperately trying to break through William's stony silence and urging him to care.

Jared realizes that he has a choice. He can finally take William's words at face value and accept his unwillingness to find a path forward—or he can keep trying to fix their broken relationship single-handedly. Jared's fear of loss is so strong that he chooses the latter. From that night on, he falls asleep with a stack of relationship books on his bedside table. He buys William lavish gifts and treats him to elegant dinners. In therapy, Jared discusses William's family history and William's fears of intimacy, hoping to learn how to make him care again. Despite William's chilly distance, Jared doesn't express any of his frustrations, attempting to create a perfectly peaceful environment in which William will learn to love him again.

Jared spends two long months trying to play God, certain that his methods will reignite love in William's heart. But when William finally ends their relationship for good, Jared realizes that his sense of control has been an illusion all along.

If someone had asked Jared what he'd been doing, the answer would have been simple: "I'm trying to save my relationship." But in truth, Jared was trying to control things that were out of his control: William's actions, feelings, and willingness to change.

PEOPLE-PLEASING IS A CASE OF MISPLACED CONTROL

Mired in the people-pleasing pattern, we become disconnected from our own sense of agency. Instead of acting from within our own sphere of power—by meeting our own needs, setting clear limits around what we will and will not accept, and honoring our own boundaries—we reach outside of ourselves, trying to control situations and change others into versions of themselves who meet our needs.

People-pleasers' attempts to control people and situations typically fall into three categories. We *micromanage others' experience of us* by people-pleasing, shape-shifting, withholding our hurts and needs, and avoiding conflict to be liked; *over-involve ourselves in others' decisions, actions, and relationships* by offering unsolicited advice, saving others from the negative consequences of their own behaviors, becoming involved in others' conflicts, and pushing others toward our preferred courses of action; and *disregard others' limits and boundaries* by repeatedly making the same requests that go unheeded, refusing to acknowledge others' unwillingness to change, and trying to convince others to take courses of action they've already rejected.

Getting Clear on Our Sphere of Control

When you get down to it, we each have control over:

- Our actions
- Our reactions
- Our boundaries
- Who we enter relationships with
- Who we stay in relationships with
- Whether we heal or grow
- Who we spend our time with and how much time we spend with them
- Who we communicate with and how often we communicate with them

We do not have control over:

- Others' actions
- Others' boundaries

- Others' reactions to our boundaries
- Others' emotions
- Whether others choose to heal or grow
- Others' relationships
- Others' addictions or compulsions

Many people-pleasers expend a great deal of energy trying to control items on the second list, while neglecting items on the first. Like Jared, instead of honestly assessing whether others' actions, emotions, or decisions work for us and setting boundaries accordingly, we try to change their actions, emotions, and decisions. When we try to control others in this way, we're not living within our own sphere of power.

We may try to control others' actions by offering unsolicited advice; using passive-aggressive cues to get them to meet our unspoken needs (such as pouting, sighing loudly, or being sarcastic); or making the same requests repeatedly, even though they've shown no interest in changing.

We may try to control others' emotions by feigning happiness or enthusiasm so as not to "ruin the mood"; staying silent instead of expressing our hurts; trying to "fix" others' difficult emotions; or being dishonest about who we are and what we feel in order to gain others' affection or admiration.

We may try to control others' unhealthy behaviors by sending them resources despite their expressed disinterest; repeatedly saving them from the negative consequences of their own actions; repeatedly trying to convince them that they have a problem when they're unwilling to acknowledge it themselves; or threatening them with ultimatums we have no intention of carrying out (e.g., "I will leave you if you don't quit drinking" or "I can't be with you if you don't work on your anger issues").

Finally, we may try to control others' relationships by playing the role of peacemaker, go-between, or moderator, involving ourselves in conflicts that have nothing to do with us.

INFLUENCING VS. CONTROLLING

It's normal to want some degree of influence over our relationships with others—but there's a difference between influence and control.

Influencing looks like expressing our thoughts, opinions, and requests, *while also ensuring* that we're respecting others' boundaries and limitations; accepting the degree to which others are willing to change; and recognizing that their decisions are their own.

Controlling looks like pushing others to change despite their unwillingness or disinterest; making our own desired outcome for them paramount even if they don't want the same thing; hiding important information about who we are and what we need to influence their decision-making; and believing that what they ultimately decide to do is up to us.

To assess whether your actions are influencing or controlling, you can ask yourself these questions. A "yes" response indicates that your actions are veering into control: Have they expressed a lack of desire to change, and am I continuing to push them to change anyhow? Am I trying to change their actions or emotions so that I don't have to face the fact that they can't meet my needs? Am I "helping" in a way that impedes their autonomy or free choice? Have they asked me to stop "helping" and "supporting" them in this manner? Am I silencing, suppressing, or neglecting my own feelings, needs, and wants in the process of trying to change them? Do I believe that I can single-handedly determine the outcome of this situation?

At my workshops, attendees often ask: "My friend keeps disrespecting the boundaries I set. How can I make her take them seriously?" or "My dad's been treating me badly for years. I tell him how it hurts me, but he continues anyway. How can I make him stop?" or "My wife has a drinking problem. She insists she's going to get help, but she never does. It's been five years. How do I make her see how serious her problem is?"

In each of the cases above, people are asking: "How do I change other people?" The answer is: "You can't." We can offer suggestions and make requests of others, but if they aren't willing, we can't *make* them respect our boundaries. We can't *make* them treat us kindly. We can't *make* them seek treatment for their addictions. Especially if we've spent a lifetime seeking refuge in the illusion of control, reckoning with the limits of our power can be painful. But by surrendering this illusion, we can finally focus on what we can control: ourselves.

Exercise: Out of My Control Inventory

Given what we've discussed so far, create a list of things that you have been trying to control but cannot. Be as specific as you can.

Jared's Out of My Control Inventory includes: *I can't control that William is unhappy in our relationship. I can't control whether he works on improving our relationship. I can't control whether he gives me the love and care I need. And I can't control whether he is willing to go to couples therapy.*

LIVING WITHIN OUR SPHERE OF CONTROL

Eventually, our many failed attempts at controlling others leave us feeling exhausted and helpless. We need a new way. Luckily, there's a simple path back to our power: taking responsibility for, and redirecting our energy toward, the things we can control.

We take responsibility for our own *needs* by acknowledging them to ourselves and taking steps to meet them; stating our needs directly instead of expecting others to mind read them; making requests of others; honoring the validity of our needs even when others can't meet them; and being honest with ourselves about whether our relationships meet our needs, and setting boundaries within those relationships accordingly.

We take responsibility for our own *actions* by doing what we want or need to do instead of what others expect us to do, and taking actions informed by our own values instead of others' judgments and guilt trips.

We take responsibility for our own *boundaries* by acknowledging our unmet needs; setting boundaries with ourselves to stop over-giving; and taking space, distance, or time in relationships that have shown us they don't meet our needs.

We take responsibility for our own *healing* by seeking support for our own mental health; breaking the people-pleasing pattern; and replacing our excessive analysis of others' emotional unavailability, avoidance, or narcissism with an analysis of why we're drawn to, or stay in, relationships that fail to meet our fundamental needs.

Finally, we take responsibility for our own *relationships* by analyzing the part we play in our imbalanced relationships; being realistic with ourselves about whether our relationships meet our needs; refusing to participate in connections that are one-sided, unbalanced, or unhealthy; and setting boundaries that enable us to participate in relationships to the extent we feel safe and comfortable.

Exercise: In My Control Inventory

For each of the items in your Out of My Control Inventory, determine how you can redirect your energy to focus on what you *can* control: your own needs, actions, boundaries, healing, and relationships.

Jared contrasts what he can't control with what he can. He writes:

I can't control that William is unhappy in our relationship, but I can control *how I manage my own emotions around the fact that he's unhappy, and how I seek support from friends and family during this difficult time.*

I can't control that William doesn't want to work on our relationship, but I can control *whether I am willing to stay together if this is case.* I can also control *whether I use my therapy sessions to understand why I am so eager to continue a relationship with someone who is not interested in making it work.*

I can't control that William doesn't give me the love and care I need, but I can control *whether I choose to stay with a partner who does not give me the love and care that I need.*

I can't control that William isn't interested in couples therapy, but I can control *whether I go to therapy for my own people-pleasing.*

FINDING POWER THROUGH SURRENDER

Author Elizabeth Gilbert said: "You are afraid of surrender because you don't want to lose control—but you never had control. All you had was anxiety." At first, the idea of surrendering control might feel terrifying. But the truth is, we never had control over other people's actions and emotions; we just thought we did. By releasing this illusion, we come face-to-face with reality. We're no longer blinded by our wishful thinking or desperate hopes, and with clear eyes, we begin the process of accepting what is. The twelve-step community puts it neatly in their serenity prayer: "God, grant me the serenity to accept the things I cannot change, the courage to change the things I can, and the wisdom to know the difference."

A sense of calm accompanies us when we begin to live within our sphere of control. We no longer feel the frustration that inevitably comes from trying to control the things we can't. We drop the scheming; we drop the marionette strings; we stop trying to solve impossible problems. We realize that we don't have to wait anxiously to see if maybe, this time, others will finally change. We no longer beg others to choose us. Instead, for the first time, we choose *ourselves*, affirming: *You are worth it. I see your needs. They will be met.* This is how we step into our true power. This is the key to breaking the people-pleasing pattern—the key to feeling like our lives belong to us.

13

HOW OPPRESSION KEEPS US SILENT

Self-advocacy can be especially hard for those who are deprived of power by oppressive social forces. Racism, sexism, ableism, transphobia, queerphobia, and poverty create conditions where speaking up for oneself carries the risk of discrimination, harassment, or even violence. For marginalized people, setting boundaries can be anywhere from uncomfortable to downright unsafe.

A person with limited financial resources, for example, may not be able to afford to leave a toxic workplace and seek employment elsewhere. A trans person may not feel safe reporting harassment for fear of facing further harassment from those in positions of authority. And a person in an abusive marriage may not feel safe setting boundaries with their spouse for fear of retaliation.

In cases like this, people-pleasing is literally a survival strategy: a way to stay safe in the face of inequality, oppression, and possible violence. When staying silent is equivalent to staying unharmed, encouragement to "be your authentic self" and "just set boundaries" can ring hollow. Well-meaning advice intended to empower can do just the opposite by ignoring marginalized groups' safety concerns.

In this chapter, we'll explore the various ways that marginalized groups are more likely to face pressure to be polite at all costs; endure negative consequences for being their authentic selves; have their boundaries disregarded on the basis of their identity; and have fewer social supports as they self-advocate. We'll also explore short-term strategies to help mitigate discomfort in the face of oppression, and long-term strategies to begin eradicating the systems of oppression that cause that discomfort.

This chapter does not aim to solve the injustices mentioned; that would be impossible for any one book to achieve! However, it does aim to help us recognize the ways in which systemic forces impose people-pleasing patterns on our lives. By recognizing how our identities enable or hinder our mission to advocate for ourselves, we gain not only greater self-awareness but also greater self-compassion.

FINANCIAL LIMITATIONS

When someone fails to respect our boundaries, sometimes our only remaining option is to make every effort to remove ourselves from their environment. However, financial constraints can make leaving certain environments—particularly jobs or homes—difficult or impossible.

Ezra is a father who supports a family of five. He has a high school education, lives in a rural area with few job prospects, and has been working at the same company for thirty years. When he gets a new manager who is rude and dismissive, he is tempted to leave his job, but other jobs nearby are sparse. He can't afford to quit; his family depends on his monthly check.

Henry and Leanna are a married couple with two children, one of whom was born with cerebral palsy and requires significant at-home care. Leanna financially supports the family while Henry takes care of their children full-time. Henry is unhappy in his marriage and finds Leanna cold and critical, but he knows that divorce—and living in two separate households—would make it nearly impossible for him to maintain his children's quality of life.

Henry's and Ezra's financial circumstances put them in the position of needing to choose between their own quality of life and their family's financial security. Without a financial safety net—in the form of assets, money in the bank, health insurance, or generational family wealth—people like Henry and Ezra struggle to transition freely into new workplaces or relationships.

ABUSE

Sometimes, those in abusive situations can set boundaries by leaving. However, for many people, this is not a feasible option. Some people are financially dependent on their abusers, making it nearly impossible for them to exit the relationship safely. Some, including some with disabilities, depend on their abusers for caretaking and physical support. Others share children with their abusers and may not have the resources to support their family on their own. And still others, especially those who were abused as children, may not even recognize their abusers' behavior as abuse.

Even in the absence of financial or physical limitations, many people are trapped in toxic situations by abusers who manipulate, intimidate, threaten, gaslight, or physically harm them. Oftentimes, setting boundaries simply evokes more mistreatment. In these cases, avoiding conflict, staying silent, and appeasing your abuser may be ways to increase your chances of staying safe. (If you are in an abusive relationship, the National Domestic Violence Hotline can be reached at 800-799-SAFE.)

RACISM

Racial stereotypes create conditions where people's feelings, needs, and grievances are dismissed because of their race. For Black men, any demonstration of frustration or irritation carries the threat of being labeled an "angry Black man," a stereotype so common, it has become a popular trope in our culture. Black women, too, are often characterized as intrinsically aggressive; research shows that when a white woman gets angry, her anger is more likely to be attributed to an inciting situation, but when a Black woman gets angry, her anger is more likely to be seen as a fundamental personality trait. Meanwhile, Latina women are often subjected to the Spicy Latina stereotype, which paints them as temperamental, volatile, and overly emotional. These are just a sampling of racial prejudices that limit people of color to painfully narrow windows of "appropriate" self-expression.

In the workplace, these windows are even narrower. People of color often face pressure to code-switch: to adjust their natural clothing, hair, speech, and behavior to better fit in with their white colleagues. Code-switching may decrease the likelihood of stereotyping and increase the likelihood of professional advancement, but it comes at a steep cost: research shows that chronic code-switching leads to burnout, reduced workplace performance, and emotional fatigue. For people of color—particularly those in predominantly white communities, workplaces, or political systems—authentic self-expression often comes at the cost of emotional, physical, or financial safety.

SEXISM

Women who dare to speak up and set boundaries are often barraged with an arsenal of sexist stereotypes: they are bossy, bitchy, overemotional, unfeminine, hypersensitive, needy, clingy, demanding, a "nag." These insults are designed to make women feel like they're too much in some way (or every way), and their only appropriate response is to be more pleasing, receptive, and silent—in other words, less themselves.

In the workplace, systematized sexism makes it even harder for women to express their opinions and self-advocate. Research shows that women are far more likely than men to be interrupted and have their judgments questioned by their male colleagues. Meanwhile, women of color, LGBTQ+ women, and women with disabilities are much more likely than women overall to have their competence challenged or undermined. Women who address these inequities—or continue to speak their mind—are often subjected to retaliation; those who self-report sexual harassment at work, for example, are both less likely to be promoted and more likely to be perceived as less moral, less warm, and less socially skilled by their colleagues. When workplace self-advocacy comes at such a high cost, it's no wonder that many women choose to stay silent instead.

These sexist double standards extend from the workplace into the home. Research shows that women carry more of the mental load than their male partners and family members: the work of anticipating needs, identifying options for filling them, making decisions, and monitoring progress. When women ask their male partners to pick up the slack, they are commonly labeled "nags" and criticized for being demanding. In this way, many women must choose between silently shouldering an unequal burden, or being punished for demanding fairness. Soraya Chemaly writes in *Rage Becomes Her*, "Girls who object to unfairness or injustice are often teased and taunted. Adult women are described as 'oversensitive' or 'exaggerating.' . . . Women's anticipation of negative responses is why so many women remain silent about what they need, want, and feel." Imagine how different the world would be if little girls were taught to set boundaries as often as they were taught to be polite.

GENDER, SEXUALITY, AND RELATIONSHIP STIGMA

For LBGTQ+ and nonmonogamous people, prejudice and the threat of violence pose a potent deterrent to self-expression. Since 2020, discrimination against LGBTQ+ people has skyrocketed. Within the American justice system, protections against LGBTQ+ discrimination are being dismantled, while new bills legalizing discrimination, banning same-sex marriage, and banning life-saving medical care are being proposed. An astounding 70 percent of LBGTQ+ Americans report experiencing discrimination. Seventy-five percent of trans people report experiencing some form of workplace discrimination such as refusal to hire, harassment, privacy violations, and physical violence. For LGBTQ+ people, authentic self-expression is not a right, but a privilege. When the risks include job loss, verbal harassment, or physical violence, choosing to make others comfortable at your own expense may feel like the safest—or only—course of action.

Meanwhile, people who participate in nonmonogamous relationships—like polyamory, open relationships, and swinging—face social stigma that prevents them from authentically expressing their relationship orientation. Despite the growing popularity of nonmonogamous relationships in recent years—a 2016 study found that approximately one in five Americans have participated in one—research shows that nonmonogamous people regularly face social intolerance; ostracism by friends, family, and social groups; and even loss of employment upon revealing their nonmonogamous status. To avoid harm, nonmonogamous people report intentionally choosing not to correct others who mistakenly assume they're monogamous, or referring to their multiple partners as "friends" in order to ensure their safety.

NEURO-DISCRIMINATION

Neuro-discrimination is the unfair treatment of neurodivergent people: those whose brains process, learn, or behave differently from what is considered "normal." "Neurodivergence" is an umbrella term that encompasses conditions from autism spectrum disorder to ADHD.

In order to maintain their jobs, social relationships, and community positions, neurodivergent people often feel pressure to mask: to hide aspects of themselves and conform to neurotypical ways of interacting. Neurodivergent people may engage in social masking by interacting with others in ways that don't come naturally to them, like making eye contact, mirroring others' body language, or pretending to understand a conversation; behavioral masking by resisting the impulse to fidget or stim; or overcompensate by spending extra time on tasks to hide the fact that they're struggling. Most importantly, masking often involves repressing one's own needs and preferences in order to secure social belonging.

In a 2017 study about the effects of masking, one participant explained: "It's exhausting! I feel the need to seek solitude so I can 'be myself' and not have to think about how I am perceived by others." Another wrote, "I feel sad because I feel like I haven't really related to other people. It becomes very isolating because even when I'm with other people I feel like I've just been playing a part." Over the course of years, the side effects of masking can include anxiety, depression, fatigue, stress, and an increased risk of suicidality. However, for many neurodivergent people, masking is the cost of fitting into a world that was designed for, and caters to, neurotypical people.

COLLECTIVISM

As we saw in chapter 1, collectivist cultures like China, Korea, and India tend to emphasize conformity, social harmony, and loyalty, encouraging members to prioritize the needs of the group over those of the individual. In collectivist cultures, those who advocate for their own needs or set boundaries—both of which can be disruptive to the group at large—may face judgment and scorn from their peers and families. In collectivist cultures, the decision to take space from an overbearing parent, for example, isn't seen as a boundary: it's often seen as a rebellion against the family and an insurrection against cultural norms.

Those who immigrate from collectivist to individualistic cultures—or those who were raised by first-generation immigrants—often struggle to reconcile the values of their home culture with those of their new culture. While individualistic cultures promote self, autonomy, and boundaries, collectivist cultures promote community, togetherness, and sacrifice. Competing pressures to honor the self and honor the group can make self-advocacy particularly challenging.

FINDING SOLUTIONS

While we can't individually fix these systemic problems, systemic change can begin with individual awareness. For each of the categories listed above, we can ask ourselves the following:

- How do my identities (race, gender, sexual orientation, etc.) affect the extent to which I feel comfortable advocating for my needs and setting boundaries with others?
- How have my feelings, needs, or boundaries been dismissed based on my identities?
- In what ways have I faced judgment or discrimination for having needs that are atypical by my culture's standards?
- What messages have I received from my culture about boundaries—specifically about my ability to remove myself from, or create distance from, individuals who treat me badly?
- In what ways have I consciously or unconsciously overlooked, dismissed, or judged others' needs, wants, or boundaries based on their identities?

By reflecting on these questions, we develop a greater understanding of how oppressive systems have impacted our own attempts at self-advocacy—and begin to address how we, without even realizing it, may be perpetuating those same systems for others.

Sometimes, oppressive circumstances leave people with no choice but to prioritize safety over self-advocacy. In such cases, solutions are twofold: we can consider short-term strategies to mitigate discomfort and long-term strategies to eradicate the systems of oppression that enable it.

Easing Discomfort in the Short Term

When we can't leave a toxic circumstance, or can't self-advocate for fear of retaliation, we can take care of ourselves by finding ways to make the present moment more bearable. In the face of unjust circumstances, we can first respond with coping strategies that reduce our discomfort as much as possible. These strategies vary based on the context:

WHEN WE CAN'T LEAVE A TOXIC WORKPLACE

If we are bound to an unhealthy workplace, we may be able to ease our discomfort by:

- Requesting assistance from colleagues
- Requesting a team transfer, manager transfer, or location transfer
- Delegating tasks or responsibilities to other staff
- Decreasing the extent to which we discuss personal matters at work
- Discussing our circumstances and getting emotional support from trustworthy colleagues
- Asking Human Resources for support or additional resources
- Setting boundaries around answering work-related correspondence after work hours, if possible
- Filing an anonymous OSHA (Occupational Safety and Health Administration) complaint if our workplace contains unsafe or unhealthy working conditions

WHEN WE CAN'T LEAVE A TOXIC RELATIONSHIP

If we are bound to a family member, spouse, or other relationship, we may be able to alleviate our discomfort by:

- Tending to our basic physical needs
- Practicing deep breathing, grounding exercises, body scans, or other techniques to soothe our nervous systems
- Using the gray rock technique (see chapter 10) to mitigate unpleasant or divisive conversations
- Decreasing the length/frequency of our interactions, if possible
- Seeking support from a therapist, counselor, or social worker

WHEN WE NEED TO RELEASE STRESS

Even when we can't escape our harmful circumstances immediately, we can take steps to reduce the impact of stress on our bodies and minds. As Emily and Amelia Nagoski explain in their book *Burnout*, when we experience a challenging event—called a stressor—this provokes an internal, physical reaction, called stress. Even when we can't completely escape a stressor, research shows that we can still reduce the impact of stress by doing some sort of physical activity; deep breathing; laughing; crying; engaging in some form of creative expression like painting or dance; or having a positive social interaction with a friend or family member. These actions won't "fix" our situation per se, but they will give us moments of respite to regain our emotional and physical equilibrium.

WHEN WE NEED SOCIAL SUPPORT

When grappling with unjust circumstances, we can gain a sense of community and solidarity by seeking social support. We might call a trustworthy friend or loved one to talk; discuss our situation with a therapist, counselor, or social worker; join a support group in person or virtually; join a twelve-step program like Al-Anon, Adult Children of Alcoholics, or Co-Dependents Anonymous; use social media to find personal stories and support from individuals in similar circumstances; or write in our journal when social supports aren't immediately available.

Fighting for Social Justice in the Long Term

Community organizer Nakita Valerio said: "Shouting 'self-care' at people who actually need 'community care' is how we fail people." We cannot "self-care" our way—or "boundary" our way—out of oppressive circumstances. Short-term, individual solutions are Band-Aids that provide quick relief in painful situations—but in order to create environments that allow marginalized groups to self-advocate safely, we, as a community, must change systems of oppression that reward marginalized groups for their silence. There's no single road map to eradicate sexism, homophobia, financial inequality, and other forms of oppression, but there are tangible steps we can take to combat these forces in our communities.

Politically, we can financially support national, state, and local advocacy organizations that combat systemic oppressions; vote for officials who resolve to address sexism, racism, homophobia, and income inequality; raise awareness about our elected officials' stances on issues affecting women, LGBTQ+ people, people of color, and other marginalized groups; email or call our government representatives in support of social justice initiatives; and participate in civic organizing activities like rallies, protests, phone banks, GOTV efforts, and letter-writing campaigns.

In our communities, we can volunteer for direct service efforts like food banks, clothing drives, or domestic violence hotlines; directly donate clothing, food, housewares, or childcare to community members in need; ensure that our local school curricula address systemic oppression and injustice; support youth-led efforts to combat inequality in elementary schools, high schools, and colleges; and address discrimination in our civic groups, parent-teacher associations, and community centers.

In our workplaces, we can ensure that there are ways for employees to submit anonymous feedback regarding their experiences of stigma, harassment, or discrimination on the job; participate in advocacy efforts for paid overtime, paid parental leave, equal pay, and fair promotions; and support efforts to improve representation across genders, ages, races, ability levels, and sexual orientations throughout the workplace.

PEOPLE-PLEASING AS A SURVIVAL STRATEGY

As we affirmed in chapter 1, though people-pleasing can have many origins and expressions, one theme unites them all: the pursuit of safety. When the world has encouraged people who look, think, or love like you to stay silent and compliant, it's much harder to confidently and safely self-advocate. We can't talk about breaking the people-pleasing pattern without acknowledging how this work is drastically different—and far more dangerous—for members of marginalized groups.

3

TAKE CARE OF YOURSELF

14

WALKING THROUGH THE FIRE

"May you have the courage to sit with discomfort
like it's a dawn, not a death."

—K. J. Ramsey

As we break the people-pleasing pattern, learning how to advocate for ourselves is only half of our work. The other half is learning how to cope with, and self-soothe through, the difficult emotions that arise before, during, and after. In part 3, we will normalize these growing pains and learn how to face them with courage and self-compassion.

Sometimes making requests means facing the fear that others won't meet our needs. Sometimes setting boundaries means feeling guilty for hurting others' feelings. Sometimes releasing our illusions of control means surrendering to the grief that some people will not change. These are the growing pains that accompany our healing, and uncomfortable though they may be in the short term, they are the fires we must walk through on our way to a brighter, stronger, more confident life. Our work isn't to avoid them—that would be impossible—but to soothe ourselves through them and practice self-compassion in their midst. We can trust that we will walk through these fires—of guilt, fear, grief, anger—and emerge emboldened and transformed.

In this chapter, we will explore how to welcome our growing pains;

discuss how to understand our discomfort as a temporary prerequisite to our healing; and learn how to build an inspired vision of the future that will support us as we step into this new stage of our lives.

WELCOMING OUR GROWING PAINS

Learning how to stand up for ourselves doesn't necessarily make our lives difficulty-free; we simply get new challenges in the place of our old ones. But these new challenges are preferable because they stem from a place of self-love, self-respect, and power—and throughout, our needs are honored instead of neglected.

Growing pains can be disorienting because many of us expect healing to be a linear process. We expect growth to bring us happiness, strength, and resolve—not sadness, fragility, and fear. We see upbeat posts on social media encouraging us to be strong, set boundaries, and speak our truth, but far fewer posts acknowledging the difficulties of doing so. But rest assured: No recovering people-pleaser escapes growing pains. Every one of us faces these discomforts in one way or another.

We may face *fear* as we summon the courage to state our needs; wonder how others will respond to our requests; worry that we'll hurt others' feelings with our boundaries; and wonder which of our relationships will support this new and empowered version of us.

We may face *guilt* as we prioritize our own needs; tell others how their actions make us feel; set boundaries to protect our health and well-being; create distance and space in relationships with people who mistreat us; release relationships that no longer align with us; and stop enabling others' behavior by saving them from the consequences of their own actions.

We may face *anger* as we recognize the ways we've made ourselves small for others' comfort; as people dismiss our needs and boundaries; and as we begin to understand how systems of oppression keep our voices silent (see chapter 13).

We may face *grief* as we release the illusion of hope that others will change if we only ask them enough; create distance in relationships with loved ones who hurt us; leave relationships with partners and friends who cannot show up the way we need them to; and accept the painful reality that certain relationships have run their course.

And finally, we may face *loneliness* and *uncertainty* as we leave unhealthy relationships, but don't yet have healthier relationships to take their place; separate from old social circles, communities, and workplaces that aren't good for us; search for new connections with people who will honor and respect our full selves; and wonder if we'll ever find our people.

In the face of these difficulties, what matters most is how we relate to our discomfort. Typically, when we feel guilt, we interpret it as a sign that we did something bad. Typically, when we feel fear, we interpret it as a warning that we shouldn't proceed with our planned course of action. But when it comes to the growing pains of breaking the people-pleasing pattern, we must interpret our discomforts in a new way. They don't mean we've done something wrong; they mean we're doing something right.

TELLING A NEW STORY OF PAIN

The stories we tell ourselves about our difficult emotions matter. When I first began setting boundaries, I was racked with guilt. Years of playing the role of emotional caretaker for my friends and family had taken a major toll on my mental health, and in the hopes of taking better care of myself, I began setting limits around how available I was for others' problems.

After months of gathering the courage, I finally told a family member I was no longer willing to be put in the middle of their marital issues with their spouse. I told a friend I was no longer available for hours-long phone calls to process her toxic relationship with her girlfriend. Another friendship had become so imbalanced—so all-give and no-take—that I ended it entirely.

No matter how compassionately I set these boundaries—no matter how certain I was that they were right for me—I was leveled by guilt after every single one. My mind spun a story like this:

I can't believe I just did that. If this is the right thing, why do I feel so sick to my stomach? Sure, that relationship has been a source of pain for me for a while, but why do I feel so guilty? I can't handle this. I'm a terrible person. I should take it all back. . . .

And so on, and so on. I hadn't yet learned that it wasn't the emotion itself, but *my interpretation* of the emotion, that was causing me so much pain.

Research shows that how we interpret our emotions directly affects our experience of them. People who judge their emotions as "bad" or "wrong" actually experience those emotions more negatively, while people who accept their emotions experience less pain overall. When we tell ourselves a story that our feelings are "bad," "unmanageable," and "signs of wrongdoing," we're more likely to exacerbate our discomfort, take back our boundaries, and return to unhealthy situations.

By changing the stories we tell ourselves about our difficult emotions, we can normalize our growing pains, mitigate our discomfort, and lay the groundwork for a courageous path forward. Our new stories can include:

"This Pain Means That I'm Strengthening My Self-Advocacy Muscle"

When we feel sore after a tough workout, we don't interpret our soreness as a sign that we shouldn't have exercised. Instead, we see it as an indication that we're building strength. Our soreness isn't comfortable, but it's worth it because we know we're getting stronger. The guilt and fear we feel when we stand up for our needs are similar; though uncomfortable in the present, they're a sign that we're strengthening our muscle of self-advocacy for the future. The stronger we get with practice, the less uncomfortable we'll feel.

"This Pain Means That I'm Breaking a Generations-Old Cycle"

A cycle-breaker is someone who recognizes a dysfunctional, toxic, or abusive pattern of behavior in their family and vows to end the cycle. As we explored in chapter 1, many of us can trace the roots of our people-pleasing back to our childhoods, and if we look closely enough, we may well find that these behaviors have been transmitted down through generations.

In these cases, breaking the pattern doesn't just stop a cycle of dysfunctional behavior within ourselves; it stops the cycle within our lineage. We're daring to believe in a way of being that is new—that is healthy—and that has rarely, if ever, been modeled for us before.

"This Pain Means That I'm Finally Putting Myself First after Years of Being Told I Shouldn't"

Throughout our lives, many of us have received messages—in the form of explicit statements or others' treatment—that putting ourselves first is unacceptable. Now, it's as if the ghosts of our past are battling our new, clear-eyed conviction that we deserve better. The growing pains we feel are the dying echoes of that old core belief. Holly Whitaker, in her book *Quit Like a Woman*, observes that "saying no to people who want you to say yes—and upholding your boundaries with people who are used to you having none—will feel terrible, like a death. And it is a death of sorts: the death of the part of you that thinks you have to violate yourself in order to be loved."

EXERCISE: STAYING THE COURSE WITH VISION

As we face our growing pains, we need a reminder of why this hard work will be worth it in the end. It helps to envision how our lives will look—and how our hearts will feel—when we stop people-pleasing once and for all.

Part One: The Before

In your journal, spend one page describing your life in "the before": the time before you began breaking the people-pleasing pattern. Be sure to list the resentments you felt; the exhaustion, fatigue, and overwhelm you experienced; how it felt to be voiceless in your relationships; how your connection with yourself suffered from self-betrayal and a lack of self-trust; and the three to five most painful experiences you had as the result of your people-pleasing.

Part Two: The After

Imagine that it's been five years since you broke the people-pleasing pattern. Your growing pains are distant specks in the rearview mirror, and you're reaping the rewards of your efforts. Your life is more colorful and joyful than you ever believed possible.

Spend one page in your journal describing what this new chapter of your life is like *as if you are already there*. Be sure to describe how your relationship with yourself has changed; how you feel from day to day; the new and invigorating ways you choose to spend your time; the dreams and desires you're pursuing; the mutual and reciprocal relationships you've built; and how you may serve as a role model for your children, friends, or community.

Part Three: The Contrast

When you've finished parts one and two, take ten minutes to contrast the Before and the After, paying close attention to how starkly these versions of you differ.

This exercise reminds us that we can't let the pains of change blind us to the pains of staying the same. Before, our pain was a dead-end street: it was leading us deeper into people-pleasing, deeper into resentment, and deeper into isolation. But the growing pains we feel now are leading us toward a healthier, happier, and more vibrant life. We aren't here because it's easy; we're here because it's worth it.

In the following chapters, we will explore how to give new meaning to our fear, guilt, anger, loneliness, grief, and uncertainty. We'll discuss how to soothe ourselves through these difficult emotions and stay the course when the going gets tough. Ultimately, we'll examine how these challenging emotions are not obstacles *blocking* our road to healing, but signposts that assure us we're moving in the right direction.

15

FACING FEAR, GUILT, AND ANGER

"Choose the great adventure of being brave
and afraid at the exact same time."
—Brené Brown

In this chapter, we'll explore the growing pains of fear, guilt, and anger; normalize their presence in our healing journey; and discuss coping strategies we can use to comfort ourselves as we seek the peace and confidence that await us.

RADICAL ACCEPTANCE

To begin, we can prime our efforts for success by first laying a foundation of radical acceptance. Tara Brach, psychologist and Buddhist teacher, defines radical acceptance as "clearly recognizing what is happening inside us, and regarding what we see with an open, kind and loving heart."

Radical acceptance is a stark contrast to the way we typically approach our pain. Many of us erect fierce defenses against our challenging feelings, making every effort to intellectualize them, outrun them, bury them, or ignore them—*anything* but feel them directly. These defenses take on a frantic quality as we try to outrun the inescapable. Like monsters in the closet, our difficult feelings swell and expand in our periphery, and we often end up exacerbating the very same emotions we're trying to escape.

When we practice radical acceptance, we pause to acknowledge our guilt, fear, anger, and grief with compassion instead of self-judgment. This attentive presence transforms our discomfort from a fierce opponent to an annoying-but-inevitable companion on our journey.

The first step of radical acceptance is to simply notice and name what we're feeling. From here, we can notice how the emotion feels in our bodies: Where do we feel the sensation? Is our chest tight or our heart racing? Is our breathing shallow? Our stomach clenched? We can gently notice these sensations, putting our hand upon our heart and offering ourselves some words of tenderness: "It's okay," "I've got you," or "You are safe."

Finally, radical acceptance invites us to allow our current emotional reality to be there, *just as it is*, without changing it. We might verbalize our acceptance by saying something like "I welcome this fear because I know I am safe," "Guilt is a natural reaction to standing up for myself; this is normal," or "This is the way it is right now, and I accept that."

Radical acceptance doesn't make our feelings go away, but it does offer a calmer, grounded foundation upon which we can act. Now that we're not running in circles trying to escape our emotions, we can make intentional choices about how to soothe them.

FROM FEAR TO RESOLVE

Breaking the people-pleasing pattern is fundamentally disruptive. We're entering unfamiliar territory, and it's completely normal to be a little scared. We may fear that others won't like us if we speak up for ourselves; that our boundaries will hurt the people we love; that people will judge us if we're honest about what we need; that our relationships will feel strained after we set boundaries; or that we'll end up alone if we set higher standards for how we're treated.

These fears are entirely natural as we change the roles we play in our relationships. Whether we're asking our housemate to clean their dirty dishes or estranging from an abusive parent, we're transforming our old passivity into assertiveness.

To illustrate the path from fear to resolve, we'll look at Danica's story. Danica has been close friends with Ula since childhood. After high school, they stayed in touch when they attended college in different parts of the country: Danica in Austin, Texas, and Ula in Seattle, Washington. Now in their late twenties, they hop on the phone at least once a month to catch up.

One day, Ula surprises Danica with some news: she's moving to Austin for a work relocation. Danica is thrilled, and when Ula arrives in town a few weeks later, Danica helps her unpack and get settled in. That night, they go out for dinner and linger over their drinks till midnight. They're thrilled to be in the same city again.

As the weeks pass, Danica, a schoolteacher, spends her evenings and weekends introducing Ula to her favorite taco trucks and thrift stores. They get margaritas on Friday nights and iced coffee on Sunday mornings. Danica's friends happily invite Ula to their parties and potlucks, warmly welcoming her into the fold. The two spend most days together every week.

Eventually, Danica begins to realize that she's feeling imbalanced. Her teaching job is demanding, and she craves a few nights each week to be alone and relax. She has other friends that she'd like to spend time with one-on-one, but she's developed a routine of spending all her free time with Ula.

Danica wants to speak with Ula about dialing back their time together so she can have more balance, but she's afraid of hurting her feelings. Ula hasn't made any friends in Austin yet, and Danica doesn't want her to feel abandoned.

Remember the Pain of Staying the Same

When we're afraid, our hearts racing and chests tight, we get tunnel vision. We temporarily forget that beyond our short-term fear lies our long-term freedom. Zooming out to see the big picture—both the benefits of changing *and* the pains of staying the same—helps us gain perspective. In my workshops, participants consistently say that this is the most impactful exercise for moving past fear.

BEGIN WITH THE BENEFITS OF CHANGING

First, zoom out to imagine the *long-term benefits* of taking this action. One year from now, how will you have changed for the better? How will your life have become richer? How will you spend your time in more enjoyable ways? How will you feel more at peace in your relationships? Close your eyes and imagine this future life.

Once your visioning is complete, do the same process again—except this time, imagine that instead of one year from now, it's five years from now. And then, once you've completed that round, do it once more—except this time, it's ten years from now. How do you notice the benefits of breaking the people-pleasing pattern compounding and expanding with time?

THEN IMAGINE THE PAINS OF STAYING THE SAME

Now imagine that you obey the fear and fail to stand up for yourself. Zoom out and imagine the *long-term drawbacks* of this decision one year from now. How will your life look? How will your mental and physical health have been affected? How will your relationships have become burdened with resentment? Then, just like you did above, imagine your life five years later, and ten years later. With each jump in time, notice how the drawbacks are magnified.

Zooming out in this way makes the pain of *not* changing crystal clear. When we succumb to fear, we may get a momentary respite from discomfort, but over time, that discomfort compounds exponentially.

First, Danica imagines the benefits of dialing back her time with Ula. One year from now, she feels a sense of calm at having a few nights each week to herself again. She's also happily reconnected to her other friends from whom she's grown distant the past few months. When she zooms out further—five years, ten years—she notices how this sense of calm and balance only increases.

When Danica imagines what it would be like if she *never* dialed back her time with Ula, she has a visceral negative reaction. One year from now, she's become totally disconnected from her other friends, and she's burned-out and resentful after having so little time to herself. Over five and ten years, the resentment and overwhelm only get worse—and she grows to destest Ula in the process.

For Danica, this exercise makes her need for change abundantly clear: talking with Ula will be hard, but the side effects of not talking with her would be worse.

Remember Your Deepest Why

As we discussed in chapter 1, our Deepest Why is the most important, most heart-stirring reason we're breaking the people-pleasing pattern. It's a salve that cools the fire of our fears when we're in distress, enabling us to see beyond our short-term discomfort and imagine a more peaceful, empowered, and expansive future. In the face of fear, hold your Deepest Why close. Write it down and put it somewhere visible as a reminder to stay the course.

Channel a Role Model

When confronted by fear, channeling a role model helps us access new ways of responding to difficult situations. Consider: Who is a person—living or dead, real or fictional—that you can channel through this fear? Who possesses the bravery, courage, or steadfastness you want to embody?

The next time you face fear, envision your role model in all their color: their face, their dress, their voice, their attitude. Ask yourself:

What would they do in this situation? Take some time to imagine, from start to finish, how your role model would respond. What would they do? How would they stay strong in their decision? How might they self-soothe through discomfort? To the extent you are able, follow in their footsteps.

When Danica considers who she'd like to channel as a role model for her conversation with Ula, she imagines her friend Callie. Callie is bold, outspoken, and does not mince words—but she also expresses her love in a similarly unreserved way. Because Callie is so transparent, Danica always knows exactly where she stands with her; she trusts Callie to be honest and clear, even when it's hard. As a result, Danica feels like Callie is one of the most trustworthy people she knows.

Danica muses on how Callie would handle this conversation. No doubt, she would be clear and straightforward. Knowing Callie, she'd probably say something simple like: "Ula, now that we've got you all settled in, I need to make sure I'm taking some time for myself and my other friends, too. Want to plan to get together once every week or two?"

Danica struggles with boundaries like this, so imagining Callie's straightforward approach gives her a helpful starting point.

The next day, when Danica drops Ula off after spending the afternoon shopping, Ula asks if she'd like to go out the following evening for drinks. Danica imagines Callie and tries to channel her direct kindness as she replies:

"Now that we've got you all settled in, I realize that I need to take some time for myself and my other friends, too. Tomorrow night won't work, but want to get drinks together next week, and shoot for getting together once every week or two?"

To Danica's surprise, Ula is completely receptive. "Of course! You've been so generous helping me get acclimated, and I know you have things to do and people to see. Next week is perfect."

Danica is relieved; Ula's acceptance feels like an unexpected gift. "Okay!" she replies, smiling. "Sounds good. Next week it is!"

Be a Role Model

Though breaking the people-pleasing pattern is a journey we take independently, it can spark a profound ripple effect in our relationships and communities. Our actions may inspire others to speak up, break old patterns, and bravely pursue new ways of living. Remembering that being role models can strengthen our resolve. When facing fear, you can stay the course by asking yourself: *Who am I role modeling for?*

Perhaps we're setting an example for our children. Children don't just absorb what we verbally teach them; they watch our behavior to learn how to speak to themselves, what is acceptable, and what types of relationships they deserve. In the same way that caregivers can pass down habits of self-sacrifice and passivity, they can also pass down self-respect, assertiveness, and confidence.

Maybe we're role modeling for members of our community or workplace. By being the change we wish to see in these spaces, we chart a course others might follow in the future, and sometimes, our actions transform the group culture entirely. Alternatively, perhaps we're role modeling for other members of our identity groups, blazing new paths for people who share our backgrounds. The woman who asserts herself with her husband is a role model for other women who wish to break the stronghold of patriarchy in their marriages. The trans teen who advocates for gender-inclusive policies at their high school is a role model for all trans youth who wish to change oppressive systems.

Remembering who we're role modeling for doesn't eliminate our fear, but recalling those we're inspiring can make it feel more worthwhile.

Remember That Life Is Short

Our time on this planet is brief. We get one shot to make the most of our lives, and we don't want fear to hold us back. Bronnie Ware, a palliative care nurse, spent her career caring for patients during the last twelve weeks of their lives. During her time with them, she asked: "Do you have any regrets? Would you do anything differently if you had the chance?" After speaking with thousands of patients, the most common regret she heard was: "I wish I'd had the courage to live a life true to myself, not the life others expected of me." What could be a more powerful incentive to proceed despite our fear? When we're on our deathbed, taking inventory of how we lived, we want to be proud of our choices. One day, this fearful present moment might be a memory we recall and say: "That was very scary—but I'm so glad I did it."

FROM GUILT TO CONFIDENCE

Guilt is a challenging emotion for everyone, but for those of us breaking the people-pleasing pattern, it's particularly agonizing. We've spent our lives bending over backward to avoid upsetting others. Now that we're prioritizing our own needs, we occasionally need to deprioritize the needs of our partners, friends, and family members—and grapple with their disappointment accordingly. We might feel guilty for setting boundaries with friends and loved ones; ending misaligned relationships; asking others for more; breaking patterns of over-giving; or setting limits around our time, energy, and space.

Soothing our guilt isn't about pretending that other people will be completely happy with our new choices; it's about remembering that prioritizing ourselves is not only acceptable, but also necessary, if we want truly intimate, truly healthy relationships.

To illustrate how we can move from guilt to confidence, we'll use the case of Jeanine. Jeanine and Kyle met at a mutual friend's birthday party. They had immediate chemistry, and since then, they've been on six dates.

At first, Jeanine enjoyed their time together; Kyle was engaging, charming, and knew exactly how to make her laugh. But the more they've learned about each other, the less she wants a relationship with him. She's very driven, and he lacks a sense of direction; he's unhappy at his dead-end job, but hasn't made any efforts to find a new one. Community is also important to her, but he doesn't seem to have many friends or even acquaintances. For Jeanine, the initial spark has flickered out.

On their seventh date, she works up the courage to break the news. She says gently, "Kyle, I've really enjoyed getting to know you, but I feel like we're not a good match. I'm open to staying friends, but I'm not interested in pursuing our romantic connection further."

Kyle is close to tears. "I thought things were going so well!" he exclaims. "What did I do wrong?"

Jeanine feels his sadness like a dagger; she hates disappointing him this way. She explains that he didn't do anything wrong; their lifestyles just aren't compatible. The conversation ends abruptly, and when she gets home, she's consumed by guilt for hurting his feelings.

Remember That Every No Is Also a Yes

When we begin setting boundaries, it's common to focus on all the things we're saying no to. However, every "no" we say is a simultaneous, full-throated "yes" to something even more important: usually our needs, desires, or sense of self-respect, all of which have gone neglected for far too long.

When you notice yourself feeling guilty for saying no, setting a boundary, or creating distance in a relationship, consider: What have you said *yes* to by self-advocating in this way?

Jeanine contemplates, *When I say no to dating Kyle, I say yes to the possibility of finding someone who is a better fit for me: someone I'm attracted to and interested in. When I say no to dating someone out of a sense of guilt and obligation, I say yes to dating someone out of genuine interest, curiosity, and excitement. And when I say no to a relationship with someone who lacks drive and community, I say yes to the possibility of finding a partner who shares my values and interests.*

Empathize with Yourself

Psychologist Marolyn Wells writes that because empathy is the natural antidote to shame, people-pleasers need to learn how to empathize with themselves—not others—when they experience situations that activate feelings of guilt and shame. When we empathize with ourselves, we resist the urge to overfocus on others' hurt or frustration, and instead pay close attention to our own lived experience: why we made this decision, how we feel in our bodies, and what *we* need in this moment.

When we catch ourselves ruminating about others' hurt feelings, we can reflect: What painful, hurtful, or unpleasant interactions led us to self-advocate in this way? How was our self-advocacy a demonstration of self-respect? How does this boundary protect our needs? And how will taking this action improve our lives in the long term?

In the hours following her final date with Kyle, Jeanine is preoccupied. She keeps thinking about the surprised look on his face when she broke the news. She imagines that he's terribly unhappy with her, and the thought leaves a pit in her stomach.

As her guilt resurfaces with a vengeance, she decides to stop living in Kyle's feelings and practices empathizing with herself instead. Intentionally, she recalls her disapppointment when she asked Kyle about his dreams for the future and he shrugged in disinterest. She reminds herself that breaking things off with Kyle is the only way to fulfill her own desire for a partner who's ambitious and community-minded. Disappointing Kyle is uncomfortable in the short term, but it's the only way for her to get what she needs in the long term.

Consider the Hidden Benefits to the Other Person

Guilt is like a spotlight. It directs our attention to all we've done wrong while leaving little space for us to consider other possibilities: namely, how our self-advocacy might help the very person we're afraid we've hurt. We gain perspective by considering: How might this person benefit from our self-advocacy in the short or long term?

Here are some common ways that our self-advocacy benefits others:

- Now that I've told them what I need, it will be easier for them to meet my needs.
- Now that I've told them what I need, they won't feel pressure to guess my needs—and I won't feel resentment toward them when they get it wrong.
- Now that I've pointed out their problematic behavior, they can change it and improve their relationships with me and others.
- Now that I've told them how I really feel, they no longer need to be confused by my inconsistency and avoidance.
- Now that I'm not solving their problems for them, they can become more independent.
- Now that I've been forthright about my boundaries, we have a chance of developing a more sustainable relationship.
- Now that I've acknowledged that this relationship isn't a good fit for me, they can find friends/partners who are a better fit: who sincerely *want* to be with them.

At the bare minimum, we benefit others when we bring honesty and transparency into our relationships instead of lying, misleading, or performing to create an illusion of harmony.

Jeanine has focused so intently on how her decision hurt Kyle that she hasn't considered how he might actually benefit from it. She realizes that if they'd continued to date, she would have spent their relationship silently wishing that he were different. Kyle deserves a partner who appreciates him for who he is, and now that they've separated, he has the space to find that. The more Jeanine thinks about it, the more she realizes that the truly unkind thing to do would have been to stay in their connection purely out of guilt, preventing them *both* from finding satisfying relationships elsewhere.

Talk with a Cheerleader

When our guilt feels all-encompassing, social support can remind us of our goodness and affirm that we're right where we're supposed to be. There's no shame in needing a pick-me-up from a friend, therapist, or support group to get us through the darkest waters of guilt.

You may tell a confidante that you're trying to break the people-pleasing pattern and ask if they'd be open to chatting about it from time to time. Perhaps you have a couple of friends who are also working on self-advocacy, and you decide to start a group text to share your respective wins. After making difficult requests or setting challenging boundaries, get in touch with your cheerleader to celebrate.

Move Your Body

As we explored in chapter 13, when we face a challenging external event—called a stressor—we have an internal physical reaction called stress. Stress makes our hearts race, chests clench, and breath shorten, and it's common to feel the physical discomfort of stress alongside the emotional discomfort of guilt. Research shows that physical exercise is the most effective tool to move stress out of our bodies.

Jeanine decides to go for a run, and with every footfall, her rumination about Kyle slips further away. By the time she finishes her three-mile loop, she feels grounded in her body again. Her guilt hasn't entirely disappeared, but now it feels less like her entire emotional landscape and more like a speck on the periphery.

FROM DESTRUCTIVE ANGER TO CREATIVE ANGER

The more we speak up for ourselves, the more we recognize how small we used to become in others' presence. We begin to understand how deeply it affected us when we were punished or shamed for expressing our needs in the past. So many times, we exchanged our comfort for those who didn't have our best interests at heart.

Often, a tsunami of anger accompanies this realization. We may feel anger at caregivers whose neglect, abuse, emotional immaturity, addictions, or mental health struggles contributed to our development of the people-pleasing pattern; at people who dismissed or mocked our feelings; at partners who decried our reasonable needs as "too much"; at workplaces and institutions that exploited our lack of boundaries; at systems of oppression that forced us to be silent in order to stay safe; or even at ourselves for staying too long in toxic situations.

At first, anger can feel like a destructive force: urgent, ruinous, and vengeful. But even when anger is the fuel that powers our engine, we are still the ones in the driver's seat: we still get to decide where we go. Studies show that anger is a powerful motivator for change; it's typically accompanied by an effort to remove obstacles, rectify injustices, and create better conditions for ourselves and others. Whereas anxiety and sadness make us feel small and fearful, anger makes us feel fiery, fierce, and engaged. Ultimately, anger can propel us toward a new way of living.

As we heal, we must honor our anger. It is holy, white-hot, and purifying: it is the righteous indignation of our innermost selves coming alive. We must let it alchemize us into a new version of ourselves that does not settle for less. Honoring our anger doesn't mean yelling at others, treating them poorly, or seeking revenge (though at times, we may be tempted to do just that!). Instead, we can harness our anger's energy to advocate for better treatment for ourselves and others. We can consider: How might we use the energy of our anger not to destroy or ruin, but to grow, create, and generate?

We might use our anger as motivation to set necessary boundaries; leave toxic relationships; help people who face the same struggles we once faced; begin a physical routine (running, weight lifting, dance, yoga, stretching) that connects us to our strength; or create a piece of art or music that shares our story.

A year into my work breaking the people-pleasing pattern, I was accosted by a tremendous anger. In therapy, I had begun to rewrite old stories from my past; I was slowly shifting my beliefs from "I'm too much" and "I'm too sensitive" to "I'm worthy of love as I am" and "Being sensitive to mistreatment is normal and healthy."

This shift in beliefs sparked an unexpected rage toward people who had minimized my needs in the past. I was furious at family members who had said I was too uptight for being hurt by their cruel comments. I was angry with ex-partners who had said I was "too needy" for requiring minimal consistency and affection in my relationships. I was upset with friends who had used me as a sounding board for their problems while offering little curiosity in return. Most of all, I was furious at *myself* for believing I needed to be smaller and less opinionated to be worthy of others' love.

My anger burned like wildfire inside me. I needed an outlet for it, so I began writing poetry on a blog. Under a pseudonym, I wrote scathing verses about my arguments with my exes; about the way sexism silences women's voices; about the brutal pain of always feeling like I needed to be less. I intended my blog as a space for personal catharsis, but with every new post I shared, strangers commented with thanks. They could relate, they said; they'd been there, too; my poetry gave them words for frustrations they'd never expressed before.

Finding catharsis for my anger this way was healing. It helped me feel less alone in my experiences. I couldn't undo my past, but through my poetry, I could offer companionship and affirmation to people going through something similar.

SOMETIMES, IT JUST SUCKS

While the tools presented here can help us soothe the growing pains of fear, guilt, and anger, there is no magic bullet that completely relieves our difficult emotions. Sometimes, there isn't a quick fix. Sometimes, it just sucks.

Surprisingly, we can find some relief in this acknowledgment. Sometimes, there's nothing more to *do*; we just have to radically accept the fact that breaking the people-pleasing pattern is hard. We can take solace in the fact that this discomfort won't last forever. Yes, there are seasons in our lives that aggravate and challenge us; there are also seasons that nourish, refuel, and restore us. We can trust that with every truth spoken and boundary set, we are edging closer to a season of strength and self-respect.

16

OUTGROWING RELATIONSHIPS

Recovering people-pleasers outgrow relationships more often than most because we're stopping the self-neglecting behaviors that made those relationships possible in the first place.

As we begin taking up more space, relationships that fit perfectly before begin to feel confining. We may discover that our partners don't care to hear our needs; they preferred us when we were deferential. We may realize that our friends don't know how to hold space for our emotions; they only know how to interact with us when we play the role of their sounding board or therapist. We may begin to see the destructiveness of certain patterns in our families, and find ourselves needing distance from parents, siblings, or other family members.

Some of these relationships are simply a mismatch: they don't feel aligned with who we're becoming as we step into our power. Others are actively harmful, and our newfound commitment to self-advocacy requires that we end them. We show great courage when we give ourselves permission to outgrow relationships that are unhealthy; that leave us feeling chronically unseen and unknown; and that are detrimental to our health and well-being.

In this chapter, we'll explore tools for navigating these difficult transitions. We'll discuss how to shift our relationships to better suit our needs or, when that isn't possible, how to exit them entirely.

MAL'S STORY

Mal, forty-five, moved to New York City three years ago after a painful divorce. Eager to find community, she arranged to link up with a friend of a friend—Jodi, a publicist—and ever since, the two have met up for drinks every couple of weeks.

From the start, Mal noticed that Jodi was a character. She could be funny, but also scathing, unafraid to make biting comments about her clients between sips of her martini. At first, Mal was drawn to Jodi's larger-than-life personality and endless repertoire of entertaining stories. But the more time they spend together, the more Mal recognizes what a poor listener Jodi is. Every time Mal volunteers information about her own life, Jodi quickly pivots the conversation back to herself. As the years have passed, Mal has begun to feel more invisible—and more resentful—with every interaction.

One Friday, Mal gets a text from Jodi: **Drinks tonight?** Mal agrees, but as the workday wanes, she begins searching for excuses to cancel her plans. *I could say I have a headache*, she considers. *Or I could say the entire office got food poisoning after lunch. . . . Or maybe I could tell her my cat fell off the fire escape and needs to go to the vet.*

As her schemes become more outlandish, Mal interrupts herself: *You're a forty-five-year-old woman, for God's sake. Cut the playground shit. It's time to tell Jodi how you really feel.*

That night, Mal arrives at the bar feeling jittery. She orders a cocktail and waits until Jodi walks through the door, resplendent in a tight blue dress.

"You would not *believe* what just happened," bursts Jodi, throwing her purse down at the bar. She signals the bartender as she launches into a dramatic retelling of a phone call she had with an infamous client.

Mal nods distractedly. When Jodi pauses for a sip of her drink, she seizes her chance. "I was actually hoping to talk with you about something," Mal says. She takes a deep breath to calm her nerves and continues: "Jodi, I've been feeling like things between us are . . . imbalanced. I'm happy to listen to your stories, but when it's my time to share, you don't pay much attention. Usually, you turn the conversation right back around to yourself."

Mal takes a sip of her drink and clears her throat. "The truth is, I tend to leave our time together feeling unseen, and I don't want that. I'd love if we could have more balanced conversations."

Jodi simply stares, taking a long sip of her drink. A few beats pass. Suddenly, she bursts out in laughter. "Mal, what are you *talking* about?" she chortles. "Honey, you've told me all about your crappy ex-husband . . . Your boring job . . . Your *cats*." Jodi rolls her eyes. "I mean . . . It's just all kind of depressing, isn't it?"

Mal stares back, speechless.

"I work with famous people, okay? My stories are hilarious. And *interesting*. We want to laugh, not have a pity party, right?"

Jodi signals to the bartender for another drink.

"Anyway, that reminds me: I've been meaning to tell you what happened last week," Jodi goes on, leaning in conspiratorially. "Did you hear . . ."

The evening proceeds in a haze, Jodi talking a mile a minute as Mal sits there, dumbfounded. After they say goodbye, Mal walks back to her apartment, amazed that anyone could be so inconsiderate. She wonders: *I feel so hurt by her reaction, but maybe I'm being too sensitive. Maybe she's right—maybe the problem is that I'm too depressing.*

TAKING STOCK OF THE RELATIONSHIP

Like Mal, when we first feel dissatisfied in a relationship, we might doubt ourselves or deny the severity of the disconnection we're feeling. We may try to ignore our instincts that this relationship (in its current form) isn't a good fit; dismiss our feelings as signs that we're just "too sensitive," "too demanding," or "not interesting enough"; or distract ourselves from our dissatisfaction by over-involving ourselves in our work, personal projects, or other relationships. The following reflections can help us take stock of the relationship with clear eyes as we decide how to proceed.

What Changes Have Occurred Since This Relationship Began?

Generally, we outgrow relationships because we change, they change, and/or our circumstances change. Identifying these specific changes helps us put the feeling that we're outgrowing the connection into context.

Consider: *Since this relationship began, how have I changed? How have they changed? And how have our circumstances changed?*

As we see through this reflection, outgrowing a relationship doesn't have to involve fault or blame. Many connections simply come to an end because developments over time have led to a mismatch in needs, desires, or values.

Mal contemplates these questions. She reflects first on how she's changed: *Well, I'm trying to stop people-pleasing, so I've started paying more attention to my needs. I've tried to assert myself more, too. I've also done a lot of healing from my divorce, and that process has made me more aware of relationships that make me feel disrespected.*

When Mal considers how Jodi has changed, she can't think of anything specific. As for changing life circumstances, Mal notes that she's been living in New York for three years now. At first, when she was a stranger to the city, she was desperate for friendship wherever she could find it. Now she has an assortment of friends and a sense of community, which enables her to be more particular about which relationships really work for her.

These changes put Mal's feelings of discontent into context. Her frustration with Jodi isn't just a fluke; it's an understandable culmination of the shifts that have occured over the last three years.

What Chronic Patterns Aren't Working for Me?

What repeated behaviors, differences, or conflicts are making your relationship a source of stress? All relationships include mistakes and momentary hurts, but when a painful behavior becomes a chronic pattern, it can be a sign of deeper mismatch.

Perhaps they rarely show you affection; perhaps your conversations are always imbalanced; perhaps they're always trying to change you; perhaps you can't give them as much support as they need; perhaps they don't take accountability for their part in conflicts; perhaps your needs for togetherness and separateness are mismatched; perhaps you can't tolerate their heavy drinking anymore; or perhaps your sex life is dissatisfying.

For every pattern, consider your underlying unmet need. Does this relationship leave you craving more connection? Reciprocity? Independence? Affection?

Mal considers the chronic pattern that isn't working for her: *Jodi monopolizes our conversations, and I feel unseen whenever we spend time together.* Beneath this pattern, Mal identifies that her unmet needs are balance, reciprocity, to be heard, and to matter.

What Has My Body Told Me?

Our bodies are an oft-overlooked source of intuitive wisdom. How our bodies react in the presence of others can offer us key information about how safe, respected, and comfortable we feel with them. Even when our minds dismiss our frustrations as "no big deal," our physical sensations may tell a more honest story.

When spending time with, communicating with, or even thinking about the person in question, we can check in with ourselves: *What do I notice in my body right now? Do I notice a tightening chest or a racing heart? Shortness of breath? Tension in my stomach? Numbness? Do I leave encounters with this person feeling energized or depleted?*

Mal hasn't paid much attention to her body during her time with Jodi. She takes a seat at her kitchen table, closes her eyes, and imagines that Jodi is sitting beside her, telling yet another long-winded tale about a client. As Mal watches this mental movie play out, she notices a clenching in her chest and a low, buzzing ache in her temple. She suddenly remembers that, after most nights out with Jodi, she falls into bed immediately, exhausted in the way she's exhausted after a long day of work.

Mal feels validated as she notes how her body has expressed its discontent. This isn't just a passing sensitivity in her mind; it's a full-body reaction signaling that something is wrong with their relationship.

Have I Communicated My Needs Explicitly?

Many recovering people-pleasers have a history of exiting relationships without first communicating our needs because the thought of expressing them makes us too uncomfortable.

The truth is, even if we think another person should just know what we need, we'll never know if they can meet us there unless we ask directly. (The exception to this rule is violence or abuse; you should never need to ask someone not to harm you in this way.) When we let our unspoken resentments fester and ultimately drive us away, we don't give the relationship a chance to become all it can be.

Mal is proud of herself for asking for more balance after three years of simmering resentment. Jodi's response was off-putting, but at least Mal knows that she did her part to make her needs known.

As Mal contemplates her responses to these four reflections, she feels a sense of clarity. The pattern is obvious: her body has spoken, her needs are unmet, and Jodi made no effort to show compassion following her sincere request. Mal feels confident in her conviction that something needs to change.

PS: It Doesn't Always Need to Be "Toxic."

Ultimately, we're the only ones who can determine a "good enough" reason to outgrow a relationship. This decision is highly dependent upon our own history, values, and capacity for sustaining multiple relationships at once. When we release a relationship that isn't toxic or harmful, but is simply not a good fit, other people may not understand or approve of our decision—but they're not the ones living our life.

PLANNING YOUR NEXT MOVE

Once we've affirmed that the relationship isn't meeting our needs, it's time to decide how we'll move forward. In some cases, small adjustments to a relationship will be enough to make it feel manageable. Other times, the only viable option is to end the connection altogether.

Starting with Small Changes: The Soundboard Approach

If you've ever been to a concert, you may have noticed an audio engineer standing in the back of the room making adjustments to the soundboard. A soundboard typically has hundreds of knobs and sliders, each corresponding to a different aspect of the sound (keyboards, vocals, treble, bass, etc.). When tweaked just right, the engineer can create a perfect sonic balance.

The soundboard is a useful metaphor for how we can make small adjustments to various aspects of a relationship to make the connection feel more tenable. Once we've made a request of someone and they don't change, we can't make them change—but we can ask ourselves, *How close and connected am I willing to be to this person who can't or won't meet this need?*

By shifting our degree of intimacy and connection—by tweaking and adjusting certain sliders on the soundboard—we may find a new balance that feels workable. We might adjust:

- How frequently we spend time together (once a year, once a month, once a week)
- How long we spend together each time (thirty minutes, two hours, all weekend)
- How we communicate (text message, phone call, video chat)
- Which topics we discuss (politics, religion, family, work)
- Our entanglements (sharing a home, sharing a business, sharing pets)
- How much we give (of our time, energy, money)
- Our own expectations for the relationship

We can adjust as many of these components as we need in order to make the relationship feel sustainable.

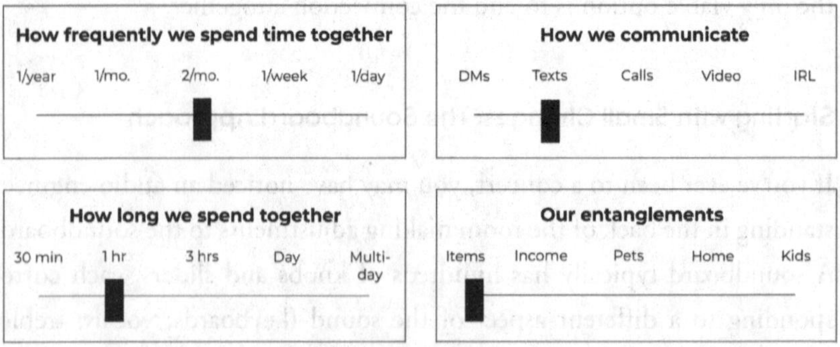

Olivia's relationship with her friend Tito has become very strained. Tito has been struggling with his mental health for years, and while Olivia is happy to support him as best she can, he wants to spend far more time together than Olivia can sustain. She doesn't want to end their relationship altogether—she loves Tito and enjoys his company, albeit in smaller doses—so in order to make the connection more manageable, she sets two boundaries: she tells him she can only meet up once every two weeks, and says she's only comfortable using text messages to coordinate plans, not to catch up.

Now that they see each other less frequently—and now that she isn't deluged with texts from him in between—Olivia has more bandwidth for his emotions when they're together. She also notices that, because she's finally honoring her own limitations, she no longer resents him.

IT TAKES TWO

By setting small boundaries around how we engage with others, we may open our relationships to levels of comfort and freedom we never thought possible—and practice asserting our needs in the process. Of course, all relationships require both people's participation. Once we've made these adjustments, the other person gets to decide if this new formation meets their needs, too. If our new boundaries don't meet their needs, the relationship may no longer be viable. If the soundboard approach doesn't go well or if the other party isn't receptive, we can move forward knowing we gave this relationship a meaningful chance to improve.

Cutting Ties with the Light Switch Approach

Unlike a soundboard, a light switch has two settings: on and off. When we use the light switch approach, we disengage entirely from a relationship. This approach works best when there is active harm or mistreatment; when *no* version of the connection would feel comfortable for you; or when the other person's behavior consistently makes you feel unsafe or uncomfortable, and they've made no attempt to change it despite your requests.

When exiting a relationship entirely, we may choose to spare the other party confusion by directly communicating our departure. We might say something like "I've given it a lot of thought, and I've come to the conclusion that this relationship isn't a good fit for me anymore," "The way we've been interacting doesn't feel sustainable for me, and unfortunately I can't continue this relationship," or "I care about you as a person, but our circumstances have changed a lot over the years, and I don't think we're compatible anymore."

Two weeks after their meetup at the bar, Mal is typing at her desk when she gets a text from Jodi: **Drinks tonight?**

Resentful, Mal doesn't respond. A few days later, another text: **Girl, where are you? Drinks tonight???** Mal just stares at her phone. She realizes she has no desire to maintain a casual friendship with someone so self-centered. The healing process Mal went through after her divorce was painful, but transformative: it taught her that life is too short to participate in such imbalanced relationships. She decides to use the light switch approach to disengage from Jodi.

Mal takes a few moments to think and then drafts a reply to Jodi's message. She writes, **Jodi, I've given it a lot of thought, and this friendship isn't a good fit for me anymore. The way you dismissed my concerns over drinks confirmed that our connection is too imbalanced for me to feel comfortable. Thanks for the time we've shared; I wish you the best.** Her heart is racing as she hits send.

TRANSITIONING WITH INTEGRITY

Outgrowing a relationship is an emotionally charged process. When we begin to recognize the ways in which we've been mistreated, denied, or ignored, it's common to feel anger, frustration, and resentment. As entitled as we are to these feelings, it's important that we handle our relationship transitions with as much integrity as we can muster. By proceeding in a thoughtful and levelheaded manner, we ensure that we won't look back later with regret that we burst out in anger, treated someone poorly, or stooped to someone else's disrespectful level.

Whether we use the soundboard or light switch approach, we can take certain steps to make sure we're acting with integrity. We might consider: Does having a direct conversation about the transition feel like the right thing to do? Should this discussion take place in person, via phone, or via email? How detailed an explanation are we willing to give them? And how willing are we to process our decision with them if they have questions?

Taking a moment for these considerations now ensures that we have as few doubts as possible about how we handled the transition later.

TRANSFORMING GUILT INTO SELF-COMPASSION

Even if we're confident that our decision to transition a relationship was right for us, it's normal to feel guilt afterward, especially if the other person expresses hurt, anger, or sadness. When visited by these discomforts, we can use the tools below—and the strategies depicted in chapter 15—to stay strong and transform our growing pains into self-compassion.

Recognize the Harms of Staying the Same

We tend to focus on how leaving relationships can hurt others, forgetting that *staying* in misaligned relationships can hurt others, too. When we force ourselves to stay in relationships that no longer work for us, our dissatisfaction emerges in unsavory ways. We might avoid their calls, messages, or texts; communicate coldly or passive-aggressively; vent about them to other people; hyperfocus on their negative qualities; become distant or withdrawn; snap at them with little provocation; or begin to lack compassion for their struggles.

These behaviors can be hurtful and upsetting. We can flip the script and imagine: *What if someone was feeling uncomfortable or unhappy in their connection with* me? *Would I* really *want them to continue in the relationship if the only thing keeping them there was a sense of obligation, guilt, or pity? Would I* really *want them to spend time with me if they spent every minute wishing they were somewhere else?*

By flipping the script, we can see that staying in a relationship we've outgrown isn't an act of kindness: it's dishonest and patronizing.

Mal considers all the ways she's reacted to her connection with Jodi: the anger and resentment; the frequent desire to fake being sick and cancel; the nights of frustrated rumination; the violent headaches after time spent together; the way she complains about Jodi's self-centeredness to her other friends. Mal asks herself: *How would I feel if I knew that a friend was having the same negative reaction to me, but was staying connected solely out of guilt?*

The thought turns Mal's stomach; she knows she would be angry at that friend for being dishonest and wasting her time in a connection that wasn't genuine. This fresh perspective helps Mal realize that, while ending the friendship may have initially hurt Jodi, in the long term, it opens space for Jodi to build relationships with people who actually want to spend time with her—not just people who are feigning connection out of fear of speaking up.

Challenge All-or-Nothing Thinking

When others react negatively to our boundaries, we may find ourselves internalizing their judgments of us. We may say to ourselves, "I shouldn't be so bothered by this," "I'm way too sensitive," "I'm such a bad friend," "I'm so selfish," or "I'm horrible at maintaining relationships."

As the examples above illustrate, our negative judgments tend to take the form of all-or-nothing thinking. By challenging these black-and-white thoughts, we can see the situation—and ourselves—in a more nuanced way. We can challenge each negative judgment by compiling a list of tangible evidence that either refutes it *or* offers more context for it. (This evidence can be pulled from as many of our relationships as we'd like, not just the relationship we're outgrowing.)

For example: If we're telling a negative story that we're "so selfish," we might recall that we generously share our time, emotional energy, food, and resources with our loved ones; that we show our friends care by being attentive and curious in our conversations with them; and that we buy our family members generous gifts for their birthdays and holidays. If we're telling a story that we're "too sensitive," we might remember that we can take a joke, especially when the person making the joke is someone who treats us well; that we can gracefully tolerate imbalance in relationships if that imbalance is short-lived; and that we're only sensitive to situations in which we feel mistreated, and that it's healthy to be sensitive to mistreatment.

By challenging our black-and-white judgments with nuanced evidence, we get a clearer, more accurate picture of ourselves and our reactions.

Remember How the Relationship Dulled Your Light

In the face of guilt, we can affirm that this was the right decision by recalling the many ways this connection hurt us, shrunk us, or dulled our light. We can reflect: What parts of ourselves were hidden in this relationship? What did we have to sacrifice in order to maintain this connection? And what if we *hadn't* ended this relationship and it carried on as usual for one year—five years—ten years? What would the long-term negative effects have been?

Mal decides to journal about the first question: *What parts of myself were hidden in this relationship?*

She writes: *I felt small in my friendship with Jodi. My other friends tell me that I'm funny and outgoing, but around Jodi, I shrank down to a shadow of myself. She never listened to what I had to say, so I grew to believe I wasn't a very interesting person. I have a lot of ideas—ideas about the world, about people, about relationships—that I never got to talk about with her. I got so little space in our conversations that I felt like I didn't have a voice at all. I began to doubt my own intelligence, my own sense of humor, my own self. At the end of the day, I was just a set of ears for her to talk at.*

Mal puts down her pen, satisfied with her response. Contemplating her answer, she feels a sense of sadness; in retrospect, it's clear just how deeply this friendship affected her self-esteem. She feels convicted that something *had* to give: carrying on in the connection simply wasn't an option.

Consider Lessons Learned

Not all relationships are meant to last forever. Some are merely teachers, briefly entering our lives to help us grow. Seeing our relationships as teachers gives them meaning, purpose, and utility; even if they're over, they played an important role in our lives.

To distill the lessons we learned, we might consider: What did the relationship teach us that we need in order to be truly happy and satisfied?

What red flags should we watch for in future relationships? What did we previously think was a *want* that this relationship taught us was in fact a *need*? And are there certain needs we downplayed in this relationship that we want to emphasize in future relationships?

IN WITH THE NEW

Ultimately, outgrowing relationships isn't just about letting misaligned connections go; it's about opening up space for newer, healthier connections to form. When we're stuck in unhappy relationships, we, like Mal, are plagued by resentment, distracted by anxiety, and afflicted with self-judgment. We struggle to muster the energy, desire, and self-confidence we need to form new, nurturing connections with other people.

But by removing ourselves from these relationships, we gain the space—and the peace of mind—to find more supportive connections. We prove to ourselves through our actions that we deserve the balanced, reciprocal, and respectful relationships we seek; we will no longer settle for less.

17

ALLOWING GRIEF, TRANSITIONS, AND NEW BEGINNINGS

"To be ourselves causes us to be exiled by many others, and yet to comply with what others want causes us to be exiled from ourselves. It is a tormenting tension and it must be borne, but the choice is clear."
—Clarissa Pinkola Estés, *Women Who Run with the Wolves*

As we break the people-pleasing pattern, the changes we make to our own perspectives and behaviors lead to changes in our relationships, workplaces, and communities. We may find ourselves going through a breakup or divorce; leaving a friendship or a community; transitioning out of a career; leaving a faith; or releasing an old belief system. Sometimes, we choose these endings; sometimes, they're foisted upon us. Either way, they're disorienting, leaving us grieving and untethered.

But for the recovering people-pleaser, these endings and transitions offer an unexpected gift: an opportunity to prioritize ourselves and build new connections upon sturdy and self-respecting foundations. In this chapter, we'll explore the many forms grief takes as we outgrow old relationships; normalize the loneliness of the period between when we set higher standards and when our lives become filled with people who meet them; and discuss practical tools for coping with the challenges that accompany endings and transitions.

MINA'S STORY

Mina and her husband, Gavin, have been married for eighteen years. When they first met, she was attracted to his charisma and drive, and he was drawn to her kindness and empathy. The two spent countless nights daydreaming about their future together, imagining the places they would travel and the home they would create.

Eighteen years later, everything has changed. They have two children: Christopher, seventeen, and Eliza, fourteen. Not long after Christopher's birth, Mina and Gavin began to have problems. With children, Mina felt more anxious than ever before; it was terrifying to think that two small beings were entirely dependent upon her. But when she tried to share her feelings with Gavin, seeking comradery and support, he would shut down. He was stressed, too, he said, and raising kids was more than he had bargained for.

As the years went on, more seeds of resentment were sown between them. Six years ago, Gavin's father passed away, and the loss plummeted him into a deep depression from which he never surfaced. Already distant, he became terse and uncompromising. He began to drink more heavily, always maintaining a steady buzz.

At first Mina tried to support him in his grief. She would cook his favorite meals, offer him back rubs, and check in on the state of his heart. Sometimes, for a day or two, she would feel connected to him again—he would climb out of whatever dark space he was in, and they would share a day of laughter and ease—but then, like clockwork, he picked up the bottle and retreated back into himself. When she'd suggest that he consider therapy, he'd leave the room and wouldn't speak to her for hours.

For the past six years, Mina's tried not to acknowledge just how lonely and bitter she has become. Memories of her early days with Gavin are too painful to recall. Countless times, she has asked him to help more with the kids—to drink less—to show her *any* affection at all. Sometimes, he gets defensive and ignores her entirely; sometimes, he makes a show of effort for a day or two before returning to his normal ways. At first, she clung to these kernels of hope desperately, thinking, *This is it! He's finally hearing me!* But after so many false starts, she is beginning to accept the painful reality that he isn't changing.

As Gavin's drinking continues to worsen, Mina's beginning to come to terms with the fact that this marriage isn't a healthy environment for her or her children. After months of sleepless nights, she works up the courage to tell Gavin that she wants a divorce. The conversation is even harder than she expected; for the first time in months, she sees genuine emotion flicker across his face. He doesn't beg her to stay or ask her to try again; he listens quietly, and when she's said her piece, he walks out of the room.

The next four months pass in a flurry of logistics and grief. Gavin moves out; Mina hires an attorney, talks to the kids, and breaks the news to her family and friends. She knows she's making the right choice, but that doesn't make it any less painful.

GRIEF IS COMPLICATED

We tend to relegate grief to the realm of death, but it can apply to any loss or ending: divorce, estrangement, leaving a workplace or community, religious disaffiliation, a friendship's demise, and more. Even when we end connections that we *know* are unhealthy for us, we may feel a strange combination of loss, pride, sadness, resolve, despair, and relief. We may feel pleased with our decision one day and flooded with nostalgic memories the next. Instead of demanding allegiance to any single feeling, we can recognize that these mixed emotions are completely natural and gently soothe ourselves through them all.

Common Companions to Grief

When we make the brave choice to leave a relationship or community, our grief may be compounded by others' negative reactions to our decision. We may encounter:

THE PAIN OF CYCLE-BREAKING

In dysfunctional families, friend groups, and communities, the person who sets boundaries around the dysfunctional behavior is often made out to be the dysfunctional one. When we finally set boundaries around a family member's addiction, a partner's abuse, or a community's toxic patterns, we may find that we're scapegoated as the problem. By addressing the unhealthy dynamic head-on, we force the dysfunction into the spotlight, and other members of the group aren't always ready or willing to face it. If they're not, they may displace their discomfort onto *us*, blaming us for rocking the boat instead of keeping the peace.

THE ACHE OF OTHERS' JUDGMENTS

The decision to leave a relationship or community is highly personal. It's often the result of hundreds of sleepless nights, tearful heart-to-hearts with trusted confidantes, and desperate attempts to make the unworkable workable. For this reason, it can feel particularly wounding when others—especially trusted others, like family or friends—do not support the boundaries that we've set.

They may say we're "overreacting" when we estrange from an abusive parent, or "not trying hard enough" when we finally end a dissatisfying marriage. These judgments can turn on a slow, leaky tap of self-doubt: *Are they right? Did I overreact? Am I a terrible person? Did I make a huge mistake?*

In these moments, it's important that we remember that other people don't experience the lived reality of our relationships the way we do. They may see the public side—the photos on Instagram, the wide smiles at social gatherings—but behind closed doors, we are the only ones who know how these relationships affected our self-worth and our mental health.

GRIEF FOR OUR PAST SELVES

Sometimes, we can't acknowledge the severity of our suffering until we have distance from our old circumstances. Sometimes, we need to leave a relationship in order to see how it harmed us. Sometimes, we don't realize how hard we had it until, years later, we share our story with a friend and see our pain reflected in their eyes.

Making the courageous choice to leave a relationship or community can spark a wave of grief for our past selves. Finally liberated from the toxic cycle, we can pause, breathe, and take stock of our circumstances. In this unfamiliar spaciousness, we may feel a deep ache for the version of us who stomached that toxicity for so long.

Grief for our past selves, though painful, is in fact a sign of deep healing. It may be the first time we've truly allowed ourselves to *feel*, with unfettered hearts, how much suffering we've been through. This pain is an affirmation that our past selves deserved better. We can't change our past, but we can use our grief to solidify our commitment never to disappear into people-pleasing again.

COPING WITH GRIEF

If we spend our lives avoiding grief, we will stay stuck in relationships, communities, and environments that hurt us. Painful though they may be, the fires of grief are necessary as we embrace the initiation that is our healing: this courageous foray into the next chapter of our lives. These tools can help soothe us in our grief:

One Day at a Time

When swimming in the black ocean of grief, it can be tempting to seek quick solutions to our pain. We may read endless articles, scour self-help books, digest hours of podcasts: anything to make it go away, and fast.

But there is no quick fix. Release the idea that you need to work harder to find a solution to this pain. You can take solace in the fact that feeling your grief is the only "work" you must do—and you don't have to feel it all at once. When the pain feels like too much, you can borrow an adage from the twelve-step community and remember: you only need to get through one day at a time. When one day feels like too much, it's one hour, or one minute, at a time.

After Gavin moves out, Mina is tidying up the house while the kids are at school. She goes into her bedroom and sees his half of the closet empty and his bedside table barren. The emptiness hits her like a gut punch: *My God, it's really over*. She falls to her knees in a wave of grief. Memories flood her unbidden: her early dates with Gavin, when everything felt possible; the rare, good days when they and the kids would sit around the kitchen table, laughing.

She sobs, letting the grief wash over her. *How am I going to get through this?* she thinks. *When will this pain end?*

When she catches her mind spinning out to the future, she encourages herself to move one day at a time. Today, that means tidying up; picking up Eliza from softball practice; cooking dinner; and doing whatever she needs to do tonight to feel okay, whether it's a hot bath, some mindless television, or calling up a friend for a good cry. She takes a deep breath. Focusing only on today makes the grief a little more bearable.

Remember What You Gained

In the throes of grief, our attention is trained squarely on all we've lost. It's easy to forget that, through this transition, we have also gained something: ourselves.

Consider: What else have you gained through this decision? Have you gained a sense of agency over your own life? A deeper sense of self-respect or self-trust? Mental or physical well-being? The possibility of forming healthier, more reciprocal connections?

The next time Mina finds herself lost in reverie, reliving her good memories with Gavin, she asks herself: *What have I gained from this decision?*

She reflects on her recent years, remembering how hollow she became in her marriage. Her relationship with Gavin was a constant source of pain and stress; she spent most days preoccupied with how much he was drinking, how little he'd done around the house, and his temper when speaking to the kids. She realizes that, in his absence, she certainly feels grief, but beneath it, she also feels an unfamiliar peace of mind. She's no longer preoccupied with his actions or decisions: she has only herself and the kids to think about.

Mina's marriage also made her feel undesired. She couldn't help but interpret Gavin's distance and disinterest as something *wrong with her.* Many times over the years, she thought to herself: *If only I were more beautiful, that would keep his attention. . . . If only I were more interesting, he would care what I had to say. . . .* These negative thoughts played on a loop in her mind. Now she realizes that choosing not to settle for distance, disinterest, and imbalance was a powerful act of self-respect. It is painful, yes, but also oddly empowering: by removing herself from her marriage, she showed herself that, yes, she does deserve better. It's still too early for Mina to consider dating, but she recognizes that only by leaving Gavin could she make herself available to, maybe one day, find real love again.

Hold a Grief Ritual

When we find ourselves touched by grief in our healing, we can honor the significance of our loss by setting aside time for a ritual. Grief rituals help us to normalize, systematize, and traverse our mourning, and research shows that they actually reduce its potency.

We might honor our loss by lighting a candle in dedication to what's ended; writing what we're releasing on a piece of paper and casting it into a fire; gathering photos that represent our loss; making a pilgrimage to a place that held special significance in the relationship; writing a eulogy for this chapter that is ending; or offering a time of silence in meditation or prayer.

Document the Ebbs

Like tides at the seashore, our grief ebbs and flows. We might cry with our morning coffee but find a spring in our step by lunchtime. At dinner we may feel morose again, but an hour later we're laughing along with our favorite comedy. Ebbs in our grief help us remember that it's possible to feel another, better way.

Savor these ebbs. Notice your lightness; your uplifted perspective; your ability to think positively about the future. Write a short letter or record a short video for your future self that you can review when you need a reminder that these brighter moments are, indeed, possible.

One day, Mina and Christopher pick up Eliza from softball practice. It's a warm May evening, and for the first time all year, lightning bugs flicker over the fields. Eliza asks if they can stop for ice cream on the way home, and though Mina has tried to be frugal since the separation, she thinks: *What the hell. We all need this.*

As they wait in line outside the ice cream parlor, Eliza is in good spirits, bouncing on her toes as she describes a home run she hit at practice. Mina half listens with a smile, enjoying the hue of the fading pink sky. She is amazed to realize she is, in this moment, genuinely happy. She wraps her arms around her kids and they both moan, mortified at their mother's public display of affection. "Mom, *please*," grimaces Eliza, "there are girls from my school here." Mina laughs, undeterred.

Later that evening, she documents the day. She writes down as much detail as she can remember: the pink sky, the brightness in Eliza's laugh, Christopher's awkward smile, the lightning bugs. Mina closes her entry with *I know there will be hard days. . . . But the next time you're in the throes of grief, just remember that happiness like this is possible.* She closes her journal and promises herself to return to this entry when she needs a pick-me-up.

REFRAMING ENDINGS

Often, the very best things in our lives are born of endings. Consider something that you feel proud of or happy about today, and then consider the many chapters that needed to *end* for that thing to be possible.

Perhaps you needed to experience that painful breakup in order to find the love of your life. Perhaps you needed to get fired from your old job to discover your current, more fulfilling career. Or maybe you needed to leave your old social circle to find the friends who were truly a match for you. At the time, some of these endings may have felt unbearable. But in hindsight, it's clear that they were necessary to get where you are now.

The losses we face as we break the people-pleasing pattern are the same: painful but essential milestones. Holly Whitaker, who writes frequently about the space between endings and new beginnings, explains: "At some point it becomes clear that what we think of as a wrong turn, a mistake, a backslide or a period of inertia was not some kind of departure from the path but actually an indispensable part of it, and sometimes the most important one. But it's never that way when you're all smooshed up against it. We never live through the hell fires of an astonishing transition and think it's supposed to be happening—we only think that about pleasant, wanted things."

What if this transition—and its accompanying grief—are, in fact, *supposed* to be happening? What if this anxious and uncomfortable time is exactly where we're meant to be right now?

WELCOME TO THE VALLEY

When we start setting higher standards for our relationships, there's a period between when we set those standards and when our lives become filled with people who meet them. I call this limbo the Valley.

The Valley is the liminal space that sits between the past and the future; between our old selves and our new selves; between the familiar and the uncertain. We may find ourselves in the Valley as we change:

- **Our relationships:** "I used to be connected with them, but now I'm alone."
- **Our communities:** "I used to be a member of that group, but now I don't know who my people are."
- **Our careers:** "I used to do that job, but now I don't know what my calling is."
- **Our faiths/belief systems:** "I used to hold those beliefs, but now I don't know what I believe in."

One of the most difficult aspects of the Valley is the loneliness we feel when old connections end, and new, healthier connections have yet to form. Since we have based so much of our identity on other people—helping others, pleasing others, getting validation from others—we may feel awkward, incomplete, or purposeless during these times of disconnection. We may feel as if we're on an awkward first date with a stranger, and in some ways, we are: the stranger is the self we've long neglected.

During these dark nights of the lonely soul, we may begin to doubt our self-advocacy. We may wonder if we're being "too picky" by requiring reciprocity, respect, and kindness from our relationships. (We're not.) We may wonder, "Should I have just settled for less?" (No!)

We must remember that if we renege on our standards, we will continuously find ourselves in connections that disappoint. The loneliness we feel now is a prerequisite to experiencing the joy and reciprocity we seek in communion with others. As we break the people-pleasing pattern, we're no longer catapulting into a relationship with every person who shows the slightest interest in us. We're no longer letting our hunger for validation drive us to feed on scraps of attention. Now we're holding out for a feast.

Mina, Revisited

It has been six months since Gavin moved out. While Mina believes the heaviest throes of grief are behind her, she is now untethered and lonely. She's not sure where—or with whom—she belongs.

Mina and Gavin keep in touch about the kids, but when they talk, they maintain a cordial distance. She used to be close with Gavin's sister and mother, but since the separation, they've been distant, too; Mina knows they wish she'd tried harder to make things work. Even Mina's friendships have been in flux; many of her friends were couples that she met during her marriage, and since the separation, she can tell that they feel pressure to pick sides.

Mina feels like almost every aspect of her life is in transition. She can't shake the feeling that she's waiting for her new life to begin, but so far, all she has are vestiges of her past.

TOOLS TO MAKE THE MOST OF THE VALLEY

Though we look forward to emerging from the Valley, this time contains important gifts we cannot find anywhere else. Only here can we see new possibilities with unclouded eyes. Only here can we unabashedly prioritize ourselves in ways we couldn't before. Here are four tools to help us make the most of this time:

Give Your Time Here a Purpose

As we discussed in chapter 15, the stories we tell ourselves about our difficult emotions affect how intensely we feel those emotions. Judging our discomfort or loneliness in the Valley as "wrong" or "a sign that we'll be alone forever" only hurts us unnecessarily.

Instead, we can give our time here a purpose. We can consider how our time in the Valley is a chance to deepen our relationship with ourselves after years of self-neglect; an opportunity to find meaning in a new hobby or passion; a chance to prioritize our own physical well-being, mental health, or creative pursuits; or even an invitation to explore our spiritual lives with solitude and intention. Ultimately, we can shift our understanding of the Valley from a time of disconnection with others to a time of *reconnection* with self.

In Mina's case, the past seventeen years were defined by caring for Gavin and her children, and she likes the idea of using the Valley to deepen her relationship with herself and rebuild her confidence. She hasn't had the time—or the energy—to prioritize her own wants or needs in years, and the thought makes her smile. There are *so* many things she spent her marriage wishing she'd had time for. The piano that she bought when Eliza was a baby sat untouched in the family room; the massage gift certificate she received for Mother's Day last year waited, unused, in her wallet; a few old college friends had reached out to get together, but she never had the time.

It's your turn, Mina tells herself. She checks her calendar for a day to use her gift certificate, and reaches for her phone to send a text to her college friend.

Distill Your Lessons Learned

Our time in the Valley enables us to look back at the relationships we've outgrown with sharp, discerning eyes. This is an excellent vantage point from which to take stock: to assess what worked, what didn't, and what we learned from our experience. Behaviors we previously accepted as normal may now seem intolerable. Ideas we accepted as truths may now feel flimsy and immaterial. We may even feel astonished by our old patterns as we recognize, for the first time, how we minimized ourselves for the sake of others' comfort.

These insights would not be possible without the fresh perspective of the Valley. Here, we might explore: What are some things we normalized then that we now see as unacceptable or unhealthy? In what ways did we shrink ourselves to make that relationship work? How did that experience prevent us from being our fullest selves? What did that experience teach us about what we need from future connections? And knowing what we know now, what self-abandoning patterns should we guard against as we pursue new connections?

Commit to New Boundaries and Bottom Lines

In the Valley, we get to establish new bottom lines. Detached from the pressures of our old situation, we can instate new boundaries without worrying about others' negative reactions. One benefit of our loneliness is that it offers us a blank slate; we have an opportunity to design our own lives on our own terms.

To discover these new boundaries, we might ask: How did we overextend ourselves in the previous situation? What aspects of our lives did we neglect *then* that we don't want to neglect anymore? What did we say *yes* to that we want to say *no* to in the future? And what are our new bottom lines: behaviors or patterns we absolutely will not tolerate anymore?

After a few months in the Valley, Mina feels like she's ready to start dating. The thought excites her and scares her at the same time; she wants to meet someone new, but her marriage was so painful that she's afraid of repeating old patterns.

She takes some time with her journal to reflect on her new boundaries and bottom lines for future romantic partners. She writes: *No heavy drinking. Freely shows me verbal and physical affection. Actively tends to their mental health. Is able and willing to have conversations about emotions: mine and theirs.*

Then Mina considers how she overextended herself in ways she doesn't want to anymore. She writes: *In future relationships, I won't be the only one who takes initiative to coordinate date nights and time together. I need reciprocity. I won't assume complete responsibility for household tasks and childcare; they need to be shared. I won't apologize for my partners if they're being rude or belligerent in public. They're adults, and they are responsible for the consequences of their own actions. And I won't be the only one to pick up the pieces after every argument. I need a partner who is able and willing to repair after disagreements.*

Reviewing her answers, Mina feels a sense of security—like she has her own back for the first time.

Prioritize Gentleness

For all the lessons it offers, the Valley isn't the easiest place to be. Its uncertainties can tax the body and the heart, and it's important that we're gentle with ourselves while we're here.

Spending time in the Valley automatically sparks inner transformation, so we don't have to constantly "work" toward change. In fact, tending to ourselves with gentleness and care might be such a departure from our old ways that gentleness itself is the inner transformation. While in the Valley, consider how you might relax your expectations of yourself; make ample time for rest and relaxation; spend time in nature; or savor the care and support that loved ones give you.

A few weeks after she begins dating, Mina is sitting at home on a Friday night. Both of her kids are out, and in the silence, she feels disquieted. She's proud of the life that she's building—she's been on a few promising dates, connected with a couple of old friends, and spent a lot of time playing the piano—but sometimes, it still feels hard. She ponders how to spend her night. She considers reading a self-help book, but honestly, she's tired of treating herself like a self-improvement project. She's just tired.

In the silence, she says: "This is hard." Her voice echoes in the empty kitchen around her.

Emboldened, she repeats, "This is *hard*!"

Something about acknowledging her struggles feels validating. *Tonight*, she decides, *my only job is to take care of myself.* She calls up her best friend, Reese, who lives a few states away. Reese picks up on the first ring.

"Hey," blurts Mina, "I'm having the lamest Friday night, and I'm feeling sad as hell. Want to drink wine with me and talk about *The Bachelor*?"

Reese laughs and agrees. An hour later finds Mina in pajamas and slippers, wineglass in hand, laughing at something Reese said. Mina knows she won't be in the Valley forever, and lighthearted moments like this are enough to keep her moving forward.

NEW BEGINNINGS ON HEALTHY FOUNDATIONS

As we open our hearts to new beginnings, we can remember that they don't always arise with fanfare; sometimes, they present themselves in the most serendipitous ways. William Bridges, author of *Transitions*, writes:

> Think back to the important beginnings in your own past. You bumped into an old friend that you hadn't seen for years, and he told you about a job at his company that opened up just that morning. You met your spouse-to-be at a party that you really hadn't wanted to go to and that you almost skipped. You learned to play the guitar while you were getting over the measles, and you studied French because the Spanish class met at eight A.M. and you hated to get up early. . . . The lesson in all such experiences is that when we are ready to make a new beginning, we will shortly find an opportunity.

New friendships, romantic relationships, careers, communities, and belief systems may enter our lives subtly. They may appear in a chance encounter; a flyer on the community billboard; a smile from a stranger. And how rewarding it is to build strong new connections upon this hard-won foundation of confidence, self-trust, and self-respect.

4

ENRICH YOURSELF

18

THERE'S NO WE WITHOUT ME

In part 4, we will explore the many ways our lives become richer as we leave people-pleasing behind. One of the greatest gifts of breaking this pattern is finally being able to form genuinely intimate relationships with others. When we were people-pleasing, we lived behind a mask: we never gave others the opportunity to truly know us. We silenced our opinions, avoided conflict, and abandoned our needs, hoping that our efforts would deliver us love, happiness, and belonging. But in truth, our people-pleasing inhibited us from intimacy. No matter how much people adored our mask, we were constantly haunted by the sense that we were fundamentally unseen and unknown.

The word *intimacy* is derived from the Latin root *intimus*, meaning "innermost." Opening ourselves to intimacy requires letting our innermost selves be known by another. It requires that we share the depths of our own passions and dreams. It demands that we are honest about what we feel and need, even when it's hard. Ultimately, accepting the invitation to intimacy means bringing *more* self to our relationships after years of bringing *less*.

In this chapter, we'll explore three keys to cultivating real intimacy in our relationships. We'll debunk the myth that playing small is the key to attracting relationships; challenge the idea that we should avoid conflict at all costs; and dispel the notion that compromise is always a good idea.

TAKING UP SPACE ATTRACTS THE RIGHT RELATIONSHIPS

For the past two years, Ciara has been striving to break the people-pleasing pattern. It's been challenging, but rewarding; she's far more comfortable making requests and setting boundaries than she's ever been before. When it became clear that her partner, Chad, couldn't meet her emotional needs, she ended their relationship. That was six months ago, and now she's ready to date.

Like so many recovering people-pleasers, Ciara has a history of dissatisfying romantic relationships. When dating in the past, she strived to be as accommodating and unobtrusive as possible. She would listen silently as men spoke about their jobs, their hobbies, and their friends. When her dates volleyed questions back to her, she would self-consciously deflect: *Oh, my work is boring, not even worth talking about. Anyway, what do you do on the weekends?*

Ciara lavished the men she dated with compliments, feigned interest in their hobbies, and spoke little about her own feelings, needs, and dreams. As a result, the partners she attracted were verbose, charismatic, and domineering. They enjoyed having a partner who devoted her attention to them so completely and required so little in return.

Ciara always began to feel overshadowed in these connections. Like many people-pleasers, she craved partners who wanted to know her; who valued reciprocity; who took as much interest in her as she did in them. In retrospect, Ciara sees how playing small to find love did just the opposite; it attracted relationships with people who couldn't love her the way she needed.

Playing Small Attracts the Wrong Relationships

When we were young, many of us received rewards—in the form of safety, security, affection, gratitude, or care—for suppressing our needs, hiding our feelings, and merging our interests with others'. With time, many of us came to believe that self-suppression was the key to garnering connection. We relied on these old strategies as we built new relationships with potential friends and partners, and in some ways, our methods were successful. Playing small *did* garner new connections—but usually, they weren't the connections we needed.

Take a moment to reflect on the times you suppressed your needs and feelings to win others' affections. Did your efforts lead to friends and partners who made you feel truly seen, understood, and appreciated? Did you finally get the reciprocal relationships you'd been waiting for? Or, like Ciara, did it leave you feeling invisible? Resentful? Trapped in relationships that were all give and no take, thinking: *If they knew what I really felt and needed, they wouldn't stick around?*

Our relationship histories are all the proof we need that playing small attracts the wrong relationships. The people we attract when we never take up space with our voices are *attracted* to our lack of voice. The people we attract when we don't have any boundaries are *attracted* to our lack of boundaries. Ironically, shrinking our needs in order to be lovable often leads us directly into the arms of people who can't, or won't, love us fully.

By changing how we show up to new relationships—by making ourselves known from the outset—we can find friends and partners who accept us as we are.

We Are People, Not Mirrors

One of the most common ways people-pleasers play small is by becoming mirrors in our relationships. Instead of bringing ourselves fully to the table—wants, needs, stories, opinions, and all—we simply reflect back what others want, need, and believe. We tailor our interests to others' interests, align our dreams with others' dreams, and slowly become eclipsed by others' personalities entirely. Psychotherapist Esther Perel asserts that real intimacy cannot come from this sort of fusion; it can only come from the interplay between self and other. She writes in *Mating in Captivity*:

> Our need for togetherness exists alongside our need for separateness. One does not exist without the other. With too much distance, there can be no connection. But too much merging eradicates the separateness of two distinct individuals. Then there is nothing more to transcend, no bridge to walk on, no one to visit on the other side, no other internal world to enter. When people become fused—when two become one—connection can no longer happen. *There is no one to connect with.*

As we break the people-pleasing pattern, we begin to understand that building intimate connections requires us to bring our individuated and authentic selves to our relationships. So, as we form new connections with friends and partners, we take up space with our own stories. We voice our own opinions. We share our own interests. We begin to occupy the 50 percent of our relationships that are rightly ours.

In the same way that playing small attracted people who liked us when we played small, taking up space attracts people who *like* that we take up space. Expressing our feelings attracts people who *like* that we express our feelings. Bringing our authentic selves to our relationships attracts people who *like* our authentic selves.

Over time, this dazzling dance of self and other enables our relationships to become more expansive, colorful, and vibrant. For the first time, they feel like relationships—not just echo chambers.

We Are Not Meant to Be Compatible with Everyone

If someone doesn't like us when we're being our authentic selves, that doesn't mean we shouldn't have been authentic. It just means that we're not compatible—and we're not meant to be compatible with everyone.

Back when we were people-pleasing, we reacted to others' disinterest by thinking, "How can I shrink my needs to get them to like me?" or "How can I hide the parts of me they don't like?" Now we react to others' disinterest with gratitude or, at the very least, acceptance. Ultimately, they saved us the effort of building a relationship with someone who wouldn't have been able to hold space for our feelings and needs.

When we release the drive to be liked by everyone, we finally give ourselves permission to be genuine—and it's only by being genuine that we can find the people who will appreciate us for who we *are* instead of who we pretend to be.

Ciara's Story

Ciara vows to leave playing small behind as she embarks on this period of dating. Over dinner, she doesn't just ask questions; she shares about herself, too. She talks about the pros and cons of her job at a nonprofit; she tells stories about her friends; she opens up about her dreams to travel the world. At first it feels nerve-racking to take up space in this way, but it also feels good.

Certain dates show curiosity and interest in what she says. They laugh along; they ask follow-up questions; they share their own stories in response. In these moments, Ciara feels like she's building genuine connections; she is letting herself be seen, and others are enthusiastic about what they see. A few of her dates are, unfortunately, dismissive. Some can't seem to empathize with her feelings; others patronize her interests. It hurts to take a risk and be dismissed, but she reminds herself: *They wouldn't have been a good match anyway.*

As the weeks pass, Ciara goes on a second date—then a third, and then a fourth—with Nathan. He is charismatic and kind, and as they grow closer, Ciara notices how foreign it feels to receive abundant affection and consideration.

Nathan invites Ciara to see his band play a show. A few weeks later, she invites him to be her plus-one at the nonprofit's benefit dinner. He handles himself confidently in a room full of strangers, and when they walk home hand in hand, he whispers: "That was a hit. I'm so proud of you."

Six months later, Ciara and Nathan are happily partnered. They've met each other's friends; they've gone to each other's favorite restaurants;

they've opened up about their anxieties and fears. Their connection feels so satisfying, so loving, that Ciara has to resist disbelief: *Can a relationship really feel this good?* she wonders.

But one day, something happens that makes Ciara question whether Nathan really cares for her as much as he claims to.

CONFLICT IS INEVITABLE IN INTIMATE RELATIONSHIPS

Every summer, Nathan's college friends get together for a day of river rafting and barbecue. When Nathan asks Ciara to join them, she's excited; she's heard him mention this event before, and she appreciates this opportunity to connect with his friends.

When they park at the riverbank, ten cars full of Nathan's friends are already there, unloading their gear and blowing up their rafts. Nathan makes his way around the group, exchanging greetings and hugs, while Ciara waits awkwardly for an introduction. When it becomes clear that he's caught up in conversation, she introduces herself and starts unloading the car on her own.

When it comes time to float the river, the group gathers in a huddle to strategize how to share the rafts. Nathan slings his arm around his friend Joe. "We'll bunk up together," he announces, punching his friend in the chest. "It'll be just like rooming together sophomore year."

As members of the group begin pairing up, Ciara feels forgotten. She doesn't know any of Nathan's friends; she wishes he were making more of an effort to include her. She ends up tagging along with two women, Lauren and Sage. As they float down the river, she enjoys making small talk with them and treasures the sun on her skin—but she is preoccupied.

The rest of the day unfolds in the same manner. After rafting, the group settles down at a picnic site for a barbecue and bonfire. Nathan is immersed in his friends; he's hardly talked to Ciara all day. She's upset. *Why did he even invite me if he wasn't going to pay me any attention?* she wonders. *Does he even want me here at all?*

When the night finally comes to a close, everyone makes their way back to the parking lot. As Nathan and Ciara drive home, she feels a tug in her chest.

"What a day," Nathan says happily, his hands on the wheel. "You should've seen it: Joe and I were headed straight for the river rocks at one point! It was a narrow miss."

Ciara tries to put forth her brightest smile. "Oh yeah?" she replies. "What happened?"

She tries to focus as he tells the story. They arrive at his house and make their way through the front door.

"Well, what did you think?" he asks her as he removes his jacket. "Pretty fun, right?"

She isn't sure what to say. She's hurt, yes, but she's afraid of spoiling the evening. Plus, they've never argued before; she worries that a disagreement could mark the end of their blossoming relationship.

Avoiding Conflict Hinders Intimacy

Few things terrify the recovering people-pleaser more than conflict. Historically, we've avoided it at all costs, censoring our feelings, silencing our needs, and bottling our grievances to keep the peace. We've exchanged our wholeness for the illusion of perfect harmony, and over time, it took a toll. Not only did we feel painfully silent in our relationships, but at times, we also felt painfully *alone*: we were the sole occupants of a hidden world of unspoken resentments. To avoid conflict, we hid parts of ourselves away, and in doing so, we avoided the potential for true intimacy.

Conflict is not only normal but also inevitable in our intimate relationships. We will certainly hurt others' feelings, and others will hurt ours; we are human, and humans make mistakes. In the face of these inevitable mistakes, mismatches, and differences, we have a choice. We can avoid conflict, stay silent, and bury our hurts beneath the surface—or we can speak up, be honest, and trust that *even when it's hard to hear*, those who care for us want to hear what we feel, what we need, and how we hurt.

This doesn't mean they will always agree with our feelings, meet every need, or respond perfectly to our grievances. But in healthy relationships, people prefer uncomfortable honesty to dishonesty because dishonesty breeds distrust and resentments that fester with time. Only when we are honest can we assess, as a team: *Where can we mend? Where can we compromise? Where can we find common ground? How can we move forward?* In truly intimate relationships, conflict resolution is a collaborative process, not a process that one person secretly undertakes in silence to keep the peace.

How Conflict Is Handled Is What Makes the Difference

According to research by the Gottman Institute, the appearance of conflict isn't what predicts the success or failure of a relationship; what matters is how conflict is managed. Certain methods of handling conflict are destructive: they exacerbate disagreement, reduce the likelihood of resolution, and amplify ill will. Other methods are generative: they create possibilities for mutual understanding and increase the chance of finding common ground.

According to the Gottman Institute, these four behaviors—known as the Four Horsemen—exacerbate conflict and even predict early divorce among married couples:

- **Criticism:** Expressing negative feelings about the person's *character or personality* as opposed to a specific *behavior* or *event* (e.g., "You are so lazy," as opposed to "I'm upset that you didn't help me prepare for the party").
- **Contempt:** Expressing discontent from a position of disrespect and superiority over the other, often in the form of sarcasm, cynicism, eye-rolling, or mockery (e.g., "So blowing up a few balloons was all you could manage, huh? I should have known better than to expect anything more from you").

- **Defensiveness:** Taking a victimized position to reverse the blame (e.g., "Why are you always nagging me? I can't do anything right").
- **Stonewalling:** Withdrawing in order to avoid conflict and convey disapproval (e.g., in the middle of a discussion, one person looks down at their phone, avoids eye contact, and remains silent).

Many recovering people-pleasers are familiar with the Four Horsemen because this is the only model of conflict we've ever known. Many of us witnessed criticism, contempt, defensiveness, and stonewalling in our families of origin and came to expect these behaviors from partners and friends in adulthood. It's no wonder we came to believe that we should avoid conflict at all costs.

Now, as we build healthier relationships, we begin to understand that conflict can be an opportunity for both people to hear the other's concerns, take responsibility for harm caused, and rebuild trust—which gives our relationships the chance to become resilient through discussion, negotiation, and repair. A conflict that ends in repair can be profoundly healing: a visceral teaching that we do not need to abandon ourselves in order to be loved.

How Others Respond to Conflict Is Important Information for Us

What about when conflict doesn't go well? What about when others engage in criticism, contempt, scorn, or judgment? What about when others use conflict to further hurt our feelings or knock us down?

When others react negatively to conflict, it doesn't mean we shouldn't have expressed ourselves; it means we've gathered important information about where we may need new boundaries and how compatible this relationship is in the long term. Conflict helps us learn whether they can respect our needs and feelings even when those differ from their own; whether they can accept responsibility for the harms they cause; whether they can work together with us to find compromise (more on this soon); and whether they can apologize and admit their mistakes. Gathering this information allows us to assess whether their way of handling conflict is compatible with our needs and boundaries.

Ciara's Story

Ciara knows that if she doesn't share her feelings with Nathan, they will fester and become resentments. She shrugs off her jacket. "I really enjoyed meeting your friends," she begins. "They're so sweet and fun." *Now the hard part,* she thinks. "But I want to be honest with you: I'm feeling a little hurt."

Nathan pauses as he takes off his shoes. He turns to face Ciara.

"Hurt?" he asks, a look of concern on his face. "Why?"

She clasps her hands. "Because I felt left out," she explains. "I wish you had introduced me, or invited me to join your raft, or paid attention to me during the barbecue. I didn't know anyone there and I felt awkward . . . It made me wonder if you wished I hadn't come."

Nathan is silent, his expression pained. Ciara holds her breath.

Is this the part where he calls me too sensitive? she worries.

Finally, he lets out a sigh. "Ciara," he says, "I didn't even realize. Come here."

He opens his arms, and she walks into his embrace, her heart pounding.

"I'm sorry," he says. "For the record, I *really* wanted you there. I was so excited to see my old friends that I sort of forgot about everything else."

"Thanks," she says in a small voice.

He squeezes her tight. "I feel like an asshole," he says. "Why didn't you tell me sooner? If I'd known you were feeling that way, I would have done more to help you feel included."

She grimaces and pulls away. "I mean—there wasn't really an opportunity to talk with you alone," she explains self-consciously. "Plus, it's embarrassing to have to ask your boyfriend for more attention in front of his friends, you know?"

"Yeah, I get that," he concedes. "How about this: in the future, I'll make *much* more of an effort to help you feel included. But also, you know me. I'm really outgoing, and sometimes I get distracted."

She nods; this is true. His charisma and sociable nature are part of what drew her to him in the first place.

"If you ever feel left out again when we're in public, will you let me know?" Nathan asks. "It doesn't have to be a big conversation. You can just come up and put your arm around me, or whisper something like 'I NEED MORE LOVE NOW' in my ear."

He's joking—partly. She laughs and rolls her eyes.

"Okay," she agrees. "Yeah. I can do that."

He squeezes her tight, and she relaxes in his arms, overcome with relief. She's grateful to him for being so receptive to her feelings, and she's grateful to herself for saying something. Now that they've successfully worked through a hard conversation, she feels even closer to him than she did before.

After this first conflict, Ciara and Nathan continue to deepen their intimacy. There are a few bumps in the road, but for the most part, they continue to respect each other's feelings and accommodate each other's needs as best they can.

Now, together for two years, Ciara and Nathan have reached another difficult moment in their relationship. They just moved in together, and cohabitating has raised new concerns about how they spend their time. Ciara's job at the nonprofit is socially demanding; each day, she has a packed calendar of meetings, and when she gets home, she's tired. Her ideal evening is decompressing with Nathan while watching TV. Meanwhile, Nathan works from home as a data engineer. He sits at his computer running complex code all day, and when five o'clock rolls around, he's eager for social stimulation. In his ideal evening, they would go out to dinner together, attend a concert, or enjoy a night out with friends.

Before they moved in, these differences were not an issue; they typically just spent the weekends together. Now that they're cohabitating, they want to hang out during weeknights, too, but their mismatched needs make doing so a challenge.

KNOWING WHEN TO COMPROMISE

In the past, Ciara would have over-accommodated Nathan's preferences and become burned-out over time. Now she knows she needs a different way forward.

All Relationships Require Compromise

No two people share identical needs, wants, values, or dreams. If we wish to sustain our relationships through inevitable differences and mismatches, we must be able to identify: *What am I willing to compromise—and what am I not?*

Before we started breaking the people-pleasing pattern, everything was up for compromise: our needs were malleable, our wants were expendable, and our values were moot. We were willing to contort ourselves into whatever shapes our relationships required of us: anything to maintain others' affections. Now we understand that shape-shifting in this manner doesn't lead to satisfying or reciprocal relationships in the long term. (In fact, research shows that frequently over-compromising in this manner is associated with higher rates of depression and anxiety.) Now we can still compromise—but only under certain conditions.

We can practice self-respect in our relationships by only making compromises when our physical or emotional safety is not at risk; when both people are able and willing to work together to find compromise; when both people explore multiple strategies to meet their needs; and when our core needs—needs that are fundamental to our well-being, values, and life goals—are not sacrificed in the process.

1. Our Physical or Emotional Safety Is Not at Risk

Any relationship that makes us compromise our safety isn't a relationship we can healthily sustain. Core, nonnegotiable requirements for physical and emotional safety include (but are not limited to): they do not physically harm us; they do not mock, humiliate, or degrade us; they do not berate, intimidate, or threaten us; they do not criticize our appearance; they respect our sexual boundaries and do not coerce us in any way; they can apologize and take ownership for their mistakes; they operate within the bounds of our relational agreement (e.g., they don't sleep with other people if we've agreed to be monogamous); and they keep their promises and maintain their commitments the vast majority of the time.

2. Both People Are *Able* and *Willing* to *Work Together* to Find Compromise

After years of over-giving, we must be wary of relationships in which we're the only ones accommodating the other's needs, preferences, or boundaries. After all: compromise isn't compromise if we're the only ones compromising. Chronically making accommodations to sustain a relationship while receiving little to no reciprocity is a recipe for resentment.

When there's a mismatch in needs, successful compromise requires collaboration, open-mindedness, and respect from both people. Both must be able and willing to ask: *How can we,* together, *find a solution that meets both of our needs* enough? Psychotherapist John Gottman writes, "Compromise never feels perfect. Everyone gains something and everyone loses something. The important thing is feeling understood, respected, and honored."

In healthy compromises, both people acknowledge the legitimacy of the other's needs, even if they can't meet them. Both people try to understand the other's position and recognize the costs and benefits of each path forward. When one person ultimately compromises on a need or want, the other person acknowledges their decision and shows appreciation for it.

Compromise that stems from collaborative effort is distinct from compromise that results from one person's dismissal or belittlement of the other's needs. In the latter, our "compromise" comes from shame, self-consciousness, and fear of loss. Our "compromise" is really just appeasement.

Ciara and Nathan both understand the importance of the other's needs. He doesn't shame her for needing time to decompress after a long day; she doesn't minimize his desire for social engagement. They don't share the other's wants, but they can understand them. This mutual understanding allows them to seek solutions together.

3. Both People Explore Multiple Strategies to Meet Their Needs

When our needs are mismatched, we can work toward compromise by exploring which strategies would meet those needs *enough*. In this process, we recognize that we won't get exactly what we want in exactly the way we want it, but we also set boundaries to ensure that the compromise won't push us past our limits.

When Ciara contemplates "What strategies could meet *enough of* my need for rest?" she comes up with the following: *If I have most weeknights to decompress at home, I'll have enough energy to go out on Thursdays or Fridays with Nathan. When we go out after work, I'm happy to get dinner or dessert one-on-one, but I need to save more socially demanding outings (like parties with friends) for the weekends. Some nights, I can stay home and relax while Nathan goes out.*

When Nathan considers "What strategies could meet *enough of* my need for stimulation?" he comes up with the following: *If I'm planning on staying home with Ciara, I can go for a run after work to get out of the house for a while. I'm willing to spend two nights each week at home if I have the other days to go out. On the nights we stay in, doing something active—like playing a board game or cooking together—will help me feel engaged. And some nights, I'll go out with friends while Ciara stays home.*

4. A Core Need Is Not Being Sacrificed in the Process

Some of our needs are sacred; they cannot be compromised. Everybody shares certain core needs like the nonnegotiable safety needs mentioned on page 245. Other core needs vary from person to person.

For some people, living in the same city as their romantic partner is a core need. A long-distance relationship would feel too disconnected; it wouldn't offer enough togetherness and intimacy. Meanwhile, others may *wish* to live in the same city as their partner, but would be open to a long-distance relationship if the circumstances—say, a semester abroad or a job relocation—required it. It wouldn't be their ideal, but it also wouldn't be devastating.

Ultimately, each of us must determine if something is a core need or a need that can be compromised. Answering "yes" to any of the following questions may indicate that something is a core need: Would compromising on this fundamentally impact my health or well-being? Would compromising on this prevent me from reaching my long-held goals or dreams? Would compromising on this place me in opposition to my values? Or would compromising on this lead me to resent the other person in the long term?

Ciara's Story

Ciara and Nathan sit down and compare the strategies they brainstormed. Both are willing to make minor compromises on the number of nights they stay in or go out; both are willing to adjust how they spend their time together.

Ultimately, they reach a compromise. Once a week, they'll plan a date night and go out for dinner, drinks, or dessert. Twice a week, they'll spend the evening together at home, playing a board game or watching TV. And twice a week, they'll spend their evening apart: Nathan will go out with friends and Ciara will stay home and relax.

This compromise enables them to meet their individual needs *enough*, while still having quality time together. Both wish the other wanted precisely what they want, but ultimately, they understand each other's reasoning, respect each other's needs, and appreciate each other's accommodations.

FEEL THE FEAR, BUT DO IT ANYWAY

Intimacy is not for the faint of heart. After years of living behind the mask of people-pleasing, letting ourselves be truly known by another can be daunting—but this is the only path to genuine and lasting connection. We saw what our relationships were like when we shrunk our needs; we saw how repressing our feelings to keep the peace made us resentful; we saw how our well-being eroded when we over-compromised on the things that were important to us.

As Ciara's story shows, intimacy can be startlingly vulnerable and infinitely rewarding. By bringing ourselves fully to our relationships—conflict, compromise, and all—we begin to recognize that we don't need to abandon ourselves in order to be loved.

19

THE PEOPLE-PLEASING PATTERN AND SEX

Building emotionally intimate relationships requires that we express our desires, set boundaries, and speak up when something isn't working. These same lessons apply to building satisfying physically intimate relationships.

Sex offers us an opportunity to share the most intimate parts of ourselves with another. Given how vulnerable it can be, we may continue to people-please where sex is concerned even after we've successfully broken the pattern in other areas of our lives. Sexual people-pleasing often manifests as consenting to sex we don't want to have; difficulty receiving pleasure and/or faking orgasm; and not speaking up about our preferences. In this chapter, we'll explore the origins of these patterns and discuss a breadth of tools for establishing a strong, authentic connection to our own desires.

Because sexual people-pleasing is so often shrouded in a veil of shame and silence, this chapter draws heavily on interviews from people of all genders and sexualities. My hope is that their stories affirm how commonplace this pattern is, and help you feel less alone in your experiences.*

*Please note that this chapter includes discussions of sexual trauma.

SAYING YES WHEN OUR BODIES SAY NO

Many people-pleasers have a history of *consensual unwanted sex*: unwanted sex resulting from freely given consent—not coercion, pressure, threats, or guilt trips. (Sex arising from coercion or pressure falls into the category of sexual assault, which is outside the purview of this chapter. Here, we will be exploring situations arising from freely given consent.)

People-pleasers may have consensual unwanted sex because we wish to be liked, gain others' approval, or feel connected in some way. As we'll explore shortly, consenting to unwanted sex can also be a response to past traumas or gendered expectations. In these cases, it isn't necessarily obvious to our partners that we aren't enjoying ourselves. After all, people-pleasers are among the world's greatest performers; we have become skilled at feeling one way, but acting another.

Dominique, forty-two, shared her story with me: "I've been with my husband since I was seventeen. I lost count of the number of times I consented to sex with him when I didn't want to have sex," she explained. "After a certain amount of time being in a relationship, it's expected. I'd spend days sometimes trying to psych myself up and get into the mood. The act became more about my 'duty' and just getting it over with. I would find myself hoping it would just end soon and remind myself that at least it would be a little while before I would start feeling guilt about 'needing' to give him sex again."

Interactions like Dominique's are commonplace. A wife isn't in the mood for sex, but goes through the motions because it's date night. A college student hooks up with a friend in his dorm room because he feels awkward asking them to leave. A young person with a crush agrees to sex sooner than they normally would to secure the other's affections.

Kali, thirty-two, offers her experience: "In one long-term relationship, I wasn't feeling emotionally connected. My interest in sex went away, but I felt that it was my duty, as a girlfriend, to do it. It felt like my only point of connection," she says. "I became more and more numb and disconnected from my body. Over time, I stopped considering what I wanted. I lost desire. . . . I just felt a visceral sense of shutting down. It took me a long time to heal from that."

As Kali's story shows, when we freely consent to unwanted sex, our bodies don't necessarily understand our mind's reasons for doing so. Ultimately, our bodies are present for unwanted physical encounters, and the repercussions can range from mild remorse to full-blown post-traumatic stress.

Sexual Trauma without a Perpetrator

In April 2022, I shared an Instagram post about my own experience of consensual unwanted sex. Years prior, I'd been on a date with someone I hadn't wanted to sleep with, but couldn't find the courage to tell him so. He didn't pressure, coerce, or guilt-trip me in any way—but still, I smiled, convincingly feigned enthusiasm, and spent the night in his bed.

Perhaps I was afraid of disappointing him; perhaps I thought it "wouldn't be a big deal" if I ignored my disinterest and just went with the flow. But unfortunately, for my body, it *was* a big deal. In the weeks, months, and years that followed, I grappled with flashbacks, panic attacks, and other symptoms of sexual trauma. I struggled to understand my reactions, because by all measures, I hadn't been assaulted—the only person who trespassed my boundaries was me. But still, my body revolted, fearful and repulsed.

In my Instagram post, I invited my followers to share their own stories, curious if they could relate to my experience. I was floored when hundreds of comments and messages flooded in. Some people reported feeling regretful, uncomfortable, or ashamed after consenting to unwanted sex. Others, like me, reported symptoms like flashbacks, intrusive thoughts, and panic attacks, some of which lingered decades after the original encounter.

Because our experiences were *consensual but unwanted*, we had trouble finding language that accurately captured our pain and confusion. We didn't feel we'd been assaulted; we were the ones who agreed, enthusiastically, to physical intimacy, often with spouses, partners, and longtime lovers. And yet, our bodies told a story of betrayal and suffering.

One commenter wrote: "I've had the same experience and it really messed me up, but I had no way to process it. People want to have a villain to point fingers at, and if there is no villain, then harm goes unacknowledged. The man I was with isn't a villain. . . . I consented. But that doesn't mean I don't have trauma from the experience."

We rarely discuss consensual unwanted sex for several reasons. Our silence may stem from the fact that we feel shame for betraying ourselves in such a visceral way. Dominique, whose story opened this section, shares: "I didn't really have the language to discuss what was going on. . . . I was embarrassed. How did I tell anyone that I never wanted to have sex with my own husband? Clearly there was just something wrong with me."

We may also worry that discussing consensual unwanted sex could cast doubt on those who have experienced sexual assault. Chris Ash, a survivor of sexual assault who has worked in the anti-violence field for over a decade, explains: "We are afraid to introduce nuance into conversations about sexual harm because we know that nuance will likely be weaponized against survivors in courtrooms, in the media, and by their abusers. . . . It's never a victim's fault if they are assaulted. And at the same time, sometimes we don't even understand all of our own sexual boundaries, much less articulate them—especially given how little actual education about sex most of us had access to, and how few models our culture provides for how to negotiate sexual boundaries."

As Chris suggests, our culture lacks language to describe sexual trauma resulting from a consensual encounter in which there was no "perpetrator." Many of us who people-please in this manner are afraid that talking about it will unjustly cast our spouses, lovers, or sexual partners as assailants.

Despite this pervasive silence, it's important to recognize that consensual unwanted sex affects people of all genders and sexualities. It's especially common among those who were raised to believe that sex was their duty—namely, women raised in cultures and religions with traditional gender norms.

It can feel incredibly frustrating and confusing to give consent for a sexual experience we don't want. Hours, days, or years later, we may look back and think: *Why did I do that?* Research sheds light on a few compelling explanations:

Because We Have a History of Trauma

Some who endure trauma develop the fawn response, a reaction to stress in which they seek safety by merging with the wishes, needs, and demands of others. When confronted with a situation that provokes anxiety—like wanting a crush to like them back, or worrying they'll hurt someone's feelings by being uninterested—a person who fawns may agree to intimacy they have no interest in.

Additionally, some who experience repeated abuse early in life develop learned helplessness, a state in which they feel powerless to affect their circumstances. These people learn that their only form of escape is within their own minds. Bessel van der Kolk, a psychiatrist and trauma expert, explains that survivors of sexual abuse are "vulnerable to develop 'emotion-focused coping,' a coping style in which the goal is to alter one's emotional state, rather than the circumstances that give rise to those emotional states." Instead of expressing disinterest in sex or setting a boundary, those with trauma histories may enter dissociative states, removing themselves mentally from situations where their bodies are still present.

Fawning isn't always a reaction to danger in the present moment; like people-pleasing generally, it can be an outdated coping mechanism that we developed in response to danger in the past. We may be interacting with loving, kind, and attentive sexual partners with whom we feel completely safe, *and still* fawn as a reaction to past traumas.

Because We Feel Constricted by Gender Roles and Sexual Scripts

Sexual scripts are pervasive beliefs about how the genders "should" behave in sexual situations. Western sexual scripts depict men as always craving and initiating sex, while depicting women as more passive and sexually ambivalent. These scripts can be painfully restrictive, often leaving out trans and nonbinary individuals entirely, and reinforce the notion that there is a very narrow window of acceptable sexual behavior.

"MEN ALWAYS WANT SEX"

Ron, thirty-eight, shared with me: "Two years ago, I was walking a woman home from our third date. We had great chemistry, but we hadn't slept together yet. I walked her to her door, kissed her good night, and turned to walk away, when she grabbed me by my shirtsleeve and asked: 'Don't you want to come in?'

"I like to take things slower when it comes to sex, but I felt like, as a man, I should be eager to sleep with her by the third date. There was this underlying pressure, not from her, but from *me*: I really liked this girl, and I didn't want her to think I wasn't interested. Instead of telling her I'd rather wait, I ended up going along with it, but I didn't feel good after. . . . I felt like I'd rushed myself and pushed myself further than I was comfortable with."

Ron's story isn't unusual. A 1994 study found that straight men who experienced unwanted sexual contact expressed concerns about their own heterosexuality if they resisted the advance. A 2019 study of eighty-seven boys in middle school, high school, and college found that more than half felt a "consistent" and "omnipresent" pressure to engage in sexual activity from parents, family, friends, teammates, and the media. As sexuality researcher Michele Clements-Schreiber explains, it is "culturally unacceptable for a man to receive a sexual opportunity with anything less than enthusiasm." For straight men, feigning enthusiasm about an unwanted sexual encounter may feel like the only way to preserve their masculinity and "prove" their heterosexuality.

"GAY MEN ARE SEXUALLY INSATIABLE"

Similarly, sexual scripts that position gay men as "hypersexual" or "promiscuous" often leave them feeling pressured to perform their queerness through sex. One 2021 study of twenty-four gay, bisexual, and queer men found that most regularly engaged in unwanted sex because they felt pressured by the expectation that they would have "unlimited sexual appetites."

One study participant said, "I tried to avoid having sex, but then I kind of felt, like, obligated to because I just didn't know how to bow out without feeling so embarrassed, if that makes sense? And so I ended up having, well, you know, having sex but not really being very engaged at all and wanting to leave very quickly." Another study participant explained, "I've probably had friends that liked me in that way and I didn't like them, and I just kind of went with it because I didn't want to hurt them, but [I] knew it wasn't going to be good."

For gay men, feigning enthusiasm about unwanted sex can feel like a requirement to affirm their queerness, secure social belonging, and attain a positive reputation in the gay community.

"SEX IS A WOMAN'S DUTY"

Many women describe sleeping with their male partners out of a sense of duty and obligation. A 2009 study found that many women in long-term relationships expressed concerns about "losing love, trust, or the relationship" if they refused to have sex. Study participants cited beliefs like "If my partner wants sex, it's my responsibility" and "It's a woman's responsibility to satisfy her man."

Likewise, women may also have unwanted sex in order to secure a new partner's affections or avoid being labeled a prude. Ella, thirty-four, told me, "About half of the people I've had consensual sex with, especially in my teen years and into my early twenties, weren't people I actually wanted to sleep with. It's not that there was deliberate pressure or coercion, but when I was younger I always wanted to be 'the cool girl,' and there was an unspoken social rule that if you found yourself alone in a room with a guy, especially after you've kissed, you would be expected to have sex with him. Otherwise, you're a tease or a prude."

Because We Want Emotional Intimacy

Some of us agree to unwanted sex because we wish to instill closeness, repair broken affections, or deepen our emotional connection to our partners. Sex, when genuinely desired, can be a powerful way to deepen intimacy, but it becomes problematic when we regularly bypass our bodies' disinterest to make these emotional gains.

Karen, fifty-five, explained: "My ex-husband and I spent a few years teetering between getting divorced and trying to make it work. We would have these massive arguments, walk on eggshells for a few days, and then, like clockwork, he would approach me and give me a wordless hug. Minutes later we'd be in bed. I didn't really want to have sex, but so much distance had come between us by that point. . . . I guess I felt like having sex was the only way to rebuild. For those few minutes afterward when his arms were around me, everything felt okay again."

Research shows that those who feel anxious in their relationships often soothe their concerns by using sex to gain a partner's reassurance, get a partner's approval, or avoid rejection. As a result, they rely heavily on sex to meet their emotional needs, and are more likely to have unwanted but consensual sexual experiences both within and outside of committed romantic relationships.

Understanding the origins of consensual unwanted sex can help us override shame and develop self-compassion. Like all forms of people-pleasing, this pattern is breakable with practice and intention. In addition to the boundary-setting tools depicted in chapter 10, the following exercises can help us honor our sexual boundaries:

Try: Preparing the Language in Advance

If you struggle to set sexual boundaries in the moment, it helps to practice the language in advance. You might try phrases like "This is fun, but I don't want to go any further," "Let's stop at kissing tonight," "The connection I feel with you is more friendly than sexual," "I don't want to be intimate," or "I don't want to have sex."

Once you've found a few sound bites that feel authentic, practice them aloud. You might rehearse them in the mirror, role-play with a friend, or practice with your therapist.

Quinn, a nonbinary college freshman, is feeling frustrated after a string of hookups they didn't really want. On campus *everyone* is always hooking up, and it feels easier to simply go along with expectations than have an awkward conversation.

Quinn is committed to strengthening their sexual boundaries, so they pick a simple phrase—"I'm not feeling a hookup tonight"—and practice it in the mirror. They even recruit their roommate, Hayden, to role-play; they laugh as Hayden uses as many corny pickup lines as he can, and Quinn answers, over and over: "I'm not feeling a hookup tonight."

By the end of the week, Quinn has said the phrase so many times that it's ingrained in their mind. They don their favorite outfit and head to a party in a nearby dorm. Lo and behold, a few hours later, Quinn is talking to a fellow nonbinary student, Jay. Jay places their arm around Quinn and asks, "So . . . Do you want to come back to my room?"

Quinn feels a twinge; they're enjoying the conversation, but they don't feel any sexual desire. Though Quinn's heart is racing with nerves—they can't remember the last time they turned down a hookup—they say at light speed: "I'mnotfeelingahookuptonight."

Jay looks at Quinn quizzically. "Sorry, I didn't catch that."

Quinn takes a deep breath, stilling their heart, and says more slowly: "I'm not feeling a hookup tonight."

"Oh," says Jay. "Okay. Got it."

Jay politely ends the conversation shortly after. While Quinn feels some residual guilt at rejecting Jay, they also feel unusually light—almost *giddy* with the realization that they stood in their power. Later, when Quinn returns to their dorm room, they put on a pair of comfortable pajamas and climb into bed, smiling and blissfully alone.

Try: Setting Proactive Boundaries

If you're still concerned about your ability to set sexual boundaries in the heat of the moment, experiment with setting them in advance, over a text message, over the phone, or in person before things have gotten heated.

You might send a message that says "Just so you know, I don't want to have sex tonight," "It's hard for me to set boundaries in the moment, so I wanted to let you know in advance that I want to move slow when it comes to sex," "Let's keep things friendly tonight, and if there's chemistry, we can do more another time," or "Not in a sexy mood tonight. Let's watch a movie and cuddle?"

Setting boundaries beforehand can reduce the pressure to find the words in the moment. If you'd like to move deeper into intimacy later, you can always renegotiate your boundary then.

Try: Discerning Your Motivations

If you consistently use sex as a substitute for emotional intimacy, you can practice discerning your motives when initiating or consenting to sexual activity.

Instead of automatically going with the flow, get in the habit of checking in with yourself and asking: Does my body physically want this person right now? Do I really want sex, or is sex just a substitute for something that I want even more, like affection, kindness, tenderness, or love? Am I feeling disconnected, distant, resentful, lonely, or sad? Have I spoken with this person about these feelings and the unmet needs beneath them?

If you find that your drive toward sex is masking a deeper need—perhaps for emotional intimacy, reassurance, or love—consider discussing this need with your partner.

Catherine's husband, Peter, has been out of town for two weeks on business. He travels for work often, and when he's away, he usually calls Catherine every couple of nights and texts her throughout each day. This time, he's been unusually silent; he's sent a couple of texts but hasn't made an effort to call.

By Peter's last day away, Catherine is feeling insecure. Her mind spins: *Is he mad at me? Did he meet someone else while he was gone? Did he go out with someone from the office?*

When Peter gets home, Catherine nervously greets him at the door. He gives her a kiss and places his hands on her waist. "I missed you," he says, smiling. "Want to take this to the bedroom?"

She almost agrees, but pauses and asks herself: *Do I want sex right now, or is sex just a means to an end that I want even more?* She checks in with her body and notices that her chest is tight and her jaw is clenched. She doesn't feel desirous at all; she's still feeling insecure. What she wants most is to know that Peter still loves her, that she still matters to him. She also wants to understand why he was out of touch while he was gone.

She places a gentle hand on his chest. "Let's wait," she says. "Come in and get settled, and then let's talk a bit about your trip."

After he unpacks and showers, they discuss his time away. She admits her insecurity, and though he's a little defensive at first, he apologizes for not being in closer touch. He reveals that he'd been feeling stressed about a deadline, and acknowledges that he could have told her sooner so she understood his silence.

Their conversation soothes her worries. Later that night, when they climb into bed, she feels a flicker of genuine desire in her body. She reaches for Peter in the dark. Now that she's feeling more connected, she can enjoy her sexual experience, not as a means to an end, but as a pleasurable addition to an *existing* sense of emotional security.

STRUGGLING TO RECEIVE

As people-pleasers, we tend to feel most at home when we're giving to others, which can make receiving sexual pleasure challenging. We might feel pressure to put the attention back on our partners; worry that they aren't enjoying themselves in their giving; or rush to reach climax more quickly so as not to "inconvenience" them.

Sometimes we struggle to access our own pleasure because we're overfocused on our partners' *experience of us* instead of our *own* physical experience. This phenomenon, called spectatoring, occurs when we focus on ourselves from a third-person perspective during sex instead of focusing on our own sensations or our partner. We may become so preoccupied with getting sex "right"—so distracted by how we look, smell, taste, and sound—that we can't savor the experience we're having.

Sexuality educator and writer Ella Dorval Hall describes, "I became so concerned with my partner's satisfaction and what they thought of me that I couldn't focus on the joys of sex. I spent entire sexual encounters critiquing my technique, analyzing what my partner must be thinking of me, and trying to anticipate what they wanted. The intrusive thoughts were brutal. My performance anxiety made it feel like there was an additional person in the room judging me. But that additional person was my own voice, in my own head, telling me all the ways I was failing to satisfy my partner and why they wouldn't like me because of it."

When we're distracted and disconnected from our own sensations, we have more trouble feeling pleasure and reaching orgasm. While orgasm isn't the only marker of a satisfying sexual experience, we may worry that we'll let our partners down if we don't come, which creates a self-fulfilling prophecy: the more anxious we are, the less likely we are to climax at all.

Orgasm involves deactivation of the regions of the brain associated with anxiety; in order to climax, we need to let go and surrender to sensation. Lacking the ability to truly relax, we may fake orgasm as a means of pleasing our partners. One study found that 28 percent of men and

67 percent of women reported having faked an orgasm. The four most common reasons they gave for doing so were that orgasm was unlikely; that they wanted sex to end; that they wanted to avoid hurting their partner's feelings; and that they wanted to please their partner.

In the same way that breaking the people-pleasing pattern requires us to attune to our own wants and needs, breaking the pattern of sexual people-pleasing requires us to attune to our own pleasure and desire.

Try: Practice Receiving by Trading Massages

We can slowly increase our capacity to receive by trading less sexually charged forms of touch like massages and back rubs. Set aside an hour to trade massages with your partner. While you're being massaged, focus *only* on receiving, while your partner focuses *only* on giving. Give yourself permission not to force any sounds or perform in any way. Notice how this experience differs from your typical sexual interactions.

Then switch: focus *only* on giving, while your partner focuses *only* on receiving. Knowing you will both have equal time to give and receive can help eliminate the pressure to over-accommodate your partner's pleasure. The purpose of this exercise is to simply luxuriate in pleasant physical sensations with no end goal.

Try: Take the Pressure off Getting Off

If you have difficulty reaching orgasm, consider talking about it with your partner in advance. This can relieve your performance anxiety and set comfortable expectations for your sexual experience.

For example, you might say: "I don't see orgasm as the destination of sex; I like to just enjoy the process," "Just so you know, it takes me a long time to feel comfortable enough to come during sex," or "Even if I'm having a great time, I don't usually come. It's just not how my body works."

While these disclaimers may offer your partner clarity, they're ultimately for your own benefit: they give you the space you need to relax without any pressure to reach a goal. Ironically, taking the pressure off orgasm might be precisely what you need to feel comfortable and relaxed enough to come. And if not, that's okay, too—getting off doesn't have to be the goal of great sex.

KEEPING OUR DESIRES ON THE DOWN-LOW

Being forthright about how we want to be touched can be tough—not just for people-pleasers, but for most people! Sometimes, we don't speak up about our preferences because we're afraid our partners won't like what we suggest. Perhaps we want to have rougher sex, but our partner seems to prefer gentler sex; perhaps we want to try a new toy, but we're concerned our partner won't be open to it.

Sometimes we don't mention our desires because we don't want to offend our partners. We might wish our partners kissed us more gently; we might wish they entered us at a different angle, or a different speed. While these preferences can feel hard to communicate, it's important to remember that healthy partners will *want to know* if they're doing something we don't enjoy. A short, awkward conversation is far preferable to an ongoing pattern of undesired touch.

No doubt, speaking up about our desires and giving sexual feedback can be awkward, especially since most of us weren't taught to communicate frankly about sex. However, doing so is the only way to ensure that we're having a sexual experience that both people enjoy. Our partners can't learn our body's language unless we teach them, and that includes giving feedback about what we like—and what we don't.

Try: Flip the Script

If you're feeling insecure about giving your partner feedback, take a moment to flip the script. Imagine that you were kissing, pleasuring, or having sex with your partner and, unbeknownst to you, they didn't enjoy the sensation. But instead of saying something, they stayed silent, feeling uncomfortable as you carried on none the wiser.

For most of us, this imagined scenario is mortifying. Flipping the script helps us see that we would much rather our partners tell us when they don't like something, *even if* it's momentarily awkward. We can do our partners the same service by courageously speaking up about what's working and what's not.

Try: Start the Conversation outside the Bedroom

If expressing your desires or giving feedback feels challenging in the moment, start a dialogue with your partner in a nonsexual setting. Carve out some time to chat about sex over dinner or with your morning coffee.

To kick-start a conversation about sex, you might say: "Hey, are there any new things you want to try in the bedroom? I've been thinking about it, and I have a few ideas!" or "I had a spicy idea today. Want to hear it?" or "Would you be down to have a check-in about sex? I had some thoughts I wanted to share, and I'd love to hear what you're thinking, too."

To give sexual feedback, you might say: "So I know we usually do X this way, but I was thinking we could experiment with doing it this way: ________________," or "I love the way you touch me, and I thought of one thing that could make it feel even better: ________________," or "The other day I heard about this position/toy/activity, and if you're open to it, I'd love to try it with you: ________________."

In these conversations, you might even use some of the radical transparency scripts we discussed in chapter 10, like: "I feel kind of awkward mentioning this, but if our roles were reversed, I would want you to know: ________________," or "I know trading feedback about sex can feel kind of awkward, but if you're open to it, I'd love to share one piece of feedback I had with you," or "I feel self-conscious telling you this, but there's something I've wanted to try in the bedroom: ________________."

Andrea and Cody have been casually dating for a few weeks. They have great conversations and strong sexual chemistry, except for one small problem: Andrea *really* doesn't like the way Cody kisses. He uses a lot of tongue, and Andrea prefers much less—but she has no idea how to address it with him.

After their last date, Andrea admitted to herself that Cody's kisses left her feeling grossed out instead of turned on. Now she wonders: *Should I ask him to change how he kisses me? Or should I just tell him we're not compatible and end it?*

While the thought of having an uncomfortable conversation is unappealing—she doesn't want to embarrass him—the thought of just ending things sounds worse. Andrea feels like she and Cody have real potential. She decides that one uncomfortable conversation is worth it if they can find a way forward.

The next night, Cody comes over to Andrea's place for a movie night. When he walks in the door, he wraps his arms around her and leans in for a kiss. Andrea gives herself a mental pep talk—*You're doing this for both of you!*—and gently pulls back from him.

She smiles and says, "I feel a little self-conscious about this, but can I tell you something?"

He nods. "What is it?"

"Okay so—I've just never been a big tongue kisser," she says. "For me, it's all about the lips, and less tongue is better. Could we experiment with that?"

Cody takes a moment to reply. "Oh—yeah." He chuckles awkwardly and his face turns red. "Sorry, um . . . Now *I* feel self-conscious. I hate to think that all this time you haven't liked how I kiss."

Andrea feels mortified. *Ugh, I embarrassed him—this is exactly what I wanted to avoid!* She feels herself turning red, too.

"Look: I know this is *so* awkward," she acknowledges, putting her hand on his arm. "I love spending time with you, and our physical chemistry is great. I know everyone kisses differently, and I thought that maybe if I told you, we could a find a way that works for both of us."

Cody is quiet for a few moments. Then he nods. "Okay. My ego is bruised, but I'm with you," he replies, winking. "Why don't we go to your bedroom, and you can teach me exactly how you like to be kissed?"

She laughs, feeling grateful for his open-mindedness. "Deal," she replies with a smile, taking his hand in hers. It takes a few sessions of experimenting, but eventually, they find a way of kissing that feels natural and exciting to both of them. Andrea feels immense relief, grateful that she took the risk of being vulnerable about her desires.

COMMUNICATION IS THE BEDROCK

Ultimately, our efforts to break the people-pleasing pattern reverberate throughout every area of our lives. The more we get comfortable using our voices and expressing our needs outside of sexual situations, the more comfortable we'll feel advocating for ourselves within them.

Identifying partners with whom we can communicate safely and openly is perhaps the most important step we can take on our journey to empowered sexuality. We must pay attention to how others respond to our boundaries, desires, and feedback. Someone who is coercive; who pressures us sexually; who is unreceptive to our feedback; or who shows little or no interest in our pleasure is not someone who deserves our affections. As we break the people-pleasing pattern, we learn to listen for our bodies' wants, heed our bodies' cues, and, most important, respect our bodies' limits. We come to understand that sex is not something we do "for someone else," but a shared activity borne of genuine desire.

20

REDISCOVERING PLAY

For the people-pleaser who is constantly striving, performing, and pleasing, life becomes drudgery. Our faces are chronically strained with false smiles as we expend every ounce of our energy caretaking other people. As we saw in the previous chapter, everything from our workdays to our sex lives become sites of obligation and resentment.

But after we've worked for a while to break the pattern, we begin to string together days of comfort and ease. There are inevitable bumps in the road, but overall, our needs are met; our wants are expressed; our boundaries are keeping us safe. We're no longer living in survival mode, and from this place of unfamiliar peace, we realize it has been years since we've *really* given ourselves permission to play.

Research shows that play directly increases our self-esteem and well-being. It injects our lives with levity, presence, and color, offering a revitalizing contrast to our daily obligations. Play is often relegated to the realm of children, but for the recovering people-pleaser, it's an essential antidote to self-abandonment and chronic other-focus.

Play is borne of our own unique desires. It's an embodied experience of self-prioritization. And for the person who spent years believing that their purpose was to make everyone else comfortable, doing something simply *for the pleasure of it* is a radical healing act. In this chapter, we'll explore the many forms play can take; examine why we lose touch with play; learn how to cultivate a playful mindset; and practice reconnecting with our sense of joy and delight.

WHAT IS PLAY?

Psychiatrist Stuart Brown, founder of the National Institute for Play, asserts that play isn't about doing a specific activity, but rather our mindset while doing it. All play, he says, "offers a sense of engagement and pleasure, takes the player out of a sense of time and place, and the experience of doing it is more important than the outcome."

For one person, practicing the piano might be play. Someone else might play by rowing on the river. Still another might play by collecting stamps or cooking new recipes. What unites these activities as play is the fact that they're intrinsically motivated; we play not for some future outcome, but for the sheer pleasure of the experience.

As we age out of childhood, we begin to call play "recreation," perhaps in an attempt to make ourselves sound more dignified. Curiously, the word "recreation" stems from the Latin roots *re* (again) and *creare* (to create, bring forth), and was first used in the fourteenth century in the sense of "curing a sick person." Recreation was, quite literally, to bring someone back to life. This translation feels poignant even in our modern world. We—not just those of us grappling with people-pleasing, but all of us—are suffering from a disconnection from joy, pleasure, and play. So many of us plod through our days on an unending hamster wheel of obligations.

We're evolutionarily wired for play; all mammals are. And yet, many of us feel like we don't know how to play. For some, this is accompanied by a feeling of brokenness or embarrassment: *This should come naturally to me, but it doesn't.*

WHY WE FORGET ENJOYMENT FOR ITS OWN SAKE

Hundreds of social and cultural forces conspire to inhibit us from play. Instead of thinking of playfulness as a skill we've lost, we might think of it as an innate quality within us, one that's just hard to access in our modern culture. Play has been declining among children—not just adults—since 1955. Experts have speculated a few reasons for this, including the rise of helicopter parenting, less time in nature, increased focus on schooling, and increased screen time. Repeatedly, they arrive at the same conclusion: it's hard to feel comfortable doing something you were never given permission to do.

Among both children and adults, staring at screens has become our most common pastime; we've moved from creative and engaged play to passive consumption of media. While consuming media might be leisurely (and even that's up for debate), it's not play, and thousands of studies attest to the fact that it actually makes us more anxious and depressed.

Most critically, we've lost touch with play because our culture places a premium on making money, attaining status, and being productive. A by-product of capitalism, grind culture asserts that we're only as valuable as what we produce, and in this framework, play becomes not only unimportant but also a waste of precious time. Tricia Hersey, author of *Rest Is Resistance*, writes, "Along with stealing your imagination and time, grind culture has stolen the ability for pleasure, hobbies, leisure, and experimentation. We are caught up in a never-ending cycle of going and doing. . . . We must uncover, simplify, and let go of our addiction to busyness."

This addiction to busyness and productivity leaves little room for play. As we get older, our free time is haunted by our ever-growing to-do lists. We answer emails while half-watching television; we respond to texts while waiting for the stoplight to change.

When we *do* manage to make time for play and creativity, grind culture encourages us to monetize our activities. If you're a great painter, you're urged to sell your paintings; if you're a comedian, you're encouraged to get on social media and collect followers. Suddenly, the goal of our play is no longer the experience of playing, but the associated rewards: money, recognition, and status. Transforming play into hustle erases one of the fundamental tenets of play: that the process is more important than the outcome.

Grind culture also breeds perfectionism: the idea that something is only worth doing if it's done perfectly. Many of us stop playing when we realize we'll never be "the best," and many of us can trace our disconnection from play back to a moment in time we didn't play "perfectly." We quit the soccer team when we lost a match; we dropped improv when we bombed a joke; we stopped songwriting when we got a critical comment after a performance. Perfectionism and play don't mix.

Combined, these forces perpetuate the illusion that play doesn't matter. If we struggle to play, it's not a personal failing; in fact, it's a sign that we followed society's rules perfectly, seeking to produce, achieve, and succeed. To rediscover play, we must dive beneath these ingrained attitudes to remember that play is a necessary and revitalizing force.

REMEMBERING PLAY: A REFLECTION

Take a moment to read the following passage. Then, sit comfortably, close your eyes, and take a few minutes to reflect.

Recall a memory of playing in your childhood.
Maybe you were playing outside in nature, near the ocean, or in the forest.
Maybe you were playing with a sibling or a friend in the family room.
Maybe you were playing on a sports team out under the sun.
Maybe you were simply playing by yourself, accompanied by only your imagination.
Watch this memory unfold in your mind.
Recall your surroundings: the sights, the sounds, the scents.
Pause on the image of that younger version of you.
Picture them in your mind's eye: their face, their smile, their laugh.

They were totally present in the moment.

They had no concerns.

They were fully engaged and fully alive.

Notice what you feel as you envision this younger you.

Do you feel a yearning?

A desire?

Maybe a sense of grief or sadness?

Take a moment to simply acknowledge this emotion in your heart and body.

You might even say to it: "I'm listening. I'm here."

Then, when you're ready, open your eyes.

When I offer this reflection during my public talks, I'm amazed by the audience members' visceral reactions. Some emerge from their reverie with tears streaming down their cheeks. Others open their eyes pleasantly dazed, murmuring: "I forgot how good that felt."

Suze, twenty-eight, shared her reflection with me: "In my memory, I'm six or seven years old and I'm jumping through puddles in the backyard. . . . There was a thunderstorm earlier in the day. I'm wearing my big red rain boots and splashing as hard as I can, laughing and encouraging my little sister, Anna, to follow me. . . . We develop an imaginary world together, treating every puddle like a new destination we have to splash in order to get its treasure. . . . I swear to God, we were out there for hours. . . . I'm happy remembering it, but it's also sad, too. . . . I can't remember the last time I lost myself in something so simple. I feel like that little girl is a stranger to me now."

Malik, fifty, offered his reflection: "I was ten years old when I was invited to join the soccer team. Every Sunday we gathered at the park to practice. I remember this one day in particular, it never left my memory. The breeze was strong and all I could smell was fresh-cut grass. . . . I was playing midfield, chasing after the ball, and I was running so hard I felt like I would lift off in flight. I felt . . . elated. Just completely alive. I didn't think about anything else the entire two-hour practice. Now I'm lucky if I can go five minutes without checking my email."

Through this reflection, we can sense—in a visceral way that transcends the logic of grind culture—the necessity of play. It didn't earn us money, it didn't give us status or fame, but the *feeling*—the sensation of presence, aliveness, and joy—is something we desperately crave, all these years later.

THE MANY FACES OF PLAY

Many of us worry that we're simply not the type of people who can become playful again. Some of us are more introverted, preferring the quiet company of books to the overstimulation of parties. Some of us feel like we aren't silly enough to play, don't know enough jokes, or don't have enough time.

When our understanding of play is narrow, we may feel intimidated at the very thought of it. But play doesn't look the same for everyone. Over the course of thousands of interviews, Stuart Brown identified eight dominant play personalities. These eight personalities offer a diverse understanding of how differently play can look for each of us:

- ***Collectors*** enjoy collecting objects (stamps, cars, coins, books) or experiences (like attending all of the concerts by their favorite band).
- ***Competitors*** enjoy structured games with specific rules, and they play to win.
- ***Creators/Artists*** enjoy making new things: writing songs, knitting, woodworking, painting, writing, etc.
- ***Directors*** enjoy creating, organizing, and facilitating experiences and events.
- ***Explorers*** enjoy novelty and discovery—not just of new places, but also new ideas, foods, people, points of view, etc.
- ***Jokers*** enjoy foolishness, pulling pranks, cracking jokes, and making others laugh.

- ***Kinesthetes*** enjoy moving their bodies through activities like dance, walking, yoga, or sports.
- ***Storytellers*** enjoy imagination and crafting stories through writing, dancing, lectures, magic, and other mediums.

These eight personalities give us a framework for identifying what sort of play comes most naturally to us. We may be surprised to find that certain enjoyable activities we hadn't necessarily thought of as play are already making an appearance in our daily lives.

Stuart, thirty-seven, has always been the serious type. He aced every test he took in high school, and in college, he spent most nights studying in his dorm room. He has never been interested in parties, comedy, or loud crowds; he worries he's not extroverted enough, or "fun enough," to play.

But when he reviews the eight play personalities, he feels a surge of acknowledgment as he reads about Explorers. Stuart loves learning random facts about people, places, and things; no topic is too obscure to dissuade his interest. As a child, he always watched *Jeopardy!* with his grandmother, and now, as an adult, he traverses Wikipedia for interesting facts in his spare time.

He never thought of this as play—he just enjoyed the rush of discovering something new—but now he realizes that he's an explorer of ideas. He considers how he might intentionally broaden this outlet for play.

Remembering his childhood flair for *Jeopardy!*, he checks if any of his favorite bars have trivia nights. He doesn't usually socialize in groups, but he imagines that having a shared purpose—like answering trivia questions—would make doing so more comfortable. He also does a Google search for local documentary screenings, thinking it might be a fun way to learn new information in an unfamiliar setting.

Two months later, Stuart regularly attends Wednesday night trivia at the local brewery, and he's already gone to a documentary screening in town. His life feels more vibrant now that he's making time for exploration.

Like Stuart, once we've determined our play personality, we can intentionally consider how to build a more robust repertoire of play. A competitor might look for recreational sports teams; a joker might look for an improv troupe; a creator might seek out a painting class.

WHAT ABOUT SCREEN TIME?

These days, it's impossible not to wonder: *Is scrolling through TikTok play? Is watching a new movie play? What about doing sudoku on my phone?* Screen time can be a form of play; it all depends on how we engage with it. For an experience to be play, it must be both pleasurable and either mentally or physically active. When we use screens to passively absorb information (as we often do on social media), we're not playing; we're just having leisure time.

Psychologist Mihaly Csikszentmihalyi writes in *Flow* that while leisure time is necessary in moderation, most people don't find it particularly enjoyable, and studies show that it doesn't boost our overall sense of happiness. Leisure, he explains, consists of "passively absorbing information, without using any skills or exploring new opportunities for action. As a result, life passes in a sequence of boring and anxious experiences over which a person has little control." This description, though written before the advent of social media, bears an uncanny resemblance to the way many of us feel after scrolling too long on Instagram or watching too much Netflix.

Conversely, play is active (physically or mentally), engaged, and enjoyable. It often involves challenging ourselves to some degree, which can lead to a flow state: "the state of concentration and engagement that can be achieved when completing a task that challenges one's skills." In flow, we are totally absorbed in our activity; time seems to disappear. Malik, the childhood soccer player, described a flow state: "I felt . . . elated. Just completely alive. I don't think I thought about anything else the entire two-hour practice."

Perhaps you've experienced flow for moments at a time when working on an art project, climbing a mountain, playing your guitar, or training for a marathon. These moments of timeless focus, which Csikszentmihalyi calls optimal experiences, are among the most enjoyable in life. Fascinatingly, research shows that while a sense of ego seems to disappear during a flow state, our sense of self emerges stronger after the activity is over. Flow states are particularly beneficial for those of us breaking the people-pleasing pattern because they bolster our independent sense of self.

Keeping this in mind, our screen time might be play if it's engaging and active, such as when we're using our devices to play challenging games, to create (write stories, compose music, design graphics, edit videos, etc.), or to research new ideas. If screen time already composes most of our leisure time—and for most of us, it does—we'll benefit from prioritizing forms of play that go beyond the device and into the world: our bodies, surroundings, friends, and communities.

HOW TO CULTIVATE A PLAY MINDSET

Because play runs contrary to grind culture, reconnecting with playfulness requires us to develop a new frame of mind: a play mindset. While a grind culture mindset revolves around perfectionism, achievement, and production, a play mindset prioritizes presence, levity, spontaneity, novelty, and community.

To illustrate how to cultivate a play mindset, we'll use the case of Mariah, fifty-nine, who has been working to break the people-pleasing pattern for over two years. She's become skilled at prioritizing her needs and setting boundaries, but she still has trouble making time for joy and play.

Mariah has the Creator play personality. When she was young, she enjoyed sketching, sculpting, and watercolor painting; her childhood bedroom was cluttered with artwork. But as she got older, she became disconnected from her creativity. Her parents tolerated her art, but offered abundant praise when she accomplished something academically significant, so she focused all her attention on acing tests, getting into an excellent college, and climbing the professional ladder.

After graduating, Mariah became an accountant, and ever since she launched her own business thirty years ago, work has completely dominated her time. She makes a lot of money; she has the financial reserves to cut her work hours in half and live comfortably for the rest of her life. But even so, she rarely takes vacations, skips lunch most days, and often works nights and weekends.

After thirty years of this hectic pace, she feels exhausted and hollow. Over-prioritizing work doesn't give her the rest, balance, or enjoyment she needs. She's getting older and she doesn't want her next decades to be defined by accounting, but the thought of creating simply for the pleasure of it feels totally foreign.

The Process Matters More than the Outcome

Even temporarily, it can be difficult to release our drive to accomplish and achieve. If we're struggling to release the desire for success, we can practice reframing what it means to be successful in play. In play, success isn't painting the perfect landscape, winning the comedy tournament, or writing a perfect song; it's painting, cracking jokes, and songwriting. In play, success is in the doing.

Mariah is a goal-oriented person; it's what has made her so successful. She loves the satisfaction that comes from checking a box off her to-do list. The thought of completely unstructured play makes her nervous, so she decides to block off two thirty-minute segments every week for creativity. She hopes to increase this amount later, but she wants to start small.

When it's time for her first play appointment, she sits down in her kitchen with a sketch pad. Her foot taps erratically on the ground; she bites at the end of her pencil. She almost chuckles at how awkward it feels to make time for her art. She decides to sketch her kitchen counter, and as her hand moves across the page, she struggles with self-criticism: *Look at how rusty you are! Do you even remember how to do this?*

Despite the self-doubt, Mariah keeps going; she's not the type of person to back out of a commitment. When the thirty minutes are over, she has a rough rendering of her countertop. The voice in her mind tries to whisper that it isn't very good, but she reminds herself that "good" wasn't the goal: the goal was to simply make the time for art. She closes her sketch pad, feeling a sense of accomplishment for doing what she set out to do.

Embrace the Awkward

Nervousness, jitters, and self-doubt are totally normal as we rebuild our relationship with play. Like Mariah, we can acknowledge these inner voices without letting them become barriers. We can embrace the awkward by reminding ourselves that we're doing something unfamiliar—something rarely modeled for us in our culture. We might ask ourselves: *Am I willing to suffer a little awkwardness to dramatically increase the joy in my life?*

Cultivate White Space

White space is time without input from the outside world: time when we're not looking at our phones, watching TV, reading, listening to a podcast, or talking to others. Nowadays, white space is a rare commodity. Moments like standing in line at the grocery store and waiting at the bus stop have become opportunities for consumption: of a text, a meme, a podcast. But white space is necessary to play. Instead of reacting to information, our minds get the chance to wander, explore, self-express, get curious, and create. We might be surprised by the unusual and expansive thoughts we have when we're not constantly reacting to input from the outside world.

We can cultivate white space by setting aside time—even just ten minutes—to simply *be.* We might go on meandering walks without our phones; sit quietly on the couch and daydream; or lie on our backs in the grass and stare up at the stars.

At first, Mariah does *not* like the idea of white space. She's spent the last thirty years glued to her screens. On the rare nights she wasn't working, she left the TV on mute while her favorite podcast ran in the background. In truth, she can't remember the last time she chose to do nothing at all.

She imagines that being in motion will make the white space feel more bearable, so on the next sunny day, she decides to go for a short walk around a nearby lake. Grimacing, she leaves her phone at home.

For the first fifteen minutes, Mariah's mind ricochets from work task to work task; she reaches for her phone to respond to an email, chagrined when she remembers it isn't there. She gazes out over the lake, hoping to find some distraction from her ruminating mind, and is struck by the way the blue of the water matches the blue of the cloudless sky. If it weren't for the distant line of trees marking the horizon, the sky and water would look like one endless swath of blue. She imagines painting the scene in watercolor, giving it a clever title like *Sky on Sky* or *As Above, So Below.*

It's pleasant to feel inspired by something in her environment; it's been ages since she felt moved to paint a particular scene. Mariah decides to go inspiration-hunting more often, leaving her phone behind and venturing out into the world around her.

Remember Your Own Mortality

When our minds are focused on our daily tasks, tomorrow's chores, or a work deadline, play can feel irrelevant. Why would we make time for something so trivial as taking a walk or letting our minds wander when there are more important things to do?

But when we remember that one day we'll be on our deathbeds, nostalgically recalling our time on this earth, the importance of play suddenly comes into sharp focus. Like Mariah, we don't want to reflect on our lives and realize, painfully, that they were a ceaseless barrage of emails, deadlines, and staring at our phones. We want to be able to look back on a life filled with beauty, creativity, vitality, and laughter. When we're feeling unmotivated to play, this shift in thinking can help us refocus on what really matters.

Four months after Mariah starts making time for play and creativity, her life looks—and feels—very different than it did before. When evening comes, Mariah is no longer pouring over spreadsheets in the office. Instead, she sits in the fading light of her kitchen, sketching and painting as the hours drift away. A brochure for a two-week artist's retreat is taped to her refrigerator; she sees it every morning when she brews her coffee. She doesn't feel quite ready to take that step yet, but she knows that one day, she will.

Mariah's skills aren't what they were forty years ago, but she doesn't mind; she sticks with it because it brings joy and presence into her life. These moments with her sketch pad are her respite, her chance to connect with herself and her imagination. Sometimes she feels regret that she didn't return to play sooner, but the moment she puts her pencil to her sketch pad, her worries, regrets, and concerns fade into the noiseless silence of creativity.

EXERCISES TO REDISCOVER PLAY

Once we've identified our play personality and begun cultivating a play mindset, we can reconnect with play using these exercises:

Begin with Just Ten Minutes

At first, carving out time for play can be challenging. However, it's important to remember that we don't have to radically change our lives or uproot our daily schedules to make space for play. Simply incorporating *ten minutes of playful activity* on a regular basis helps play become more comfortable and natural for us.

As you begin rediscovering play, set yourself up for success by committing to short, playful activities. Some examples (depending on your play personality) might include spending ten minutes dancing in the living room; playing catch with a friend; researching something interesting; telling your friend a joke; practicing voice impressions; doing a crossword puzzle; molding clay; playing guitar; shooting some hoops; or going for a short walk.

Javier is a single dad. He works as a consultant and takes meetings from his home office when his two daughters are at school. When the girls get home, Javier's evenings pass by in a whirlwind of activity: he cooks dinner, helps the girls with their homework, reads to them before bed, and, if he's lucky, manages to read a few pages of his own book before falling asleep.

His life is incredibly busy. The constraints of his schedule prevent him from signing up for a class or joining a team. However, he desperately wants more play in his life; he's tired of every day feeling like a never-ending to-do list.

One day while the kids are at school, he's tidying up the playroom when he spots a deck of cards under the couch. He recalls spending time with a college friend who could do all manner of card tricks, and Javier is seized by a funny thought: *What if I learned a few magic tricks? It shouldn't be too hard, and I know the girls would love it.*

He checks his watch; he has ten minutes until his next meeting. He grabs the cards, wipes off the dust, sits down in his desk chair, and opens YouTube. Ten minutes later, he's learned the basics of a simple trick. He'll need to keep working at it, but it feels refreshing to focus his energy on something light and fun.

After two weeks of these short play intervals, he shows his daughters the tricks he's learned. The girls shout, "Again! Do it again!" He laughs, thrilled by their delight. These magic nights become a casual routine: every weekend, he shows his daughters the new trick he's picked up throughout the week.

It's a small shift to Javier's schedule, but it offers him a much-needed respite from the stress of his daily life. For a few minutes every day, he gets to feel like a kid again, and the levity of those moments is enough to power him through until tomorrow.

Say Yes to Spontaneity and Novelty

After the daily demands of modern life, many of us just want to decompress with the comfort of the familiar. If we wanted to spend every night watching Netflix or scrolling social media, we easily could. But when we're trying to reconnect with play, it's important to push ourselves out of our comfort zones and say yes to the unfamiliar. Doing new and spontaneous activities is, in itself, a form of play—and when we say yes to the unknown, we might be surprised by the activities that pique our interest.

Saying yes to spontaneity can look like seeing a flyer for an event in your town and attending; checking out a new local band; exploring an unfamiliar part of town on a whim; striking up a conversation with a stranger at the coffee shop; or saying yes when a friend invites you to a hike or a beach day.

Sign Up for Group Play

After a lifetime of suppressing our playful instincts, it can feel hard to access them on our own. Playing with a group gives us inspiration, community, and routine. Even if you're brand-new to an activity, there are many groups for beginners to gather and learn together. You might experiment by joining a recreational sports team; a book club; a knitting circle; a hiking collective; a writer's group; a cooking class; an improv group; or a collector's meetup.

Spend Time with Someone Playful

When we're stuck in the quicksand of stress and overwork, spending time with someone playful can unstick us. Perhaps we have a friend or relative who's always up for a new adventure. Babies and children are the stewards of play; perhaps we have a niece or nephew we can spend time with if we don't have any kids of our own, or perhaps we can volunteer at a local organization that works with kids. Spending time with animals can also help us access a present and spontaneous spirit.

Genevieve is really struggling to play. This year has been difficult for her: she got a promotion at work, and the increased responsibility left her more stressed, and more anxious, than she's ever been before. She wishes she could play, but her anxiety makes it difficult. When confronted with the choice to go out and try a new activity or stay home and watch TV, staying home feels like the more comfortable option.

One Saturday after a harrowing week, Genevieve is curled up in sweatpants on the couch. She gets a text from her best friend, Janelle. **You around? I miss you! Let's hang out!**

The two met in college, and Genevieve was immediately drawn to Janelle's easy laugh and boisterous personality. Janelle was always the friend who coordinated plans, bought concert tickets, arranged picnics, and booked spontaneous weekend trips. Genevieve loves Janelle, but she's tempted to stay home. **I don't know,** she writes back. **I've had a stressful week and I feel like a downer. I don't want to spoil the mood.**

Janelle instantly replies: **Downer or not, I'll be over in 30! You will feel better when I'm done with you :)**

Genevieve chuckles despite herself; she can always count on Janelle to lift her spirits. Thirty minutes later, she arrives in her beat-up Jeep, blasting dance music out the open windows. Genevieve climbs into the passenger seat and is instantly soothed by Janelle's easy laughter and dry humor. They spend the afternoon in town, stopping for ice cream, browsing through the thrift store, and driving to a scenic spot to watch the sunset.

When Janelle drops her off, Genevieve realizes it's been hours since she thought about work. She feels a lightness that she'd all but forgotten in recent weeks. She promises herself that she'll make time with friends like Janelle a priority even when she's stressed, because those are the moments she needs play more than ever.

21

ALLOWING AMBIGUITY AND PRACTICING DISCERNMENT

Breaking the people-pleasing pattern gives us permission to play, create, and lean wholeheartedly into our desires. We begin to cultivate a deeper relationship with ourselves than ever before, and from this place of self-connection, we can develop the self-trust and discernment required to make difficult decisions.

Now that we've practiced the skill of putting ourselves first, we're equipped to bring more nuance into our decision-making. We know how to erect firm boundaries; now we get to decide if we want to loosen them from time to time. We know how to put our needs first; now we get to decide if we want to occasionally prioritize a loved one's needs instead.

As we break the pattern, we will confront complex situations that set our empathy against our newfound commitment to self-advocacy. People in need will ask for our help when we're already overcommitted. Our loved ones will require things from us that push us to our limits. Mismatches in values, needs, and desires may require that we compromise in order to maintain our relationships. In these cases, we are called to practice discernment: to gather multiple pieces of information to make conscious decisions that align with our values.

Before, we put everyone else first as a matter of course; we said yes because we couldn't say no. Now that we've learned to meet our own needs, protect ourselves with boundaries, and soothe ourselves through discomfort, we have our own backs, and from this place of self-trust, we can embody greater flexibility.

In this chapter, we'll explore how to make difficult decisions when our empathy and our self-advocacy are at odds; how to step away from black-and-white thinking and adopt a nuanced attitude; and how to normalize our mistakes and embrace lessons learned along the way.

JASMINE'S STORY

For two years, Jasmine was married to Leslie, a woman caught in the throes of alcohol addiction. For the duration of their marriage, Leslie's drunken exploits were a constant source of tension for the couple. She stayed out all night, slept with strangers from bars, and treated Jasmine with disdain. Eventually, Jasmine had had enough of Leslie's mistreatment. Their divorce was finalized six months ago.

Understandably, Jasmine feels angry and resentful toward Leslie, and she believes that the quickest way to heal is to avoid all communication with her. She's blocked Leslie on social media and deleted her number from her phone, and in the six months since their divorce, she's done her best to rebuild a life of her own.

One night at eleven o'clock, Jasmine hears her doorbell ring. She shuffles to the door, looks through the peephole, and there stands Leslie: confused, distraught, and clearly drunk. When Jasmine opens the door, all she can smell is the stink of alcohol.

Leslie's eyes are unfocused as she begs with slurred speech to stay the night. She claims that there's nowhere else she can go and nobody else she can turn to. Despite Leslie's drunkenness, Jasmine believes her; she knows that Leslie's addiction alienated all her friends and family long ago.

At this moment, Jasmine's values are clashing. On the one hand, Leslie caused her incredible pain; she never respected Jasmine's boundaries and treated her with unjustifiable harshness. After their divorce, Jasmine promised herself that she would never interact with Leslie again. Jasmine is flabbergasted that, after all Leslie put her through, she has the audacity to show up on her doorstep and ask for help.

On the other hand, Leslie is clearly in distress, and Jasmine worries that if she doesn't let her inside, she could end up sleeping on the street, at risk of being hurt. As much pain as Leslie caused her, Jasmine doesn't wish her any harm.

Is this a moment for Jasmine to hold firm to her boundaries—or a moment for her to compromise?

HOW TO MAKE DIFFICULT DECISIONS

In tricky situations like Jasmine's, we are called to practice discernment: to weigh the information before us and make an intentional decision that aligns with our values. We release the idea that there's a perfect set of rules we can follow to "get it right," rejecting black-and-white thinking in favor of shades of gray. Our task is to identify how to act in self-respecting ways *without* losing the compassion that makes us who we are.

The following guidelines can support us in making thoughtful and nuanced decisions:

Pause

In the heat of a difficult moment, we may be tempted to act impulsively: to do whatever it takes to resolve the challenging situation, and its unpleasant emotions, *right now*. However, impulsive action doesn't give us time to contemplate our values and assess multiple paths forward—both practices required for discernment.

We can cultivate a calmer mental landscape by pausing, taking a few deep breaths, and grounding in our bodies. Sometimes, like in Jasmine's case, we only have a few moments before we must decide. Sometimes, we have the space to postpone a decision, and we may benefit from getting a good night's sleep and coming to a conclusion the following day.

Jasmine's time is limited, so she invites Leslie to sit on her stoop while she takes a few minutes to contemplate what to do next.

Think Long Term

Complex decisions require us to zoom out and consider the big picture. How might each path forward impact not only our present, but also our future? Which path better contributes to the life we wish to lead overall?

Sometimes, the path that is best for us will include a period of short-term discomfort on the way to long-term freedom. When we're only thinking about short-term gratification, this path might not even cross our minds; we may make choices that feel great right now, but ultimately leave us feeling hollow, disconnected, or out of alignment with our values. To think long term, summon the image of your five-years-later self and ask them: *Looking back, which choice would you feel most proud of me for making?*

Release the Idea of a "Correct Answer"

When making difficult decisions, it's common to feel like there's an objectively correct answer that we'll find if we only search hard enough: the "right answer" that will lead to uncomplicated happiness and ease.

But in most cases—especially those involving relationships—there's no such thing as a perfect solution. There are simply multiple paths forward, some of which align more closely with our values than others. Typically, *all* paths involve some degree of benefit, some degree of sacrifice, and some degree of discomfort. By releasing the idea of a correct answer, we give ourselves permission to assess which path forward works best for us, right now, in this moment.

Remember That Your Path Is Unique

When we practice discernment, we remember that there's no such thing as a one-size-fits-all solution. We all have different histories, cultures, needs, wants, values, dreams, and fears. Each of these factors informs our decisions, and the path that works best for us won't necessarily work best for others. Gathering outside feedback can be helpful, but others' suggestions should only be one, small component in our ultimate decision.

Jasmine knows her friends and family would have strong opinions about how to handle Leslie's sudden appearance. Her parents, furious at the way Leslie treated their daughter, would advise Jasmine to call the police immediately. She feels equally certain that her friends from church would encourage her to give Leslie a warm bed for the night and send her on her way tomorrow.

Jasmine understands that neither group is necessarily right or wrong—they just have different experiences, values, and priorities. Ultimately, Jasmine will need to make this decision on her own.

Given the state that Leslie's in, Jasmine is tempted to let her inside—but she worries that doing so will unravel all her efforts to break the people-pleasing pattern. *I promised myself I would never interact with Leslie again*, thinks Jasmine. *If I let her stay the night, will I be sacrificing my self-respect? Will all my work breaking the people-pleasing pattern be for nothing?*

BREAKING THE BLACK-AND-WHITE BINARY

When we engage in black-and-white thinking, we view the world in extremes. We are either good or bad; decisions are either correct or utterly wrong. For this reason, black-and-white thinking is the enemy of discernment. It prevents us from seeing the world as it is: complex, uncertain, and constantly changing.

As we break the people-pleasing pattern, we may find ourselves embedded in black-and-white thoughts like "I will *never* put anyone else's needs before my own ever again," "I *never* have to explain my boundaries to anyone," "I will cut relationships off if they're not *perfect*," "If someone gets upset when I set boundaries, they're *toxic*," or "If they can't meet *every single one* of my needs, they're a bad fit for me."

At first, these attitudes may appeal to us because they unequivocally place us first. We might also find relief in the thought of a single, simple rule that applies to every circumstance we face. However, practicing discernment requires us to see past the black-and-white binary and consider that perhaps the truth is more nuanced.

Nuance in Action

Nuanced alternatives to these black-and-white perspectives include:

Black and White: I will never put anyone else's needs before my own ever again.

- **Nuance:** As I break the people-pleasing pattern, it's important that I practice putting my own needs first after years of prioritizing others'.
- **Nuance:** Occasionally putting others' needs first is necessary to find compromise and maintain relationships when we have mismatched needs.
- **Nuance:** Sometimes, abiding by my values means occasionally putting others first, especially if they are in dire need of my help.

Black and White: I never have to explain my boundaries to anyone.

- **Nuance:** I can protect myself by refusing to explain my boundaries to people who are committed to misunderstanding them.
- **Nuance:** Sometimes, an explanation can help make my boundary more palatable for others.

Black and White: I will cut relationships off if they're not perfect.

- **Nuance:** I can prioritize relationships that offer as much agreement, peace, and alignment as possible.
- **Nuance:** I accept that no relationship will ever be perfect. Even the healthiest relationships include mismatch, conflict, and compromise.

Black and White: If someone gets upset when I set boundaries, they're a toxic person.

- **Nuance:** I will remove myself from situations where others respond to my boundaries with rage, gaslighting, and guilt trips. These are unacceptable responses and I do not have to tolerate them.
- **Nuance:** It's natural for people to feel sad when I insert space or distance in our relationship. Others can have negative feelings about my boundaries while still respecting them with their actions.

Black and White: If they can't meet every single one of my needs, they're a bad fit for me.

- **Nuance:** After years of settling for relationships with people who treated my needs with judgment and disdain, I am only interested in relationships with people who want to meet my needs.
- **Nuance:** Even if someone wants to meet my needs, it's unlikely that they'll be able to meet *every single one of my* needs all the time. It's up to me to decide which of my needs are nonnegotiables and which are open to compromise.

As Jasmine reflects on her situation, she realizes that she's holding on to a black-and-white perspective: that helping Leslie would mean all her efforts to stop people-pleasing were for nothing. When Jasmine challenges herself to inject more nuance into her perspective, she comes to a few conclusions:

No single action will undo two years of work to stop people-pleasing, she thinks. *Listening to my values might mean occasionally putting others first, especially if they really need my help. . . . Plus, there's a difference between offering to help Leslie because* I feel like I can't say no, *and offering to help Leslie because I trust myself to say yes or no and* choose, *this time, to say yes. The former is people-pleasing; the latter is kindness.*

PRACTICING DISCERNMENT

As we grapple with complex situations, we may wonder: How will I know when to choose which path? How will I know when prioritizing others is self-betrayal, and how will I know when it's simply an expression of care? How will I know whether to see a relationship through a period of turmoil or let it go?

The following tools can help us find answers to these difficult questions:

Brainstorm Multiple Options

When we take the time to think creatively, we can usually find more than two paths forward in any circumstance. There are the obvious decisions—A and B—and then a variety of middle-ground options that contain some element of compromise.

From a black-and-white perspective, Jasmine has two options. She could welcome Leslie with open arms and give her a place to stay for the night; or she could reject Leslie's request and not allow her inside.

When Jasmine pauses to consider multiple options, she realizes there are more than two paths forward. She might allow Leslie inside and let her sleep on the couch, but not in the guest bedroom; offer Leslie food and water, but require that she spend the night elsewhere; call nonemergency city services (such as 311 in New York City) and request their assistance in handling the situation; call a local emergency service or shelter to house Leslie for the night; or call a selection of rehabs to see if they have any beds available for Leslie.

Contrast Two Values Wheels

As we explored in chapter 4, when faced with difficult decisions, we can contrast two values wheels to discern which path better aligns with our values. For this exercise, you will need your top eight values on hand.

1. Draw a circle and divide it into eight slices like a pizza. Write your values around the edges of each slice. This represents Decision A.
2. Create an identical circle beside it and write your values around the edges. This represents Decision B.
3. Begin with Decision A. For each value around the wheel, ask yourself: "On a scale from 1 to 10—10 being the most and 1 being the least—how much does Decision A embody this value?"
4. Based on your answer, shade in the slice from the inside out. A ranking of 10 means the slice will be entirely shaded in; a ranking of 5 means the slice is shaded halfway; a ranking of 1 means it will barely have any shading at all.
5. Go through this process for every slice on Decision A. If you can't see how a value applies to the current decision, shade it in with lines. By the end, you will have a visual representation of to what extent Decision A embodies your values.
6. Then go through the same process for Decision B. When you've finished, you can compare the two wheels to see which decision embodies your values more fully overall.

Jasmine's completed values wheels look like this:

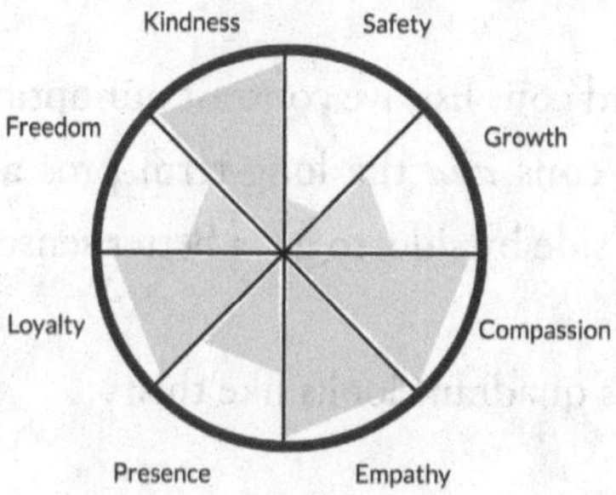

Let Leslie In

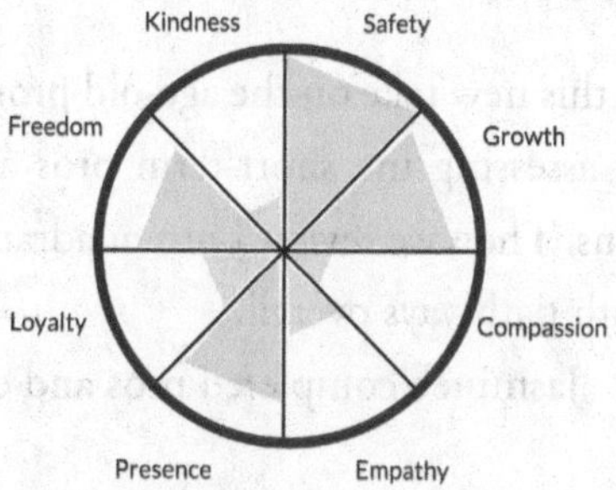

Don't Let Leslie In

Jump Forward in Time

It's normal to be tempted to choose whichever course of action will soothe our discomfort most quickly. However, choosing the path that best aligns with our integrity requires that we assess the situation *over time.*

For each option you're considering, ask yourself: If I pick this option, what will my life be like in one hour? In one week? In one year? In five years?

First, Jasmine contemplates sticking firm to her boundary and not letting Leslie in. *In one hour*, she thinks, *I'll be unable to sleep, nervous about Leslie's well-being and concerned that she's hurt. In one week, I'll be wondering what happened to her, checking the local papers and Facebook Groups to see if there are any announcements. In one year, I think I might regret this. . . . I'll worry that I let my pride get in the way of helping a person in genuine need with nowhere else to go.*

Then Jasmine contemplates letting Leslie in: *In one hour, I'll be frustrated and resentful that this person who treated me so poorly is taking refuge in my house. I'll wonder if I betrayed myself by loosening my boundary to never interact with Leslie again. In one week, Leslie won't be here anymore. I might still feel resentful that she came here, but I won't be wondering what happened to her. And in one year, this will be a distant memory.*

Fill Out a Pros and Cons Quadrant

In this new take on the age-old pros and cons list, we contrast our options by assessing the short-term pros and cons *and* the long-term pros and cons. Then we review both quadrants, side by side, to get a better sense of both pathways overall.

Jasmine's completed pros and cons quadrant looks like this:

DECISION A: I LET LESLIE IN.	
Short-Term Pros • Leslie is safe. • I won't be ruminating about Leslie, worrying if she's been hurt or injured.	**Long-Term Pros** • I won't wonder, "What ever happened to Leslie that night?" • I will be proud that I didn't let my personal baggage prevent me from helping someone in dire need.
Short-Term Cons • I won't sleep well tonight. • Being around Leslie might be triggering or uncomfortable.	**Long-Term Cons** • Helping her tonight violates my boundary of never interacting with her again. • If I help her tonight, Leslie might think I'm open to helping her again.

DECISION B: I DON'T LET LESLIE IN.	
Short-Term Pros • I won't have to deal with Leslie.	**Long-Term Pros** • I will feel like I stood my ground and honored my boundary.
Short-Term Cons • Leslie might get sick or injured. • I might feel regret or shame about my decision, especially if Leslie ends up getting injured.	**Long-Term Cons** • I will feel guilty for not helping someone in need. • I might feel regret.

Once Jasmine has thought through her options, she decides to strike a balance. She's comfortable helping Leslie this one time; doing so aligns with her values of compassion, empathy, and kindness. Jasmine isn't comfortable letting Leslie stay in the guest bedroom—that feels far too intimate—but she invites Leslie inside to sleep on the couch.

That night, Jasmine sleeps fitfully. The next morning, she wakes early, puts on her robe, and goes into the living room to rouse Leslie. She is disoriented and still mildly drunk.

Jasmine doesn't bother with pleasantries. "You came here last night asking for a place to stay, and I let you crash on the couch," she says firmly. "This is the only time I'm willing to do this. If you show up here again, I won't let you inside. Instead, I'll have to call the authorities."

Jasmine says this as much for her own benefit as Leslie's. She wants the expectation to be crystal clear: she was willing to help once, but she will not do so again.

"I need you to leave now," Jasmine says. She walks purposefully to the front door and holds it open expectantly. Leslie nods and mumbles something unintelligible; slowly, she shuffles out the door into the morning light.

Jasmine closes the door behind her and exhales a breath she didn't realize she'd been holding. She makes her way to the kitchen and checks to see how she feels about her decision. No doubt, having Leslie in the house was uncomfortable; Jasmine feels shaken up. On the other hand, Jasmine knows that if she *hadn't* let Leslie stay, she wouldn't have slept well then, either. She would have been wide awake, worrying about Leslie out on the street in the middle of the night.

Ultimately, Jasmine feels proud of the balance she struck: she went out of her way and helped someone in need, but made it clear that it was a one-time kindness. For Jasmine, the fact that it was an *intentional and deliberate* choice informed by her values made it feel entirely different than the compulsive people-pleasing of her past.

EMBRACING LESSONS LEARNED

What if, despite our efforts to be discerning, we end up choosing a path that later feels poorly aligned with who we are and what we want? Perhaps we decide to compromise on something we later realize was a nonnegotiable need. Perhaps we end a friendship due to differences in values and later wish we hadn't. Perhaps we set a boundary too harshly and later feel guilty for being so uncompromising.

As we break the people-pleasing pattern, we will all make decisions that we later regret. Not only is this normal, it's inevitable, and accepting the certainty of mistakes relieves us of the pressure to get it right every time. In fact, some of our most powerful lessons can only be learned through the making and correcting of mistakes.

The following reflection questions can help us find hidden gems of learning when we've made a mistake in our decision-making:

- How did this mistake teach me what's most important to me? How can I embody this new knowledge moving forward in my life?
- Is it possible that making this mistake was *the only way* to learn this valuable information?
- What did this experience teach me about my values? Did it uncover a deeply held value I hadn't recognized before? Did it show me that one of my values was more important than I'd ever realized? How can I embody this knowledge moving forward?
- In the future, how can I handle scenarios like this one, knowing what I know now?
- What did this experience teach me about my decision-making process? How should I refine my decision process in the future?
- How can I use the lessons learned from this experience to help other people?

Ultimately, there are no wrong choices as we confront these complex situations. In this space of ambiguity, we get to learn, through experimentation, who we are and what we value. With every decision that later feels like a mistake, we gain a new understanding of what doesn't work for us and incorporate that knowledge into our future conduct. Our experiences become our greatest teachers as we work out our own, unique blueprints for living.

After years of people-pleasing—after years of feeling like we *had* to say yes—we finally have the gift of choice. True freedom isn't always saying no. It's the ability to *choose*: to say yes or no depending on what we value, what we feel, and who we most want to be.

EPILOGUE: REDISCOVERING THE (REAL) JOYS OF GIVING

A little-known secret about breaking the people-pleasing pattern is that it enables us to experience the joy of giving anew. Strange, isn't it? You would think that leaving people-pleasing behind means giving *less*: being *less* generous, *less* kind, *less* compassionate.

But in truth, breaking the people-pleasing pattern is the gateway to a rich, new terrain of giving: a giving that is sincere, genuine, and boundaried. Now our offerings of kindness are voluntary, not obligatory. They're driven by goodwill, not by guilt. We trust ourselves to say no, so when we say *yes*, we really mean it—and our giving, instead of masking resentment and obligation, becomes an openhearted expression of care and compassion for others.

In this way, breaking the people-pleasing pattern allows us to experience the real joy of giving for the very first time: the joy of giving to others, *and* the joy of giving to ourselves.

THE JOY OF GIVING TO OTHERS

Back when I was people-pleasing, giving to others rarely if ever brought me joy. Daily, I surpassed my own limitations and "gave" even when it left me feeling bone-deep fatigue and overwhelm.

For me, "giving" was a synonym for self-abandonment. Every new commitment was another addition to the ever-increasing pile of things I had to do for others, whether or not I had the time, space, or energy—much less the desire. Time and time again, my giving left me feeling resentful toward the very people I was trying to help. My attempts to pour from an empty cup came at a high physical and psychic cost.

But now my cup is, by and large, full. I regularly tend to my own feelings, needs, and desires. I say no to commitments that would threaten my well-being. I only invest in relationships that invest back into me. I have built a solid foundation of self-care, and as a result, I have the time, energy, and emotional bandwidth to participate in *boundaried giving*: giving to others in a sustainable way without sacrificing my needs in the process.

This new relationship with giving has become a source of unexpected joy and connection with the people I love. When my friend asks if I can drive her to the airport the next morning at four o'clock, I consider: *Does my schedule allow for this? Will I be able to fit in a short nap tomorrow if I need to?* If the answer is no, I say no: over-giving (and resentment) averted. But if the answer is yes, I say yes—and the following morning at four o'clock finds me en route to SeaTac, happy to help a friend in need. As we drive the sleepy highway with coffees in hand, I feel the satisfaction of doing a good deed for someone I love.

When a loved one asks me to support them after an anxious day, I internally consider: *Do I have the emotional space for this? Do I feel resourced enough to hold space for their emotions right now?* If the answer is no, I say no. But if the answer is yes, I say yes—and as they share their anxieties with me, I am awash with compassion. I feel grateful that they entrust me with their concerns; I feel connected to them in their vulnerability. By giving within my own limits, I can embody *genuine* kindness, compassion, and generosity. And I know that this joy of giving to others wouldn't be possible if I hadn't first experienced the joy of giving to myself.

THE JOY OF GIVING TO OURSELVES

It's incredibly healing to finally give ourselves the care and attention we spent so long reserving exclusively for others. I can't say what it's like for everyone on the other side of people-pleasing, but here's what it's been like for me.

More than ever before, my time is my own. I still have to work and pay the bills, but my free time is no longer cluttered with unwanted commitments I guiltily agreed to. When I have the energy, I say yes to friends' invitations to parties, concerts, and potlucks; when I don't, I cozy up with tea and a good book.

I understand—viscerally now—that my needs are a priority, not a luxury. I schedule doctor's appointments and take regular trips to the grocery store; I go for runs, meditate, and enjoy much-needed breaks from social media. I've come to accept that I am both a sensitive person and an introvert, and after years of dismissing myself as "too sensitive," I'm no longer at war with my needs for quiet, stillness, or alone time.

Prioritizing my desires and pleasures has come less easily to me, but I'm getting better at it all the time. Last year, I finally bought myself a keyboard—something I'd wanted since I left home, and our family piano, at age eighteen. Recently, heeding my desire for more play, I spontaneously signed up for an improv class. It has become an enormous source of joy and levity in my life.

Like so many recovering people-pleasers, I've outgrown relationships as I've found my voice. Many of the connections I forged when I was making myself small were ultimately not compatible with the authentic version of me. Transitioning out of those relationships was difficult—sometimes the grief lasted for months, and I wondered if I'd ever make it out of the Valley—but in their wake, I've prioritized connections with people who accept me, and love me, for who I am.

Now, in my relationships, I make my needs known. I ask my family for support; I ask my friends for reciprocity; I ask my partner to touch me *this* way, not *that* way. In the past, it took me weeks to find the courage to make these sorts of requests. (Half the time, I never found it at all!) Now expressing my needs is second nature. It isn't always comfortable—I'm still visited by occasional guilt and fear—but having a difficult conversation feels far preferable to letting an unspoken resentment fester.

As a result, a current of honesty and genuine intimacy runs through my relationships. When others hurt my feelings, I am comfortable letting them know, and I trust that they will do the same. Sometimes, hard conversations about our hurts result in awkwardness. Sometimes that awkwardness lasts an hour; sometimes, it lasts six months. Through these experiences, I'm learning that worthwhile relationships can not only withstand—but can also grow from, and become more resilient as the result of—difficult, honest conversations.

In a similar way, I have come to learn the joy of true intimacy in love. Before, I was certain that I would only find love if I made myself small: less emotional, less opinionated, less *me*. As a result, I consistently suffered in relationships where I was the silent and doting supporting character in someone else's story. When I began making my true feelings and needs known from the start, I scared some people away—and I drew others in. Eventually, I found a partner who—to my daily surprise—wants *more* of me, not less; who *compassionately* holds space for my big emotions; who gives love freely, simply because he wants to. His acceptance of me has taught me greater acceptance of myself.

As for my family: I have the gift of knowing that if they disappeared from the face of the earth tomorrow, there would be nothing left unsaid between us. I've shared old grievances and set new boundaries that have been received with more grace and compassion than I could have ever asked for. (I recognize that not everyone has the privilege of this sort of familial healing; it's a gift I don't take for granted.) My younger self couldn't have imagined the comfort and honesty we share today.

These changes within my relationships have been profound and deeply healing—and still, none of them compare to the changes I've witnessed in my relationship with myself. Breaking the people-pleasing pattern has enabled me to discover a sense of agency, self-trust, and self-respect the likes of which I've never known.

After years of feeling like a victim of other's requests and actions, I finally recognize that I can choose what to give and what to tolerate. This doesn't mean that choosing is always *comfortable*—in fact, it often hurts!—but it does mean that I do, in fact, *have a choice*. I can say no; I can set boundaries; I can remove myself from situations that don't meet my needs. Before, I thought that power looked like getting others to change or getting others to prioritize me. Now I understand that taking responsibility for myself and owning my agency is the true gateway to my power.

As a result of exercising my agency, I finally have an unwavering certainty that I'll have my own back, even on my hardest days. With every need I've prioritized, request I've made, boundary I've set, and growing pain I've soothed through, I've shown myself that I'm not leaving me behind: *I'm not going anywhere*. Even in the face of others' judgments, I trust myself to stand up for me. Others' perceptions of me matter, but my own perceptions matter more.

As a result of building this self-trust, I have found—after years of wishing—that I respect who I am. This doesn't mean that I never feel anxious, self-judging, or self-critical—I do, and I don't know a soul who doesn't—but, on the whole, my actions align with my words, and my words align with my values. The person I am *inside* matches the person I am *outside*, and after years of being trapped behind the mask of people-pleasing, this is a degree of integrity I never dared to dream I'd experience.

Breaking the people-pleasing pattern isn't easy, but it is worth *every* difficulty—because on the other side awaits our voice, our joy, and our power.

ACKNOWLEDGMENTS

Thank you to my agent, Meg Thompson, for being the first believer in this project. I will always be thankful for your hard work finding *Stop People Pleasing* a home, and for your encouragement that bolstered me through the tougher moments. Thank you to my editor, Eamon Dolan, for bringing your keen, discerning mind to this project. Your edits brought such clarity and potency to my manuscript; I'm in awe of your mastery of the English language! Thank you, also, to Sandy Hodgman, for managing the foreign rights and helping me bring this book to readers overseas. I'm indebted to the team at Simon & Schuster for their work copyediting, marketing, promoting, and otherwise bringing *Stop People Pleasing* into the world. I couldn't imagine a better home for this book. To my earliest readers—Kali, Andi, Gerry, and Joe—thank you for helping me hone my very first draft all those years ago!

To Katie, Kali, Andi, Sarah, and Grace: Thank you for teaching me the art of building resilient friendships. I've learned, through you, that the greatest friendships can withstand hard conversations and emerge stronger and more beautiful than before. Thank you for cheerleading me through this project and keeping me afloat with many a late-night pep talk.

To my parents, Maggie and Ed: Thank you for showing me love, grace, and acceptance as I learned to use my voice, even when the things I said were hard to hear. You've role modeled an unconditional love that I can only hope to embody when I'm a parent myself one day. Thank you for always believing in me, cheering me on, and making me laugh. I love you.

And finally, thank you to Aaron, for teaching me that I don't need to be less to be worthy of love. Your bottomless support kept me afloat as I completed this project. Your acceptance of me as I am—needs, big feelings, and all—has been the greatest gift of my life. Thank you for teaching me how to love and be loved.

NOTES

1: PEOPLE-PLEASING: WHAT IT IS, WHERE IT COMES FROM, AND WHY WE'RE LEAVING IT BEHIND

7 *Walker explains that, in childhood*: Pete Walker, "Codependency, Trauma, and the Fawn Response," Pete Walker, January 2003, https://pete-walker.com/codependencyFawnResponse.htm.

7 *Walker explains that those who fawn*: Pete Walker, "The 4Fs: A Trauma Typology in Complex PTSD," Pete Walker, 2023, accessed September 5, 2023, http://pete-walker.com/fourFs_TraumaTypologyComplexPTSD.htm.

7 *Over time, many become completely disconnected*: Tian Dayton, *Emotional Sobriety: From Relationship Trauma to Resilience and Balance* (Deerfield Beach, FL: Health Communications, 2008), 79.

8 *In the 1960s, clinical psychologist Diana Baumrind*: Diana Baumrind, "Child Care Practices Anteceding Three Patterns of Preschool Behavior," *Genetic Psychology Monographs* 75, no. 1 (February 1, 1967): 43–88.

8 *Authoritarian parents are punitive*: Edward Teyber and Faith Holmes Teyber, *Interpersonal Process in Therapy: An Integrative Model* (Boston: Cengage Learning, 2010), 201.

8 *They become externally motivated, anxiously*: Ibid.

8 *Though many become hardworking*: Ibid.

10 *They believe that they're worthy of love*: Cathy W. Hall and Raymond E. Webster, "Risk Factors among Adult Children of Alcoholics," *International Journal of Behavioral Consultation and Therapy* 3, no. 4 (January 1, 2007): 494–511.

10 *Research shows that adult children*: Ibid.

10 *In the home, women perform four hours*: Gus Wezerek and Kristen R. Ghodsee, "Opinion: Women's Unpaid Labor Is Worth $10,900,000,000,000," *New York Times*, August 11, 2020, https://www.nytimes.com/interactive/2020/03/04/opinion/women-unpaid-labor.html.

10 *Psychologist Marshall Rosenberg writes*: Marshall B. Rosenberg and Deepak

Chopra, *Nonviolent Communication: A Language of Life: Life-Changing Tools for Healthy Relationships* (Encinitas, CA: PuddleDancer Press, 2015), 84.

10 *Women, more often than men, find themselves responsible*: Britni De La Cretaz, "How to Get Your Partner to Take on More Emotional Labor," *New York Times*, May 8, 2020, https://www.nytimes.com/article/emotional-labor.html.

11 *Research shows that women apologize far more*: Karina Schumann and Michael Ross, "Why Women Apologize More than Men," *Psychological Science* 21, no. 11 (September 20, 2010): 1649–55.

11 *Women are even more likely to be*: Alice Robb, "Sheryl Sandberg Is Right about the Word 'Bossy.' This Data Proves It," *New Republic*, March 19, 2014, https://newrepublic.com/article/117076/sheryl-sandbergs-ban-bossy-campaign-right-about-one-thing.

11 *Across the board, men are still expected*: Kelly Gonsalves, "Study Shows Men Still Feel Judged When They Talk about Their Feelings," mindbodygreen, October 16, 2019, https://www.mindbodygreen.com/articles/men-think-expressing-emotions-threatens-masculinity-study-shows.

11 *Denying their own needs for rest and restoration*: Nick Boettcher et al., "Men's Work-Related Stress and Mental Health: Illustrating the Workings of Masculine Role Norms," *American Journal of Men's Health* 13, no. 2 (March 1, 2019): 155798831983841.

12 *Individualistic cultures, like the United States*: Sjoerd Beugelsdijk and Christian Welzel, "Dimensions and Dynamics of National Culture: Synthesizing Hofstede with Inglehart," *Journal of Cross-Cultural Psychology* 49, no. 10 (October 2, 2018): 1469–1505.

12 *Emphasizing conformity, obedience, and loyalty*: Ibid.

13 *People who score higher on the sociotropy*: Aaron Beck, "Cognitive Therapy of Depression: New Perspectives," in *Treatment of Depression: Old Controversies and New Approaches*, eds. Paula J. Clayton and James Elmer Barrett (Philadelphia: Lippincott Williams & Wilkins, 1983), 265–84.

14 *Sociotropic people are more likely to develop*: Peter Bieling, Aaron T. Beck, and Gregory K. Brown, "Stability and Change of Sociotropy and Autonomy Subscales in Cognitive Therapy of Depression," *Journal of Cognitive Psychotherapy* 18, no. 2 (April 1, 2004): 135–48.

14 *Meanwhile, the Bowen family systems theory*: Diane R. Gehart, "Intergenerational and Psychoanalytic Family Therapies," in *Mastering Competencies in Family Therapy: A Practical Approach to Theory and Clinical Case Documentation* (Boston: Cengage Learning, 2017), 263–309.

14 *Highly differentiated people have a strong*: "Introduction to the Eight Concepts," Bowen Center for the Study of the Family, accessed September 5, 2023, https://www.thebowencenter.org/introduction-eight-concepts.

14 *More than anything, anxiously attached*: Jeffry A. Simpson and W. Steven Rholes, "Adult Attachment, Stress, and Romantic Relationships," *Current Opinion in Psychology* 13 (February 1, 2017): 19–24.

14 *Originally popularized in the 1980s*: Carrie A. Springer, Thomas W. Britt, and Barry R. Schlenker, "Codependency: Clarifying the Construct," *Journal of Mental Health Counseling* 20, no. 2 (April 1, 1998): 141–58.

15 *Psychologists define pathological altruism*: Rachel Bachner-Melman and Barbara Oakley, "Giving 'Till It Hurts': Eating Disorders and Pathological Altruism," in *Bio-Psycho-Social Contributions to Understanding Eating Disorders*, eds. Yael Latzer and Daniel Stein (New York: Springer, 2016), 91–103.

17 *Psychologists define healthy altruism*: Beth J. Seelig and Lisa S. Rosof, "Normal and Pathological Altruism," *Journal of the American Psychoanalytic Association* 49, no. 3 (September 1, 2001): 933–59.

17 *Healthy altruists gratify their own*: Scott Barry Kaufman and Emanuel Jauk, "Healthy Selfishness and Pathological Altruism: Measuring Two Paradoxical Forms of Selfishness," *Frontiers in Psychology* 11 (May 21, 2020): https://doi.org/10.3389/fpsyg.2020.01006.

17 *Research shows that healthy altruism*: Bachner-Melman and Oakley, "Giving 'Till It Hurts.'"

17 *We aren't necessarily expecting*: Ibid.

18 *Psychologists Scott Barry Kaufman and Emanuel Jauk encourage those*: Kaufman and Jauk, "Healthy Selfishness and Pathological Altruism."

19 *Research also shows that emotional suppression can contribute*: Mostafa Bahremand et al., "Emotion Risk-Factor in Patients with Cardiac Diseases: The Role of Cognitive Emotion Regulation Strategies, Positive Affect and Negative Affect (A Case-Control Study)," *Global Journal of Health Science* 8, no. 1 (May 17, 2015): 173.

2: FINDING OUR FEELINGS

25 *Psychologist Tian Dayton, author of* Emotional Sobriety, *explains*: Tian Dayton, *Emotional Sobriety: From Relationship Trauma to Resilience and Balance* (Deerfield Beach, FL: Health Communications, 2008), 153.

26 *Psychologist Hillary McBride, in her book* The Wisdom of Your Body, *explains*: Hillary L. McBride, *The Wisdom of Your Body: Finding Healing, Wholeness, and Connection through Embodied Living* (Grand Rapids, MI: Brazos Press, 2021), 137.

27 *Anthropologist Roy Grinker explains*: Roy Richard Grinker, *Nobody's Normal: How Culture Created the Stigma of Mental Illness* (New York: W. W. Norton, 2021), 27.

28 *After compiling the data, the research team*: Lauri Nummenmaa et al., "Maps

of Subjective Feelings," *Proceedings of the National Academy of Sciences of the United States of America* 115, no. 37 (August 28, 2018): 9198–9203.

28 *Anger, they discovered, is*: Ibid.

29 *When we notice an emotion*: McBride, *The Wisdom of Your Body*, 123.

3: DISCOVERING OUR NEEDS

35 *Difficult feelings like resentment*: Rosenberg and Chopra, *Nonviolent Communication*, 84.

36 *At the extreme, our self-neglect*: Suzy Braye, D. Orr, and Michael Preston-Shoot, "Learning Lessons about Self-Neglect? An Analysis of Serious Case Reviews," *Journal of Adult Protection* 17, no. 1 (February 9, 2015): 3–18.

36 *Research shows that those who practice healthy selfishness*: Kaufman and Jauk, "Healthy Selfishness and Pathological Altruism."

36 Merriam-Webster *defines a need as*: "Need," *Merriam-Webster's Collegiate Dictionary*, accessed September 2, 2023, https://www.merriam-webster.com/dictionary/need.

4: UNEARTHING OUR VALUES

47 *First, research shows that acting*: Kristine Klussman et al., "The Importance of Awareness, Acceptance, and Alignment with the Self: A Framework for Understanding Self-Connection," *Europe's Journal of Psychology* 18, no. 1 (February 25, 2022): 120–31.

47 *Second, while our feelings change*: John W. Berry, Ype H. Poortinga, and Janak Pandey, "Values," in *Handbook of Cross-Cultural Psychology: Basic Processes and Human Development*, vol. 3 (Boston: Allyn & Bacon, 1997), 77–118.

47 *And third, aligning our*: Matthew McKay, Jeffrey C. Wood, and Jeffrey Brantley, *The Dialectical Behavior Therapy Skills Workbook: Practical DBT Exercises for Learning Mindfulness, Interpersonal Effectiveness, Emotion Regulation, and Distress Tolerance* (Oakland, CA: New Harbinger, 2019), 36–38.

56 *When confronted with situations*: This exercise is adapted from Marilyn Atkinson and the Art & Science of Coaching at Erickson Coaching International.

5: UPDATING OUR SELF-CONCEPT

62 *While our values are the principles*: J. A. Bailey, "Self-Image, Self-Concept, and Self-Identity Revisited," *Journal of the National Medical Association* 95, no. 5 (May 1, 2003): 383–86.

62 *As children, we don't yet have the ability*: Raymond M. Bergner and James R. Holmes, "Self-Concepts and Self-Concept Change: A Status Dynamic Approach," *Psychotherapy* 37, no. 1 (January 1, 2000): 36–44.

63 *For example: If we believe we're unlovable*: Ibid.

63 *Due to this inner need for consistency*: Sanaz Talaifar and William B. Swann, "Self-Verification Theory," in *Encyclopedia of Personality and Individual Differences* (New York: Springer, 2017), 1–9.

63 *This phenomenon is called the self-verification*: Ibid.

65 *Research shows that the most important prerequisite*: Hazel Rose Markus and Elissa Wurf, "The Dynamic Self-Concept: A Social Psychological Perspective," *Annual Review of Psychology* 38, no. 1 (January 1, 1987): 299–337.

67 *This is because our minds use three methods*: Ibid.

68 *To counteract our habit to recall only*: Ibid.

71 *Psychologist and philosopher William James*: Gretchen Rubin, "Act the Way You Want to Feel," *Slate*, November 6, 2009, https://slate.com/human-interest/2009/11/act-the-way-you-want-to-feel.html.

6: ALLOWING OUR WANTS

77 *We experience envy when*: W. Gerrod Parrott and Richard H. Smith, "Distinguishing the Experiences of Envy and Jealousy," *Journal of Personality and Social Psychology* 64, no. 6 (January 1, 1993): 906–20.

78 *Research shows that envy can also be*: Richard H. Smith and Sung Hee Kim, "Comprehending Envy," *Psychological Bulletin* 133, no. 1 (January 1, 2007): 46–64.

80 *Research shows that breaking down our larger goals*: Szu-Chi Huang, Liyin Jin, and Ying Zhang, "Step by Step: Sub-Goals as a Source of Motivation," *Organizational Behavior and Human Decision Processes* 141 (July 1, 2017): 1–15.

8: SETTING BOUNDARIES WITH OURSELVES

107 *Research suggests that sharing your goal*: Howard J. Klein et al., "When Goals Are Known: The Effects of Audience Relative Status on Goal Commitment and Performance," *Journal of Applied Psychology* 105, no. 4 (April 1, 2020): 372–89.

10: SETTING BOUNDARIES WITH OTHERS

129 *Coined by a blogger*: Zawn Villines, "What Is Gray Rocking?," *Medical News Today*, January 10, 2023, https://www.medicalnewstoday.com/articles/grey-rock.

130 *Differentiation is the ability*: Gehart, "Intergenerational and Psychoanalytic Family Therapies," 263–309.

137 *The broken record technique is a form*: Manuel J. Smith, *When I Say No, I Feel Guilty* (New York: Bantam, 1975): 60–62.

138 *Silvy Khoucasian, a relationship coach*: Silvy Khoucasian, "Sometimes One Person's Boundaries Are Incompatible with Another Person's Needs," Instagram, 2023, accessed January 10, 2024, https://www.instagram.com/p/CwdYBUqvEb7/.

11: SETTING EMOTIONAL BOUNDARIES

141 *Emotional parents are run*: Lindsay C. Gibson, *Adult Children of Emotionally Immature Parents: How to Heal from Distant, Rejecting, or Self-Involved Parents* (Oakland, CA: New Harbinger, 2015), 70.

146 *This can feel pleasant when things*: Gehart, "Intergenerational and Psychoanalytic Family Therapies," 263–309.

148 *A popular quote widely*: Stephen Covey and Alex Pattakos, *Prisoners of Our Thoughts: Viktor Frankl's Principles for Discovering Meaning in Life and Work* (National Geographic Books, 2017), IV.

148 *Visual metaphors have been proven*: Valerie Thomas, *Using Mental Imagery in Counselling and Psychotherapy: A Guide to More Inclusive Theory and Practice* (New York: Routledge, 2015), 55–56.

12: WHAT WE CAN AND CAN'T CONTROL

165 *Elizabeth Gilbert said*: Elizabeth Gilbert, "You are afraid of surrender because you don't want to lose control," Facebook, July 12, 2020, https://www.facebook.com/GilbertLiz/photos/a.356148997800555/3234180116664081.

13: HOW OPPRESSION KEEPS US SILENT

168 *For Black men, any*: Brea Love, "NAACP Explains the 'Angry Black Person' Bias," ABC10, March 31, 2021, https://www.abc10.com/article/news/local/naacp-explains-angry-black-person-bias/103-dce57751-10bd-403e-81fd-4e7cec058671.

169 *Black women, too, are*: Daphna Motro et al., "Race and Reactions to Women's Expressions of Anger at Work: Examining the Effects of the 'Angry Black Woman' Stereotype," *Journal of Applied Psychology* 107, no. 1 (January 1, 2022): 142–52.

169 *Meanwhile, Latina women*: Dana Mastro and Elizabeth Behm-Morawitz, "Latino Representation on Primetime Television," *Journalism & Mass Communication Quarterly* 82, no. 1 (March 1, 2005): 110–30.

169 *People of color often face*: Courtney L. McCluney, "The Costs of Code-Switching," *Harvard Business Review*, January 28, 2021, https://hbr.org/2019/11/the-costs-of-codeswitching.

169 *Code-switching may decrease*: Ibid.

169 *Research shows that women*: Alexis Krivkovich et al., "Women in the Workplace 2022," McKinsey & Company, October 18, 2022, https://www.mckinsey.com/featured-insights/diversity-and-inclusion/women-in-the-workplace.

169 *Meanwhile, women of color, LGBTQ+ women*: Ibid.

170 *Women who address these inequities*: Chloe Grace Hart, "The Penalties for Self-Reporting Sexual Harassment," *Gender & Society* 33, no. 4 (May 1, 2019): 534–59.

170 *Research shows that women carry*: Allison Daminger, "The Cognitive Dimension of Household Labor," *American Sociological Review* 84, no. 4 (July 9, 2019): 609–33.

170 *When women ask their male*: Gemma Hartley, "Women Aren't Nags—We're Just Fed Up," *Harper's Bazaar*, July 8, 2019, https://www.harpersbazaar.com/culture/features/a12063822/emotional-labor-gender-equality/.

170 *Soraya Chemaly writes in*: Soraya Chemaly, *Rage Becomes Her: The Power of Women's Anger* (New York: Simon & Schuster, 2018), 14.

170 *Since 2020, discrimination*: Sarah Kate Ellis, "Executive Summary: Accelerating Acceptance 2022," in *Executive Summary: Accelerating Acceptance 2022*, GLAAD, May 12, 2023, https://glaad.org/publications/accelerating-acceptance-2022/.

170 *Within the American justice system*: "Mapping Attacks on LGBTQ Rights in U.S. State Legislatures," American Civil Liberties Union, September 1, 2023, https://www.aclu.org/legislative-attacks-on-lgbtq-rights.

170 *70 percent of LBGTQ+ Americans*: Ibid.

170 *Seventy-five percent of trans people*: Sandy James et al., "Executive Summary of the Report of the 2015 Transgender Survey," National Center for Transgender Equality, December 2016, https://transequality.org/sites/default/files/docs/usts/USTS-Executive-Summary-Dec17.pdf.

171 *Despite the growing popularity*: Elisabeth Sheff, "Polyamorous Women, Sexual Subjectivity and Power," *Journal of Contemporary Ethnography* 34, no. 3 (June 1, 2005): 251–83.

171 *To avoid harm, nonmonogamous*: Ibid.

171 *Neuro-discrimination is the unfair*: Ariane Resnick, "What Does It Mean to Be Neurodivergent?," Verywell Mind, July 5, 2023, https://www.verywellmind.com/what-is-neurodivergence-and-what-does-it-mean-to-be-neurodivergent-5196627.

171 *"Neurodivergence" is an umbrella term*: Ibid.

171 *Neurodivergent people may*: Billie Olsen, "What Is Masking and Why Do Neurodivergent People Do It?," LGBTQ and ALL, September 24, 2021, https://www.lgbtqandall.com/what-is-masking-and-why-do-neurodivergent-people-do-it/.

172 *In a 2017 study*: Laura Hull et al., "'Putting on My Best Normal': Social Camouflaging in Adults with Autism Spectrum Conditions," *Journal of Autism and Developmental Disorders* 47, no. 8 (May 19, 2017): 2519–34.

172 *Another wrote*: Ibid.

172 *Over the course of years*: Rebecca Stanborough, "Autism Masking: To Blend or Not to Blend," Healthline, November 19, 2021, https://www.healthline.com/health/autism/autism-masking#effects.

172 *As we saw in chapter 1, collectivist cultures*: Hazel R. Markus and Shinobu Kitayama, "Culture and the Self: Implications for Cognition, Emotion, and Motivation," *Psychological Review* 98, no. 2 (April 1991): 224–253.

172 *In collectivist cultures, those who advocate*: Eftychia Stamkou et al., "Cultural Collectivism and Tightness Moderate Responses to Norm Violators: Effects on Power Perception, Moral Emotions, and Leader Support," *Personality and Social Psychology Bulletin* 45, no. 6 (November 3, 2018): 947–64.

175 *As Emily and Amelia Nagoski*: Emily Nagoski and Amelia Nagoski, *Burnout: The Secret to Solving the Stress Cycle* (New York: Ballantine Books, 2019), 27–49.

175 *Even when we can't completely*: Ibid.

175 *Community organizer Nakita*: Nakita Valerio, "This Viral Facebook Post Urges People to Rethink Self-Care," *Fashion*, July 13, 2021, https://fashionmagazine.com/flare/self-care-new-zealand-muslim-attack/.

14: WALKING THROUGH THE FIRE

182 *People who judge their emotions*: Brett Q. Ford et al., "The Psychological Health Benefits of Accepting Negative Emotions and Thoughts: Laboratory, Diary, and Longitudinal Evidence," *Journal of Personality and Social Psychology* 115, no. 6 (December 1, 2018): 1075–92.

183 *Holly Whitaker, in her*: Holly Whitaker, *Quit like a Woman: The Radical Choice to Not Drink in a Culture Obsessed with Alcohol* (New York: Dial Press, 2019), 147.

15: FACING FEAR, GUILT, AND ANGER

186 *Tara Brach, psychologist*: Tara Brach, *Radical Acceptance: Embracing Your Life with the Heart of a Buddha* (New York: Bantam Books, 2003), 27.

193 *After speaking with thousands of patients*: Bronnie Ware, *Top Five Regrets of the Dying: A Life Transformed by the Dearly Departing* (London: Hay House, 2019), 42.

195 *Psychologist Marolyn Wells writes*: Marolyn Wells, Cheryl Glickauf-Hughes, and Rebecca Jones, "Codependency: A Grass Roots Construct's Relationship to Shame-Proneness, Low Self-Esteem, and Childhood Parentification," *American Journal of Family Therapy* 27, no. 1 (January 1, 1999): 63–71.

197 *Research shows that physical*: Nagoski and Nagoski, *Burnout: The Secret to Solving the Stress Cycle*, 27–49.

198 *Studies show that anger is*: Charles S. Carver and Eddie Harmon-Jones, "Anger Is an Approach-Related Affect: Evidence and Implications," *Psychological Bulletin* 135, no. 2 (January 1, 2009): 183–204.

198 *Whereas anxiety and sadness*: Ibid.

17: ALLOWING GRIEF, TRANSITIONS, AND NEW BEGINNINGS

221 *Grief rituals help*: Francesca Gino and Michael Norton, "Why Rituals Work," *Scientific American*, May 14, 2013, https://www.scientificamerican.com/article/why-rituals-work/.

223 *Holly Whitaker, who writes*: Holly Whitaker, "#34 You Are Doing It. This Is the It," *Recovering*, November 17, 2022, https://hollywhitaker.substack.com/p/34-you-are-doing-it-this-is-the-it.

229 *William Bridges, author:* William Bridges and Susan Bridges, *Transitions: Making Sense of Life's Changes* (New York: Da Capo Lifelong Books, 2019), 139.

18: THERE'S NO WE WITHOUT ME

233 *The word* intimacy *is derived*: Richard E. Sexton and Virginia Staudt Sexton, "Intimacy: A Historical Perspective," in *Intimacy*, ed. M. Fischer et al. (New York: Plenum Press, 1982), 1–20.

235 *One of the most common ways*: Pete Walker, "The 4Fs," in Esther Perel, *Mating in Captivity: Unlocking Erotic Intelligence* (New York: HarperCollins, 2009), 25.

240 *According to research by the Gottman*: "The Four Horsemen: The Antidotes," Gottman Institute, February 5, 2023, https://www.gottman.com/blog/the-four-horsemen-the-antidotes/.

240 *According to the Gottman Institute, these four behaviors*: Ibid.

244 *In fact, research shows that frequently*: Wei-Fang Lin et al., "We Can Make It Better: 'We' Moderates the Relationship between a Compromising Style in Interpersonal Conflict and Well-Being," *Journal of Happiness Studies* 17, no. 1 (October 5, 2014): 41–57.

245 *Psychotherapist John Gottman writes*: Ellie Lisitsa, "Manage Conflict: The Art of Compromise," Gottman Institute, December 28, 2020, https://www.gottman.com/blog/manage-conflict-the-art-of-compromise/.

19: THE PEOPLE-PLEASING PATTERN AND SEX

250 *Many people-pleasers have*: Lucia F. O'Sullivan and Elizabeth Rice Allgeier, "Feigning Sexual Desire: Consenting to Unwanted Sexual Activity in Heterosexual Dating Relationships," *Journal of Sex Research* 35, no. 3 (August 1, 1998): 234–43.

252 *Chris Ash, a survivor of sexual assault*: Chris Ash in discussion with the author, April 2023.

253 *Some who endure trauma*: Walker, "The 4Fs."

253 *These people learn that their*: Bessel Van Der Kolk, "Posttraumatic Stress Disorder and the Nature of Trauma," *Dialogues in Clinical Neuroscience* 2, no. 1 (March 31, 2000): 7–22.

253 *Bessel van der Kolk, a psychiatrist*: Ibid.

254 *Sexual scripts are pervasive*: Sarah Bonell et al., "Benevolent Sexism and the Traditional Sexual Script as Predictors of Sexual Dissatisfaction in Heterosexual Women from the U.S.," *Archives of Sexual Behavior* 51, no. 6 (July 5, 2022): 3063–70.

254 *A 1994 study found*: Cindy Struckman-Johnson and David Struckman-Johnson, "Men Pressured and Forced into Sexual Experience," *Archives of Sexual Behavior* 23, no. 1 (February 1, 1994): 93–114.

254 *A 2019 study of eighty-seven boys*: Kiera D. Duckworth and Mary Nell Trautner, "Gender Goals: Defining Masculinity and Navigating Peer Pressure to Engage in Sexual Activity," *Gender & Society* 33, no. 5 (July 26, 2019): 795–817.

254 *As sexuality researcher*: Michele Clements-Schriber, John Rempel, and Serge Desmarais, "Women's Sexual Pressure Tactics and Adherence to Related Attitudes: A Step toward Prediction on JSTOR," *Journal of Sex Research* 35, no. 2 (May 1998): 197–205.

255 *Similarly, sexual scripts that position*: Diane Felmlee, David Orzechowicz, and Carmen E. Fortes, "Fairy Tales: Attraction and Stereotypes in Same-Gender Relationships," *Sex Roles* 62, nos. 3–4 (January 5, 2010): 226–40.

255 *One 2021 study*: Virginia Braun et al., "Sexual Coercion among Gay and Bisexual Men in Aotearoa/New Zealand," *Journal of Homosexuality* 56, no. 3 (April 1, 2009): 336–60.

255 *One study participant said*: Ibid.

255 *Another study participant explained*: Ibid.

255 *A 2009 study found*: Rachel Jones and Elsie E. Gulick, "Reliability and Validity of the Sexual Pressure Scale for Women-Revised," *Research in Nursing & Health* 32, no. 1 (February 1, 2009): 71–85.

255 *Study participants cited*: Ibid.

256 *Research shows that those who feel anxious*: Susan M. Johnson and Dino Zuccarini, "Integrating Sex and Attachment in Emotionally Focused Couple Therapy," *Journal of Marital and Family Therapy* 36, no. 4 (September 30, 2009): 431–45.

256 *As a result, they rely*: Amy L. Gentzler and Kathryn A. Kerns, "Associations

between Insecure Attachment and Sexual Experiences," *Personal Relationships* 11, no. 2 (April 27, 2004): 249–65.

260 *This phenomenon, called spectatoring*: Paul D. Trapnell, Cindy M. Meston, and Boris B. Gorzalka, "Spectatoring and the Relationship between Body Image and Sexual Experience: Self-Focus or Self-Valence?," *Journal of Sex Research* 34, no. 3 (January 1, 1997): 267–78.

260 *Sexuality educator and writer Ella*: Ella Dorval Hall, "I'm a Recovering People Pleaser. Now That I Know What I Want and Need, I Have Better Sex," *Insider*, March 31, 2023, https://www.insider.com/enjoy-sex-healing-people-pleasing-habits-performance-anxiety-2023-3.

260 *Orgasm involves deactivation*: Johnson and Zuccarini, "Integrating Sex and Attachment in Emotionally Focused Couple Therapy."

261 *The four most common reasons*: Charlene L. Muehlenhard and Sheena K. Shippee, "Men's and Women's Reports of Pretending Orgasm," *Journal of Sex Research* 47, no. 6 (November 2, 2010): 552–67.

20: REDISCOVERING PLAY

266 *Research shows that play directly*: Tamlin S. Conner, Colin G. DeYoung, and Paul J. Silvia, "Everyday Creative Activity as a Path to Flourishing," *Journal of Positive Psychology* 13, no. 2 (November 17, 2016): 181–89.

267 *All play, he says*: Jennifer Wallace, "Why It's Good for Grown-Ups to Go Play," *Washington Post*, May 20, 2017, https://www.washingtonpost.com/national/health-science/why-its-good-for-grown-ups-to-go-play/2017/05/19/99810292-fd1f-11e6-8ebe-6e0dbe4f2bca_story.html.

267 *We're evolutionarily wired for play*: "Play Science: What We Know So Far," National Institute for Play, accessed September 6, 2023, https://www.nifplay.org/play-science/summary-of-key-findings/.

268 *Play has been declining*: Esther Entin, "All Work and No Play: Why Your Kids Are More Anxious, Depressed," *Atlantic*, October 12, 2011, https://www.theatlantic.com/health/archive/2011/10/all-work-and-no-play-why-your-kids-are-more-anxious-depressed/246422/.

268 *While consuming media*: K. C. Madhav, Shardulendra P. Sherchand, and Samendra Sherchan, "Association between Screen Time and Depression among US Adults," *Preventive Medicine Reports* 8 (December 1, 2017): 67–71.

268 *Tricia Hersey, author of*: Tricia Hersey, *Rest Is Resistance: A Manifesto* (New York: Little, Brown Spark, 2022), 73.

271 *These eight personalities*: "Play Personalities," National Institute for Play, accessed September 6, 2023, https://www.nifplay.org/what-is-play/play-personalities/.

273 *Leisure, he explains, consists*: Mihaly Csikszentmihalyi, *Flow: The Psychology of Optimal Experience* (New York: HarperCollins, 2009), 68.

274 *These moments of timeless*: Marino Bonaiuto et al., "Optimal Experience and Personal Growth: Flow and the Consolidation of Place Identity," *Frontiers in Psychology* 7 (November 7, 2016): https://doi.org/10.3389/fpsyg.2016.01654.

274 *Fascinatingly, research shows*: Csikszentmihalyi, *Flow*, 49.

21: ALLOWING AMBIGUITY AND PRACTICING DISCERNMENT

287 *When we engage in*: Dan Brennan, "Black and White Thinking," WebMD, March 30, 2021, https://www.webmd.com/mental-health/black-and-white-thinking.

INDEX

ABOUT THE AUTHOR

HAILEY MAGEE is a certified life coach who helps people around the world stop people-pleasing and find their power. Her refreshingly nuanced perspectives on boundary-setting and self-advocacy have captured the attention of millions on social media, and her public talks and workshops have welcomed tens of thousands of participants. Certified by Erickson Coaching International, Hailey is dedicated to offering clear, research-supported strategies for change, helping recovering people-pleasers rediscover not only their power and agency, but also their pleasure, joy, and sense of wonder. She lives in Seattle, Washington. You can find her at HaileyMagee.com or on Instagram at @HaileyPaigeMagee.

www.ingramcontent.com/pod-product-compliance
Lightning Source LLC
LaVergne TN
LVHW041207061126
851857LV00018B/1964
* 9 7 8 1 6 6 8 0 6 5 3 2 7 *